The 5 Dharma Types

"This work has opened doors of insight and perception, allowing me to see our species in a fresh and hopeful light. I hope people will read this book more than once, and slowly."

ROBIN GILE, COAUTHOR OF
THE COMPLETE IDIOT'S GUIDE TO PALMISTRY

The 5 Dharma Types

VEDIC WISDOM FOR DISCOVERING YOUR PURPOSE AND DESTINY

SIMON CHOKOISKY

Destiny Books

Rochester, Vermont • Toronto, Canada

Destiny Books
One Park Street
Rochester, Vermont 05767
www.DestinyBooks.com

Text stock is SFI certified

Destiny Books is a division of Inner Traditions International

Library of Congress Cataloging-in-Publication Data
Chokoisky, Simon.
    [Dharma types]
    The five dharma types : Vedic wisdom for discovering your purpose and destiny / Simon Chokoisky.
        pages cm
    Originally published in 2013 by Upaya Publications under the title The Dharma Types: Secrets of the Five Ancient Castes That Will Transform Your Life!
    Includes index.
    ISBN 978-1-62055-283-4 (pbk.) — ISBN 978-1-62055-284-1 (e-book)
    1. Spiritual life—Hinduism. 2. Dharma. I. Title.
    BL1237.32.C55 2014
    294.5'48—dc23
                                                                    2013034050

Printed and bound in the United States by Lake Book Manufacturing, Inc. The text stock is SFI certified. The Sustainable Forestry Initiative® program promotes sustainable forest management.

10 9 8 7 6 5 4 3 2 1

Text design and layout by Virginia Scott Bowman
This book was typeset in Garamond Premier Pro and Helvetica with Parma Petit and Helvetica used as display typefaces

To send correspondence to the author of this book, mail a first-class letter to the author c/o Inner Traditions • Bear & Company, One Park Street, Rochester, VT 05767, and we will forward the communication, or contact the author directly at **www.spirittype.com** or **siddhadeva@yahoo.com**.

*My grateful acknowledgment to Mantriji,
Dr. Vasant Lad, Hart de Fouw, and all keepers of
ancient wisdom the world over.
Special thanks to my wife, Ventzi, for her love
and support, without which this book would never
have come to fruition!*

Contents

PART TWO

Authentically Living Your Dharma Type

Preface

This work is a practical manual intended to help you attain fulfillment in your personal, social, and spiritual life. It is not a treatise on religion, philosophy, or academics, all of which offer relative truths to a specific culture, age, and environment. Instead, it is distilled from all of the above to present universal truths pertinent to humanity in the modern age. In today's global society, where humankind's understanding of reality is muddled by distinctions of race, color, and creed, it is ever so difficult to find one's place. The mundane world is a cacophony of sound, and the song of the spirit is difficult to discern for the multitude of contrary voices pulling us this way and that. This guide is intended to help you find your voice in the chorus of the many, and perhaps more importantly, to develop your ear that you may better hear and harmonize with the world about you. It is designed to help you know your purpose, and understand that of others, and by doing so to live in the world in a way envisioned by our most cherished prophets and mystics.

This book is best read in its entirety, as you will discover things about your dharma type, as well as those of others in your life, by reading even the sections that don't appear to apply directly to you. Reading only those parts that reference your type will prevent you from fully integrating it, as we must understand all five types in a symbiotic system that mirrors Nature, where one entity feeds another, which feeds the first in turn.

When each of us fulfills our destiny we empower others to do the same, and when they fulfill their destinies we are benefited in turn. This is the basis for mutual respect, sharing, and responsibility—the foundations that pave the way to wisdom. May this be a useful guide to such wisdom and of service to all who use it!

Note to the Reader
on the Use of Sanskrit Terms

This book is not a translation but an original work that makes use of Sanskrit terms with no real English equivalents. Where appropriate these have been plainly spelled out rather than transliterated. This is for two reasons. First, readers new to the material may find it cumbersome to decipher transliterations along with the plethora of new vocabulary and concepts. Second, readers who are already familiar with diacritical marks or even conversant in Sanskrit should know the proper spelling and pronunciation of these words. Thus, no great need is served by introducing transliteration here.

Introduction and Self Tests

Dharma kshetre Kuru kshetre . . .* begins that well-known and beloved classic of spiritual wisdom, the Bhagavad Gita. In India's Vedic tradition[†] it was customary to open an important work with an auspicious word that served both to set the tone as well as to give readers an idea of its content. With *dharma* at its fore we can understand the Gita to be a treatise on purpose, duty, and Natural Law. Dharma is also the subject of this book. In the West we are familiar with terms like *karma,* but there is less understanding of dharma, our purpose in the world. Life without purpose is meaningless. Our modern Merchant society tries to provide meaning by giving us wealth and possessions to strive after, but material things cannot answer those most basic questions: "Who am I?" and "Why am I here?" Material objects can sustain us on our quest, but what we have come to do remains a mystery.

The Gita tells us that we must embrace dharma, our purpose, in order to find happiness in life. But how can we do this if we do not know what our purpose is? How are we to walk the path of fulfillment without a map to show us the way?

It is the role of society to organize people in such a way as to foster their optimal self-expression. Over the last several thousand years humankind has tried to invent and reinvent social structures that befit the free expression of our destinies, but our inventions are limited in

---

*"On the battlefield of Destiny, on the battlefield of the Kuru clan . . ." (Bhagavad Gita 1:1). (See page 72 for a variant of this quote.)

[†]The Vedas are the oldest scriptures of the teachings from India.

1

scope and knowledge. As Paul writes in Corinthians, "We know in part and we prophesy in part." What is needed is something that addresses our core essence to align us with the Natural Laws of the universe. Myth and archetypes do that very thing.

> "That which is beyond even the concept of reality, that which transcends all thought—the myth puts you there all the time, gives you a line to connect with that mystery which you are."
>
> JOSEPH CAMPBELL, *THE POWER OF MYTH*

If you do not think that myths are important, consider that we pour ourselves into mythic molds every day without realizing it. Fashion, movies, sports, family, and social dynamics all furnish different identities, casting us into roles like "boss," "parent," "chic girl," or "Lakers fan," thereby affecting how we behave and what we expect from life. But most of these roles are poor complements to the fullness of who we really are. The dharma types, on the other hand, are personal myths that have existed since time immemorial and will continue to be useful so long as humankind exists because they are the unseen matrices that guide how human beings express their destinies. Though invisible, their effects can be readily determined: a Warrior behaves like a Warrior and a Merchant like a Merchant in organized, predictable patterns.

MATTER AND SPIRIT

A person's archetype is like an operating system, the internal software that runs a computer. Regardless of the color, size, or manufacture date of its hardware it is the OS that gives a computer its most basic expression and instructs it to work. Likewise, the dharma type informs every human being regardless of race, sex, age, or nationality. In this book we shall consider five dharma types, or operating systems, and how they affect us in specific ways. To get the most out of the systems we were born with we must become familiar with how they work. To that end, this is an instruction manual detailing the inner workings of each type in practically every area of life, from how to maintain health to how to make money.

The dharma types are Individual Archetypal Myths, the "I AM" identity inside that guides each of us in subtle but definitive patterns. Today we associate the word *myth* with something unreal or untrue, but to our ancestors, myths spoke to an enduring truth that lay beyond the ken of the senses. Consider that our everyday world is in perpetual flux—coming into being, changing form, and dying. In Sanskrit, the ancient language of India, this was termed *samsara,* "constant movement, constant change." But myth is eternal, driven by the intelligent blueprint that underlies the mundane world of name and form.

Our ancient ancestors thought in mythic terms not because they were primitive, but because in many ways they were advanced. They understood that what would survive their bodies, societies, and even civilizations was made not of earth and stone but of something more subtle and permanent. Their personal myths helped them to find purpose and obtain an everlasting life beyond the parenthetical existence of the human body. The dharma types are alive today even as they lived 5,000 years ago, here for us to access if we only know how.

Like the laws of gravity or flight archetypes existed before they were harnessed by the conscious mind, and they have been around as long as the universe itself. Accordingly, they are considered *apaurusheya,* a Sanskrit word that means "not invented by the mind of man." And to this day, though it may be impossible to localize one's Warrior or Educator genes (perhaps because no one has looked for them), these continue to influence our lives in every sphere—from the most mundane, such as relating to a lover, to the most spiritual, such as relating to God.

In this context "spirituality" does not equate to religiosity. Myths delve deeper than religion, and spirituality here simply means that:

1. There is purpose to life.
2. There is order and justice in the world.
3. There is more to it than material existence.

These three points—called *dharma*, *karma*, and *duhkha* in Sanskrit—separate the ordinary believer, or the materialist, from the true spiritual seeker.

Duhkha, which means suffering, suggests that it is impossible to have lasting peace from physical existence alone because of the difficulties inherent to balancing the material needs of life. Ayurveda, the Vedic science of holistic healing, illustrates this by depicting three bodily humors constantly vying to pull us out of balance and states that health is tantamount to skillfully juggling them to minimize their effects. Physical duhkha is evident in how much cleansing, movement, nourishment, rest, and maintenance the body requires. Without attentive daily care it breaks down into disease—and even careful maintenance only prolongs the inevitable. Nothing is permanent in the physical world, and nothing endures; change is the only constant. Duhkha.

The next concept, karma, means universal justice—nobody escapes the laws of cause and effect. Knowing this a wise person practices the Golden Rule—*Do unto others as you would have them do unto you*—not out of some pious obligation but from an earnest desire to have an optimal life experience, and ultimately, to free him- or herself of samsara. Everything you do rubs off on you. Karma.

> "A certain order prevails in our universe. This order can be formulated in terms of purposeful activity."
>
> **MAX PLANCK**

Finally, dharma is the sense that there is purpose to life. Without purpose there is only chaos and entropy in the universe. Without dharma life is a series of random moments ungoverned by any sense of natural order. The eventual question that a self-inquiring person asks is: "Do I live in an orderly universe, or in a world of random chance?" Our ancient ancestors were secure in their belief that there was more to life than the transitory material (duhkha), that life was governed by inextricable laws (karma), and that these laws were organized to serve the purpose of our evolution (dharma). These three elements of spirituality, the tripod of all Vedic philosophy, are developed throughout this book.

WHY VEDIC?

From Norway to Nigeria, from the Native American "Indians" to the Indians of the Asian subcontinent, archetypes are universal human attributes. They do not belong to any culture or religion any more than Earth's atmosphere belongs to one country. Nonetheless, some traditions have nurtured them longer and more successfully than others. This work is based on the Vedic lineage of India. The dharma types do not belong to India, though it has done much to develop and, in the modern age, corrupt them. We shall see the reasons for this in the following chapter, and explore the pure essence of these types divested of any cultural dogma.

The word Vedic here is used not in an academic sense, tied as that is to historical timelines and geopolitical considerations, but rather to describe a living tradition that, while rooted in India, has spread its branches across time and territory to offer its fruits to the modern Western world. Vedic refers not to an individual tree planted in antiquity along the skirts of the Sarasvati (an ancient river in northern India), but to the lush garden that has flourished from its fortunate seed and continues to grow, though the waters that fed it have long disappeared from the earth. Today the Vedic lineage is evident in the fruits, flowers, and even weeds that comprise the culture of the Indian subcontinent. Its branches are known to anyone who has taken a yoga class or who practices meditation. From healing herbology to Vedic astrology, the implications of Vedic thought have spread around the world and common words like *nirvana, guru,* and *pundit* have become part of our lexicon.

The West appreciates function when it sees it, and the litmus test for success in a capitalist society is the ability to generate money. From religion to relaxation, Vedic imports like yoga and meditation are multimillion-dollar industries in America, which is all the more astounding since they are essentially free in India! But beyond their economic success there is a reason that Vedic transplants have found a rich soil in the West, and a people hungry for their harvest. That is because they offer an unbroken link to our ancestral past, and beyond that, to our divine roots. Therein lies the difference between modern personality measurements and the Vedic archetypes, between systems based in the last century and those with roots that probe deeper into the reaches of time: the latter recognize one's connection to a sacred Self that is primordial, ancient, and unseen, though very much governed by Natural Laws.

Many self-help strategies that exist today cover some portion of the human experience, but none have the breadth and depth of the dharma type. None go so deeply into the spiritual component of existence or trace their lineage back as far into the ancient past. Self-help strategies are recent inventions of an industrialized world, while archetypes and myth have been around forever and speak to a more lasting aspect of life: our dharma.

The introduction of the Vedic body of knowledge, *vidya,* to America in the 1800s began a process of seeding this knowledge into new earth, and since then it has provided an opportunity for others to appreciate it anew: Indians have been taking a fresh look at their own cultural treasures since these sprouted in America. Yoga, vedanta (Vedic philosophy), and ayurveda enjoy an ever-increasing popularity today because people find in them something deep and real—an unbroken connection to the past that brings them in contact with their authentic selves.

BE YOURSELF

It is painful to be anything but yourself. "It is better to be bad at what you do than good at what is bad for you,"* which is why so many peo-

---

*This warning from Krishna in the Bhagavad Gita in Sanskrit reads: "Shreyan svadharmo vigunah, paradharmat svanushthitat."

ple today are fraught with anxiety, and no wonder feelings of being overwhelmed and dis-ease rampant. Life is stressful and empty when we are unaware of our destinies, for no amount of wealth, food, or entertainment can fill us like a tiny grain of purpose. The Vedic tradition asks, "Why chase after different destinies, when it is hard enough to find your own?" Helping people find their purpose was crucial in ancient cultures, and it is a multibillion-dollar industry in today's global Merchant society. From self-help books and seminars to religion (the original self-help methodology), everyone seems to have a different answer. But the truth is deceptively simple—love, prosperity, and God are on your path: find *that,* and you find them all! We are so busy looking for these things that we ignore the fact that they are synchronous with our journey. Our job is simply to anchor our selves to our dharma; everything follows therewith.

> **Love, prosperity, and God are on your path;**
> **find *that,* and you find them all!**

People pray for what they think will make them happy, like a certain amount of money, a certain job, or a certain partner. But how do we know that what we pray for is indeed our highest good? Even if we get what we desire, how much of our time is wasted yearning for things that do not pertain to our highest destiny, or worse, that distract us from our paths? When we follow dharma we are assured not only of our own prosperity but the good of everyone around us. The more we follow our purpose in the world, the more we lift up others in the process. There is more than enough fulfillment to go around for everyone on the planet because fulfillment is not a material resource like coal or water but a limitless side effect of dharma. Spiritual treasure is not tied to the rules of natural selection and competition: the more we give of it, the more we obtain.

If fulfillment were based on limited resources there would always be haves and have-nots: those who hold the resources and those who do not. Great misery is tied to this belief, especially when people do not know another way. The dharma types state that everything you need is already inside you. Your dharma is wired in you just as the oak is present in the seed; it needs only to be watered and guided by the hand of an able gardener while Nature takes care of the rest. There is no need to step on others to get to where we want to go—competition now arises to challenge and inspire people rather than dominate them. Imagine relating with people without needing to *get* anything from them. Imagine relating to people not as obstacles but as allies, helping each other obtain fulfillment.

> **Relationships are the test and temper of any person,
> philosophy, government, or religion.**

Relationships are the test and temper of any person, philosophy, government, or religion. How we behave toward others reflects our evolution and refinement. We may be great at balancing our checkbooks or have mastery of the latest Neuro-Linguistic Programming technique, but if in our daily life we cannot do something as simple as treating others as we treat ourselves (the Golden Rule), then we are really only compartmentalized beings, not whole—unholy. Improving relationships with others begins by improving the relationship with ourselves. This entails understanding the dharma of the individuated self, and ultimately merging it with the larger Self, the Self of All. Love dawns when you know yourself, and compassion begins when you know the Self of All. When your "I am" becomes the I AM of everyone, all conflicts cease and misunderstanding fades like darkness before a torch.

Self-improvement in the Vedic sense is really Self-actualization; the Self is already perfect and cannot be improved upon. It is a question of realizing that essence, which in reality has no distinctions—the silent, pure witness living in the present moment. It is devoid of labels like dharma type, man/woman, human being. It simply *is*. Abiding in that, you have no need for a book like this. But books like this offer specific instruction to help you find your essence. Aligning with your purpose makes it easier to be yourself. And being one's self translates into *being-one-self*. And that is the goal of spirituality, no matter what system you use. All that changes is the words—from Georgia Baptists to Greek Orthodox Christians, from Theravada to tantric Buddhists, and from Kashmir Shaktas to Krishna Bhaktas, the goal is the same: to know one's Self, in turn knowing all things that can be known.

Once you understand that the Self is the doer, and you in fact do nothing, then what else is left to do? The answer is your dharma, that which is required by virtue of your birth. Every being that is born must act. From breathing, talking, and eating to moving and even thinking, action is incumbent on us as a Natural Law. These are general actions germane to the species. But there are actions specific to your individual nature that must be done; if you perform these you receive the maximum of desirable karma and minimize undesirable karma. What these are and how they are to be performed is the subject of the remainder of this book.

THE SEARCH FOR HOME

Whether we choose a secular or sacred path, the human mind is always searching for its source—people look for this connection in their genetic heritage, their country, and their religion, among other things. This search for belonging is evidenced by our attachment to everything from sports teams and ethnic cuisine to the vernaculars we speak. We may love Italian food because somewhere in our genes our Mediterranean ancestors desire to be fed. Something latent inside wants us to remember who we are and whence we came. People want to be connected to their own kind, and even within one country a state, city, or neighborhood differentiates itself from neighboring states, cities, and streets in order to carve out its identity.

When this search for belonging becomes perverted it turns into racism, prejudice, and ethnic cleansings. When our search for purpose is derailed and we cannot find who we really are we become attached to our race, profession, social status, and other temporary labels. In fact it is important to honor our genetic traditions—we owe much to the body we use, and the physical inheritance it brings us through gender, race, and cultural heritage. Part of our duty on this planet is to discharge the karma of our ancestors, to fulfill the dharma of our sex, and to abide by the customs and traditions of our clan and country. These are all obligations we must deal with if we want to survive and prosper, but the dharma type offers us a way out of mere survival into an expression of our true selves—a relationship with the world that is based on the ecumenical principle of unity.

Ecumenical, which means "of worldwide scope, universal, concerned with establishing unity among churches or religions," comes from the Greek word *oikos,* meaning "home."* Our home lies in the unity of our species, by the understanding that we are related by the dharmas we share. More expressive than the role of "parent"—and deeper than gender, profession, or race—is your archetype. In that, all Merchants are related regardless of the expanse of language, custom, or geography that separates them. All Warriors share the common bond of their dharma, no matter how it expresses in the world. Today through DNA mapping people are exploring their genetic heritage many generations into the past to discover their roots, to find their country of origin. But in the modern world, where nations and borders come and go and national identities change, the role of the dharma type remains constant. This is the real meaning of the root *dhri,* from which the word *dharma* originates: "to remain fixed, constant, centered in reality."

It is that connection we all seek when we identify ourselves with our sports team, our local restaurant, or our favorite song—but as we know, these things lose their meaning and grow stale in time, and the search for belonging continues. But those who are fixed in the eternal dharma of their archetype remain at home wherever they go.

---

*The word *catholic,* which means "liberal, universal, of interest to all," contains the same root.

DISCOVER YOUR DHARMA TYPE!

So let us now discover your dharma type. In Self Test 1 choose one answer that describes you best, though you can pick up to four for each multiple-choice question if you are unable to decide. Next, read the paragraphs in Self Test 2 and choose two that describe you *best*. Not all of their qualities have to fit, though they should at least elicit a gut reaction of "yeah, that's me"—even if you don't necessarily like them! There are two paragraphs for each type. If it is difficult to decide, you may pick as many paragraphs as you like, and narrow the results later. Check the answer key at the bottom of each test to tally your choices; the one that receives the most answers is most likely your dharma type.*

Your type will also become clearer to you upon reading the descriptions that follow in this book, which will make sense in light of your own life experience. Ultimately, it is useful to have friends or relatives help us with the tests and descriptions. Often we see ourselves differently from how the rest of the world perceives us. We may also be in a cycle that makes it difficult to access our essential dharma type. Life cycles can tint our basic expression like different colored lenses—some enhance our light while others sometimes diffuse it—so take your whole life into consideration when reading the following descriptions, and have a friend or relative help you in the process. Looking at yourself from childhood to now will provide a complete portrait that should help determine your type, or at least narrow it down sufficiently to make a determination when you read the descriptions in part 1 of this book. *Enjoy!*

---

*Another way to find your dharma type is to consult your Vedic Life Map, requiring an accurate birth time and place, though it is often possible to use general information such as "around 10 a.m." This technique zeroes in on not only dharma type, which remains the same, but also on the sequence of life cycles (different periods experienced as we travel through life and assume different roles and karmas), covered in detail in chapter 15. Dharma type practitioners can be found at www.spirittype.com.

◆ *SELF TEST I*

Circle the answers that best apply to you. You may choose more than one answer for each question if applicable. Try to think of qualities that are permanent in you, how you have always been, rather than how you are at times or during recent changes in your life. Tally them up at the end to determine your dharma type.

1. **Circle the word that means the most to you or describes you best.**
   a. Freedom
   b. Loyalty
   c. Wisdom
   d. Honor
   e. Prosperity

2. **Circle the phrase that means the most to you or describes you best.**
   a. Independence and Bliss
   b. Love and Devotion
   c. Worldliness and Knowledge
   d. Discipline and Perfection
   e. Entertainment and Fun

3. **Circle the phrase that means the most to you or describes you best.**
   a. I love being alone. Sometimes I hate people, sometimes I like them, but they usually don't understand me.
   b. I don't mind being alone as long as I have something constructive and productive to do.
   c. I love being alone. I like people but I need time to spend by myself for quiet contemplation and rejuvenation.
   d. I don't mind being alone, as long as I have a goal to accomplish.
   e. I hate being alone. I prefer the company of people, even if I don't know them.

4. **Circle the phrase that means the most to you or describes you best.**
   a. I like strange, dark, or wild and remote places no one has ever thought of or been to.

b. I like the plains and wide expanses of earth. I like living close to the ground, on ground floors rather than high-rise apartments.

c. I like high and remote places. I like upper floors, high-rise buildings, and living above others looking down.

d. I like challenging places, places that are high, but not so high as to be remote. I like fortified and strong places.

e. From the Beverly Hills to gently rolling slopes, I like places where the action is, places that are easy to get to, but also exclusive. I like living in the middle ground, not too high, not too low, where there is activity and access to the world.

5. **Circle the sentence that describes you best.**
   a. I am the rebel or black sheep of my family. As a parent, I give freedom to my kids and let them individualize themselves from others.

   b. I am deeply bonded with my family. As a parent, I nurture my kids by making sure they are well fed, healthy, and content.

   c. I tend to teach my family and urge them to improve themselves. As a parent I make certain my kids learn how to think for themselves, get a good education, and understand the world.

   d. I am the strong one in my family. As a parent I lead by example and earn my kids' respect with discipline and order.

   e. I actively support my family with shelter and resources. As a parent I provide for my kids and make sure they understand the value of money, self-effort, and making your way in the world.

6. **In religion I *most* value the following:**
   a. Going my own way.
   b. Faith and devotion.
   c. Study and scripture.
   d. Penance and discipline.
   e. Rituals and observances.

7. **In marriage I *most* value the following:**
   a. An unconventional spouse, one who understands my particular quirks and desires.

    b. A dutiful spouse who is loyal and provides for me: a woman who cooks and cleans/a man who brings home the bacon.

    c. A sensitive, intelligent spouse.

    d. A challenging spouse with whom I can do activities.

    e. A beautiful spouse.

8. I mainly watch TV for:

    a. Horror, alternative political and spiritual viewpoints, science fiction (like the Sci-Fi, FX, Indie, and Alternative channels).

    b. Family, drama, history, and community programs (like soap operas, reality TV, daytime shows, cartoons, entertainment gossip, and reruns).

    c. Educational, thought-provoking, human-interest stories and entertainment (like National Geographic, PBS, Sci-Fi, and documentary channels).

    d. Sports, action, news, and politics; adventure stories and entertainment (ESPN, CNN, etc.).

    e. Fun programs, drama, music, comedy, game shows, financial and motivational stories and entertainment (like HBO, the Comedy Channel, and Spike).

9. Under stress I tend to:

    a. Bend the rules or lie to get my way; feel invisible and self-deprecate.

    b. Become lazy, close down in my own space, and worry a lot.

    c. Be scatterbrained, feckless, and wishy-washy.

    d. Become anger prone, inattentive, and reckless.

    e. Be moody, depressed, loud, and restless.

10. At my best I am:

    a. A revolutionary, an inventor, a genius.

    b. A devoted friend, a hard worker, a caregiver.

    c. A counselor, a teacher, a diplomat.

    d. A leader, a hero, a risk taker.

    e. An optimist, a self-starter, a promoter, an adventurer.

Answer Key

Tally your answers now. The most selected letter likely reflects your dharma type. For confirmation you should now move on to Self Test II.

      A. Outsider

      B. Laborer

      C. Educator

      D. Warrior

      E. Merchant

 SELF TEST II

Select *two* paragraphs that describe you best. Then refer to the answer key at the end to determine your type.

1. Sometimes I think no one really understands me, and no one ever will. I love freedom and need to feel independent and free most of all. Although I can fit into many crowds, I never really feel a part of any of them. I wear many hats but none of them defines me. People may see me as secretive or mysterious, but I am just the way I am—different. By fate or choice I am attracted to foreign lands, cultures, religions, and values and have embraced some of these. I have talents and abilities that are not always recognized, and it can be hard to make a living if I do not compromise with my society. My ambitions are somewhat unique, and I have a quirky way of seeing the world. Sometimes I feel lost and don't know what my true purpose is, but when I look at others I am reminded of what it is not: I can't conform to somebody else's lifestyle just for the sake of security, even though I may not have found my own.

2. I have often dreamt of owning my own business and being financially independent. From an early age I have felt a need to provide and be provided for. I have a strong sense of the value of money and I don't mind working long hours to generate security for myself and family. I don't pay much attention to my body, unless it is part of my business

or I have the leisure time. I like giving and the feeling that it creates, but in this competitive world it is most important to secure my own and my family's needs first. I have a good practical sense and know how to take care of mundane obligations. I believe that anyone can make it in today's society if they're willing to apply themselves. I am motivated and self-driven and can't understand idealistic or so-called spiritual people who deny the importance of financial security.

3. I like to protect those who cannot protect themselves. I believe in standing up for a good cause whether it is social, environmental, ecological, etc. Money is less important to me than securing justice in the world. I have strong convictions and character, and people often look to me for leadership. I have an inner strength that drives me to achieve. I can usually outperform others by sheer force of will. I have an eye for deception and can tell when someone is lying. I admire wisdom and like to associate with smart and educated people, though I may not have the time or opportunity to cultivate these qualities in myself. I can be highly disciplined and therefore acquire skills quickly. At my best I am courageous, noble, and self-sacrificing, but I can also be distracted, anger prone, and judgmental.

4. I love the camaraderie of working with others to construct something useful. I am handy, skilled, practical, and not averse to work. I am devoted to friends and family, and though not an intellectual I have a good sense about things, though I can't always explain it in words. My needs and tastes are simple, and it doesn't take a lot to make me happy: good food, good company, and a solid roof over my head are the essentials in life. I like being of service and feeling needed. Being useful to someone is more important than how much money I make, though I don't like to be cheated. I believe in hard work and don't understand lazy people. I can be superstitious and have deep-seated beliefs about things that often stem from my childhood and cannot be easily rationalized.

5. I prefer intellectual work to physical labor. I can be idealistic and focus on

concepts and philosophies rather than living in the real world. I become disheartened by the ugliness and injustice of life and often lack energy to change it. I have always been smarter and more perceptive than most of my peers, though not inherently practical. I like to counsel others, though I don't always practice what I preach. I have a knack for encouraging and finding the best in people, and as a result people come to me for advice. I don't have a killer instinct and that's a disadvantage if I try to compete in physical or other cutthroat professions. I like to live in a peaceful environment, rather than the hustle and bustle of the busy world. I often know what needs to be done but don't necessarily have the energy or skills to do it. It is often easier for me to tell others what to do rather than to do it myself.

6. I set strong standards for myself and expect to live up to them. I love competition, debate, and testing my limits. I even compete with myself when others are not around. I have a huge heart, and my generosity sometimes gets me in trouble. I like to lay down the law in my family and with others. From early on I was blessed with physical and mental strength, though I often abuse these by pushing too much—I play hard and party hard. I like to care for those who cannot fend for themselves: the innocent, the elderly, and the underprivileged.

7. I hate constrictive social, religious, and moral institutions, and I feel it is my right to speak and act out against them. I also feel justified in flouting an unjust law and not conforming to artificial regulations. I am physically, emotionally, and/or spiritually different from others, and because of this I find it hard to fit in. I can see through people's bullshit, and that makes me want to run away from society. Sometimes I resent normal people who were born with opportunities that I don't have. I would rather overthrow the status quo to allow fresh growth than try to patch things up piece by piece. I respect an authority that allows me to be who I am and understands the gifts I have to offer.

8. I am a devoted, loyal, patriotic person and have a deep connection to the things that are dearest to me: my family, friends, God, and country.

I believe it is important to abide by the codes and principles of my country, church, and society. I love to build community. I guess you could say I'm sentimental about the things I value. A dutiful worker, I believe in getting a job done right and am faithful to my word. I am also very good at what I do and specialize in well-developed skills. I secretly admire widely read and cultured people and wish I were a bit more like them, but I just don't have the time to waste on that and prefer to be better at what I do than to know a lot of trivia. I have to touch, see, hear, or feel something; otherwise it is not real for me.

9. I love attention and being the life of the party. I am quick and clever and find it easy to get along with others. I can be very likable, though I don't necessarily like other people and am more attached to the few people I can really trust—myself and my family. I am naturally glib and gregarious, and people tend to believe what I say. I have good taste and appreciation for the finer things in life, things that have beauty and value. However, I sometimes feel an emptiness that I have to fill with outside things, though it is never really filled until I give or do something for others. Sometimes I feel that I am not worth anything, and that if people really knew me they wouldn't like me. Because of this I respect those who have raised and supported me, and I work hard to pay back their love in return. I am also very emotional and can go to extremes of depression and elation. This volatility may cost me in relationships and in my health, and I sometimes like to numb it with drugs, sex, and entertainment. I enjoy all sorts of fun, from performing for people and being the center of attention to watching others do the same.

10. I consider myself a rather cultured, mild-mannered person. I don't tolerate vulgarity or crass behavior. I have special food preferences and daily regimes that require me to be alone for parts of the day so I can tend to my rather delicate constitution. I tend to be solitary in my personal habits and prefer losing myself in a book more than engaging in the hustle and bustle of the world. I like the realm of ideas and

concepts, though I am rarely able to embody them in the real world. I don't have abundant physical energy, though I enjoy sports, games, and being in Nature for their recreational and inspirational value.

Answer Key

1 and 7: Outsider

2 and 9: Merchant

3 and 6: Warrior

4 and 8: Laborer

5 and 10: Educator

RRIOR•EDUCATOR•OUTSIDER•LABORER•MERCHA

RCHANT•WARRI OUTSIDER•LABO

ORER•MERCHANT•WARRIOR•EDUCATOR•OUTSID

CATOR•OUTSIDER•LABORER•MERCHANT•WARRIO

PART ONE

The Roles
of the
Dharma Types

1

Merchant Society
and the Dharma Types

From Celts to Polynesians, from Nordic to Vedic lands, different cultures in different climes have stamped and coined their unique version of the dharma type. But the archetypal gold from which dharma types are made remains universal, valuable in the steppes and the cities, the marshes and the marketplaces of the world. Unfortunately we have left behind the gold standard of the archetype for the paper currency of believing that our jobs, education, possessions, or the changing fashions of society define us, rather than the other way around. Ancient cultures recognized that people have unique personality types that inform every facet of their individual expression. Nowadays, the homogenization of society has blended distinctions between people to such a degree that it has become increasingly difficult to distinguish ourselves from others around us. Information and cultural exchange make it easy for anyone to access the trends of popular culture. We are increasingly becoming members of a consumer-driven global society, and while this has encouraged integration among nations and neighbors it has also made it more difficult to find our own destinies amidst the many choices that beckon us in different directions. More choice brings less certainty, and less certainty makes people confused about how they are supposed to live.

More choice has made casual relationships easier, but lasting union more elusive; it has made money more available, but diminished the satisfaction it brings; it has made food plentiful, but good health a rarity. As illustrated by the panoply of dating, employment, and health and wellness websites we have a greater choice in partners, professions, and even diets. But studies show that divorce rates, poverty, and health are no better than they were fifty years ago, and are, in fact, worsening. We need a map to help us navigate the ever-increasing avenues of choice to their purported end—happiness and prosperity. If we are ever to reach that hallowed place romanticized by phrases such as "the American dream" or "the end of the rainbow" we must have direction, and a navigation system to lead us there. The ancient dharma types are just such a system, more useful now than ever, which can help us reach our destinations and steer us away from the storms and ill winds that threaten to divert us from our course.

FOUR TYPES

Our ancestors in the ancient world sought to condense the variety of natural phenomena into underlying principles that described the whole of creation in concise, yet profound, categories. In a way this is evidenced today in Newton's laws of motion or Einstein's $E = MC^2$, seemingly simple formulations of Natural Law that yet have had a profound influence on our lives, from microwave ovens to rocket travel. One of the many ways the ancients classified the world of matter and energy was according to four great elements: Earth, Water, Air, and Fire (figure 1.1). These described matter in its solid, liquid, gaseous, and transformative states and helped us understand the world by condensing its amazing variety into four irreducible principles.*

---

*There are other categories of four in Vedic philosophy, such as the four seasons of life, four aims of life, four great ages, and four Vedas, all of which are discussed in this book. The number four relates to stability and solidity and was often used in the ancient world to categorize material reality. Four right angles make a square, the most stable human-made shape according to the Vedic practice of spatial arrangement, *vastu shastra*.

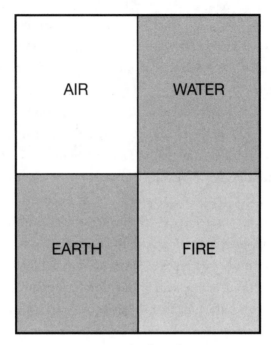

Figure 1.1. The four elements.

Corresponding to the four perceptible elements are four basic archetypes: Laborer, Merchant, Warrior, and Educator (figure 1.2). Not surprisingly, just as these types relate to an element, they also correspond to one of the four aims of life, in Sanskrit called *purusharthas* (figure 1.3).

The Vedic seers' explanations for any living creature's actions in this world were categorized into four basic drives:

1. **Dharma:** The drive to live according to the Natural Law of one's being, and to obtain one's rightful purpose in the world. Dharma, sometimes called "natural destiny," is the foundation of any Vedic philosophy and the cornerstone of this book.
2. **Artha:** The drive to win security and sustenance for self and family. From plants to human beings, all creatures have a built-in desire to secure their existence.

Figure 1.2. *The four elements and their corresponding dharma types.*

| AIR
EDUCATOR
FREEDOM | WATER
MERCHANT
ENJOYMENT |
| EARTH
LABORER
SECURITY | FIRE
WARRIOR
PURPOSE |

Figure 1.3. *The elements, dharma types, and aims in life.*

3. **Kama:** The drive to obtain enjoyment resulting from one's attainment of purpose and security.
4. **Moksha:** The drive to gain freedom from any type of bondage or restriction.

Although they bear Sanskrit names these principles are universal and express themselves at all times and places in the world. They were mirrored in the Declaration of Independence as "life, liberty, and the pursuit of happiness," which correspond to artha, moksha, and kama, three of the aims of life the Vedic seers deemed vital to mankind. Conspicuously absent from the Declaration is the concept of dharma—though in formulating his masterful civic document Thomas Jefferson drew heavily on Enlightenment philosophy, he did not have a tradition to describe dharma and how to ensure it for all people. Perhaps as a result American society to this day continues to live out the legacy of slavery while its citizens struggle to find their rightful place in society. America, though arguably the most secure, free, and enjoyable country in the world, nevertheless lacks its rightful purpose, which is perhaps why it is both loved and hated by its global neighbors. Dharma inspires trust, leadership, and confidence. Lack of dharma inspires anxiety, stress, and fear. Like a person, a society inspired by dharma knows where it stands and has clear direction. A society infiltrated by *adharma* (dharma's opposite) lives on the edge of fear and stress, grabbing its enjoyments where it can while living in a dog-eat-dog reality. It is rarely sustainable for very long and inevitably crumbles under the weight of its own irresponsibility and self-indulgence. However, it is not just America that lacks an internal compass—America is conspicuous only because of its prominence in today's world. Most other countries fare no better, and often do worse when it comes to defining a standard of dharma for their people. Countries like France and Brazil that emphasize kama (enjoyment), or cultures like Japan or Germany that idealize economic welfare, all miss the mark when it comes to defining a standard of dharma. Perhaps Bhutan comes closest to this aim by taking pains to guide its citizens along lines of purpose and Natural Law, even ensuring a "Gross National Happiness" index. There is a lesson in this for other nations, for happiness does not come about through the pursuit of enjoyment and security alone but through the development of all four aims of life, particularly dharma.

Though every creature expresses these four drives, each dharma type has an affinity with one of the aims of life. For example, life on Earth is impossible without food, shelter, and security—what John Locke called "the right to property," a founding principle of any enlightened society. These are the drives and talents of the Laborer type. On the other hand, even with security life is dull and depressing without beauty, joy, and laughter. Sharing these is the drive of the Merchant type. Enjoyment without proper respect for Natural Law and order loses its purpose and turns to pain in the end. Preventing this anarchy of lawlessness is the purview of the Warrior. Finally, life without an understanding of the freedom inherent to the Self can never realize its full potential and has no context or higher inspiration. The desire to evolve into something higher, something better, to release oneself from the restrictions of a base existence, is represented by wisdom and the Air Element. Teaching this wisdom, which is the key to personal freedom, is the drive of the Educator type.

These categories of four were used to describe much of the physical world in ancient times. The Greeks used them to formulate everything from personality types to four physiological humors, but in borrowing from the older Vedic culture much was lost in translation. A prime example: though the four elements effectively describe the physical world, a fifth exists, Space, which is not discernible by the senses. This is akin to the difference between Newtonian and particle physics: one admirably describes the function of material reality but breaks down when confronting subtler realms of existence. Just so, a fifth dharmic archetype exists that, like space, encompasses the other four: the Outsider (figure 1.4). Five is the number that takes the stable categories of four (four cardinal directions, four discernible elements) and spiritualizes them, by introducing the *unseen* into the equation.

Space is imperceptible and difficult to quantify. It is both the most subtle *and* the most abundant element—which makes it mysterious, a quality it shares with the Outsider type whom it typifies. While not traditionally part of the fourfold Vedic social hierarchy, the Outsider is particularly relevant in our age and must be understood if we are to adapt this system to modern usage. The great yogi Vivekananda said that we must revise *smriti* (secular knowledge) and reinterpret *shruti* (sacred wisdom). We must adapt human-made laws to our time and place and reinterpret eternal laws in light of present need. Like the fifth element Outsiders are the most subtle, pervasive, and influential type in today's world precisely because they are also the most abundant, a fact that we will explore in the chapters that follow.

Though the Air Element is the most free of the four traditional elements Space ultimately best represents freedom, or moksha, since space is not bound by the rules that govern air. Thus, Educators become more indicative of wisdom and self-awareness, and Outsiders freedom and liberty, as we shall see when we discuss the symbolism of the elements in part 2.

Western thinkers from Plato to Jung have used and modified the four basic archetypes over the ages to suit their needs and levels of understanding. However, few philosophers or psychologists knew the source of these types and the context in which they were fashioned. Some people today confuse the ayurvedic classification of mind/body types (Vata, Pitta, and Kapha) with the dharma type. The first are physiological humors used almost exclusively for treating diseases of the body and mind, while the latter have far wider applications, like fulfilling the four aims of life. Thousands of years before Jung, and even Plato, these four archetypes enjoyed a lively existence in Vedic society and more than gauging temperament, or even healing, were

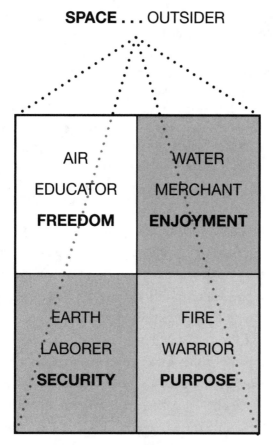

*Figure 1.4. The four elements in relation
to the Outsider element, Space.*

designed as beacons of dharma. Failing to understand this we relegate
them to a mere remedial function, like turning an iPod into a paper-
weight, and sit in silence when we could be dancing to the rhythms
of our lives.

However, while many societies have used a version of the dharma
types to celebrate the soundtrack of humanity, their recordings over
time have become denatured, and none survive today untainted.
Even the Vedic archetypes, though produced in the spirit of harmony, were remixed over time into the discordant caste systems of
modern day.

"The Satya [Golden Age] was the age in which righteousness was eternal, when duties did not languish nor people decline. No efforts were made by men, the fruit of the earth was obtained by their mere wish. There was no malice, weeping, pride, or deceit; no contention, no hatred, cruelty, fear, affliction, jealousy, or envy. The castes [dharma types] alike in their function fulfilled their duties, were unceasingly devoted to one deity, and used one formula, one rule, and one rite. Though they had separate paths, they had but one Veda and practiced one duty."

FROM THE MAHABHARATA

Although in Latin *castus* means "pure," societies in the current age have strayed from the original intent of that word—we cannot say that one type is better than another any more than we can claim water superior to air; both nourish us in different ways. In fact living creatures all require food, water, light, oxygen, and freedom to survive—represented respectively by the Earth, Water, Fire, Air, and Space elements. Likewise every dharma type nourishes society with separate but equally valuable contributions. Society works best when it accounts for and accepts all five personality types by delegating appropriate duties to each—helping to productively channel their natural, inborn talents. But when stratification becomes a source of discrimination, it can degenerate into tyranny. What we have seen in the world's caste systems over the last few thousand years is just such a deterioration. India is not alone in this; examples of caste degradation can be seen in every culture that has tried to uphold this system in modern times. In Hawai'i, for example, commoners were regularly required to debase themselves before the *ali'i*, or ruling warrior caste.

Ultimately, neither Indian nor Polynesian society is to blame for this; it is a function of the current age that these systems are so corrupted by literalism and materialism—a fundamentalist adherence to precepts we no longer understand and do not know how to apply. The aim of this book is to wipe away the false accretions of prejudice, intolerance, and control, revealing the spirit of a system that embraces equality *and* individuality, freedom as well as righteousness—and far beyond just social categories, one that portrays the complete destinies available to each type regardless of race, culture, or sex. Understanding requires radical re-vision, seeing the vibrant truth again behind the grimy veil of time and depredation.

In a moment we shall take a look at the types in detail—not just as members of a social class, but as personality types whose destinies are uniquely their own. But before we do, let us observe the archetypes through the lens of sacred history and see how they have devolved over time. This is a view of the world over thousands of years that describes a cycle of Golden, Silver, Bronze, and Iron ages, and is less concerned with dates and battles than with the changing of mores in Earth's societies. In Sanskrit it is called the *chaturyuga,* the four great ages.

THE FOUR AGES

Today we consider ourselves at the apex of a human history that dates back in a straight line to our ape-like ancestors and beyond, all the way into the primordial peptide pools where evolution began. Many sacred societies, however, propose a different view. They not only provide a cosmology connecting humankind's origins to a sacred divine source but view time itself as a cyclical, nonlinear event. They describe a sequence of great ages that come and go in intervals governed by Nature, intervals that witness the growth as well as destruction of civilization as mankind moves from age to age. They propose a sacred history that is radically different from the standard scientific model. We can still find hints of this mysterious history in the implacable faces of the megalithic structures some of these civilizations left behind. From the pyramids of Egypt and the Americas to Stonehenge, cosmic signposts still survive today that provide an insight into our ancient ancestors, suggesting these structures were built by civilizations that were far from primitive. However, despite our best estimations, we can only guess at why these monuments were placed and what they are really trying to say.

The living lore of the Vedic tradition has preserved vital records of previous civilizations in a sacred history that dates back into the mists of our origins. Records carved not of stone but etched into the minds of vessels fit to carry them over the ocean of time. This history states that world cycles are inextricably tied to the dharma type, showing how the dharma type describes not only the life span of individual personalities but the life span of Earth itself over ages that range from thousands to millions of years. It describes a gradual *devolution* of civilization that is marked by the higher and lower qualities of the four basic types. For example the Silver Age is associated with the higher Warrior qualities of truth and honor, while the Bronze Age takes on the Warrior's lower qualities of violence and power.

While the spirit of the archetypes states that everyone is created equal, the Vedic record informs us that there is a natural cycle of ages during which each type successively becomes important in dictating the tenor of the age by virtue of its relevance to society. For example during the first, or Golden Age, there is an emphasis on peace, harmony, and spirituality. Societies are small, and Educators take an active role in creating and organizing an idyllic order. In a Golden Age Educators rise to prime importance, though every dharma type tends to follow its dharma and there is little conflict, misunderstanding, or jealousy. Instead people lift up and support each other by the natural dispensation of their duties. All are anchored to their purpose and work together to attain the highest personal, social, and spiritual virtues. This is a Garden of Eden in which people walk hand in hand with their Creator, and Educators are revered for their ability to interpret the word of Spirit for the benefit of all.

In a Golden Age people are longer lived, healthier, and more tuned in to spiritual values. From the Bible to the Vedas we see references to a distant past in which people lived for hundreds, even thousands of years, in communion with Spirit and Nature. Yet the actual duration of these ages is hotly debated. For example, from 4,800 to 1,728,000 years are allotted to the Golden Age by different sources.* And though there is a case to be made for each of these, we propose the figures in table 1.1 (page 34) as the most useful to the purposes of the dharma types. That is not to say that larger or smaller timelines are not correct, but that a reckoning in the millions of years describes events that are beyond the scope of this book to detail. By moving the decimal point two places we get a timeline that is more relevant to the human experience on this planet. Most authorities agree that today we are in the Iron or Dark Age, in Sanskrit called the Kali Yuga. This yuga is said to have begun in the third millennium BCE, remarkably close to the beginning of another now well-known cycle: the Mayan calendar.

Though they last for thousands of years every age must end and give way to its successor, as cycles of time bring about a revolution in human consciousness. It should be noted that though these cycles describe the movement of human mores through history, they are also closely connected to Earth's movement through space. It is likely that the great ages are caused by Earth's relationship to its greater galactic home and reflect cosmic as much as personal phenomena. As Earth moves through its cosmic shadow it becomes successively darker and darker, until it reemerges into the light of another Golden Age. As the saying goes, "As above, so below." Ultimately the full story that links what is above and below is known only to those ancient *rishis* (sages) who passed down the chaturyuga concept to mankind. Time and space are mysteries that become fully realized only in the consciousness of the enlightened seer.

---

*The former figure comes from Dr. David Frawley via Sri Yukteswar, famed guru of Paramahansa Yogananda. The larger is the more readily accepted number referenced in Sanskrit texts. However, for our purposes it is less than ideal since cycles of millions of years hardly describe the human career *as we know it*, and they are difficult to relate to on a modern human scale. Our figures move the decimal point two places to make them relevant to a discussion of the dharma types, thus maintaining the numerological essence of the figures (the number 9, base nine numerals are mystical) while adapting them to our proximal history. Thus, 1,728,000 years become 17,280 years. For more on Dr. Frawley's unique reckoning of the ages, visit www.vedanet.com.

TABLE 1.1. FOUR AGES AND THE DHARMA TYPES

AGE	SANSKRIT NAME	DHARMA TYPE AND QUALITIES	DURATION*
Golden Age	Satya Yuga	Higher Educator Qualities: peace, religiosity	17,280 years
Silver Age	Treta Yuga	Higher Warrior Qualities: justice, organization, law	12,960 years
Bronze Age	Dvapara Yuga	Lower Warrior and Merchant Qualities: dominion, power	8,640 years
Iron or Dark Age	Kali Yuga	Lower Merchant, Laborer, and Outsider Qualities: materialism, greed, depravity	4,320 years

*Total duration of one Great Cycle is 43,200 years. After this time the ages repeat again; thus after the Kali Yuga the Golden Age, or Satya Yuga, begins anew.

It was these rishis who organized society in a distant Golden Age many thousands of years ago. That is the role of the Educator—to teach, inspire, and guide, while seeking inspiration from above. But as societies grow and become increasingly complex, and able hands are needed to keep public order, Warriors gradually step forward to seize the reins from Educators. This is the dawn of the Silver Age, when divinely appointed Warrior heroes take control of an ever growing culture whose complexity is beyond the Educator's energy to manage. Truth, honor, and purity become ideals, and though the Educator still commands respect it is the kings and heroes of the world who take center stage. Educators prefer to give maxims to people and remove themselves from the fray. In the Silver Age they appoint Warriors as their successors to justly enforce order and carry out the precepts of Natural Law. Educators pass down their supernal wisdom and the right to rule to Warrior kings—here is the myth of the ideal king and his guru like Rama and Vashishta, or Arthur and Merlin, the pure-hearted knight and his erudite counsel. Whatever the tradition and geography, Silver Ages are ruled by Warrior types whose job is to sacrifice themselves for the good of the community they are sworn to protect.

In the period that follows, the Bronze Age, Warriors continue to rule but instead of honor and virtue their ideal becomes power and possession. As societies become ever more wealthy and materialistic Warriors are challenged to hold on to their power by the increasing strength of the Merchant class. Warriors are not naturally inclined toward making societies profitable; their role is to protect people and enforce justice. When the complexity of society exceeds their ability to keep up they are tempted to seize power by the only means they know—force. Thus in a Bronze Age we see a struggle between Merchants and Warriors, with the latter prevailing as dictators and tyrants. Now, instead of exalting the divine right of kings, petty Warriors succumb to the lure of greed and enact through violence a revolution of "might is right." Kings make good their claims to kingship by violence, not wisdom. And though vestiges remain of the Silver Age, great valor and terrific exploits go hand in hand with terrorism and murder as warlords become the rulers of a Bronze Age. The Vedic epic Mahabharata recounts the events of the last war of the Bronze Age, and how all the rules of conduct in battle were abrogated by both sides in order to attain victory. This is a foreshadowing of the current age in which dharma is least protected, and the virtues of good conduct are all but forsaken.

> **"In Kali Yuga property alone will confer rank; wealth will be the only source of devotion; passion will be the sole bond of union between the sexes . . . and women will be objects merely of sensual gratification."**
>
> FROM THE *VISHNU PURANA*

The selfish thirst for name, fame, and possessions naturally degenerates into the final period of a Dark or Iron Age in which Merchants finally overtake Warriors, and all hell breaks loose upon the earth. In an Iron Age Merchant clout overwhelms Warrior might and money prevails over brute strength to rule. But because ruling and organizing society is not the dharma of a Merchant type the other classes also revolt, and their lower traits become evident as materialism, greed, and profanity become the norm. Since its inception these qualities have ruled the Kali Yuga, but with the advent of the industrial era in the last two centuries there has been a rapid acceleration of production and commerce, increasing the importance of the Merchant to the world. As a result the past century has generated a powerful Merchant society, whose values are primarily *economic*, not *ecumenical*. With possession (wealth) as the foremost virtue, social order has become skewed to favor any concept that has profit potential and to reject such goods and information that do not. While this has favored a few, most people have had to conform themselves to a system that does not promote their highest good. In *The Marriage of Heaven and Hell* William Blake, living at the inception of the industrial era, cried, "One law for the lion and the ox is oppression."

In chapter 14 we will discover what promotes personal growth for each type in its profession. For the Merchant, fulfillment comes from enjoying and sharing the resources of the world with others, including wealth and luxury. These are fine goals that serve the purpose of the Merchant, who works very hard to attain them. But when they are systematically imposed on every type a kind of tyranny is born out of which only a few types find happiness, while the rest struggle to adapt and survive. Unlike the tyranny in the age before, this does not emanate from one person, a king, but is systemized throughout society. From the South Pacific to the Americas its effects can be seen in aboriginal societies where "work" used to take up no more than four to five hours of the day. The rest of the time was devoted to self-development, family, leisure, and rest. Perhaps that is one reason that aboriginal cultures—those anchored to older sacred traditions—have had a hard time integrating into Merchant society. Such hours are almost laughable today and hardly make up a part-time schedule, much less an adequate schema for full-time employment.

Today the Merchant system is designed to keep most people occupied with securing their welfare—paying the mortgage and feeding their kids while taking their rest when they can—rather than promoting self-study, play, and family time. Perhaps this is why we are so fierce about being entertained in today's America. From the largest big-screen 3-D, HD, LCD TVs to the most outrageous displays of weekend party heartiness it is almost as if we are trying to catch up on the leisure and self-cultivation we miss by stuffing it into the few remaining hours we have. This is also why we like weekend seminars and quick fixes: we don't have time for anything more. And although we are rewarded with many kinds of entertainment as a release from the stress of the long days we slog through to provide for our families, these must also be paid for, which continues the cycle of spending and earning, earning and spending.

> **"The only problem with capitalism . . . is the capitalists."**
> **HERBERT HOOVER**

While the Merchant system is not inherently evil, it is ill suited to the just rule of people and society. When it becomes inextricably woven with government, as discussed in chapter 9, iniquities are born that provoke environmental and humanitarian calamities. What promotes profit does not necessarily encourage safe working conditions, what improves productivity does not advance personal freedoms—in fact, it is usually the contrary. As a result Merchants do not make the best political leaders. This is not out of any deficiency, as Merchants are great material benefactors of society when well evolved. But a system built to maximize profit and production does not see the need to optimize human rights, environmental sustainability, and equitable relations with its neighbors. We have but to look at the wars and abuses that owe their existence to issues of ownership as proof of this. The lust for sugar, diamonds, oil, gold—and now paper money—has drained the blood and sweat of billions, yet this thirst remains unquenched.

The Vedic system takes another road: it shows separate avenues of fulfillment for each of the five dharma types and allows each one to express freely without detracting from the others. It teaches how society must be run for the optimal integration of its constituents. When each type evolves it becomes a boon to its neighbors. This way the competition for resources that characterizes the material world becomes obsolete, as there is enough money, success, truth, happiness, and excitement to go around for every type according to its nature.

PAST AND PRESENT

Wisdom, justice, power, and greed reflect the four yugas. But just because a Golden Age is more pure than a Silver does not make Educators superior to Warriors, Warriors to Merchants, and so on down the line. Readers should not construe the sequence of the ages as a hierarchy of one type over another. When a dharma type expresses itself at the highest level it enacts qualities of the Satya Yuga regardless of where and when in history it might be. Later we'll explore how everything from music styles to political systems correlate with individual archetypes; for now we have matched them with the yugas because their lower and higher qualities best reflect the tenor of their age.

Whatever we decide about their duration, the ages eventually revolve so that after the Kali Yuga there again follows another Golden

Age of truth and wisdom, though it may be preceded by a time of great tribulation—there is always upheaval before regeneration, death before rebirth. When such a period is likely to recur is a matter of debate. Experts differ on the timing of sacred history and some even believe that such changes are due in our lifetime, but whatever the case it is the purpose of the dharma types to align us with our higher destinies. This way we are ready to receive them, and should nothing change, we continue to live our highest truth.

> **"Educator" is a universal term, and it belongs as much to India as to Indiana, to Amritsar as to America: what makes one a given dharma type is one's natural disposition thereto, *not* a cultural or familial milieu.**

CONCLUSION

Here is a summary of each type: Educators are the designated teachers, though they are not really meant to rule or enforce policy. They are also referred to as sages, priests, or philosophers. In India they are called Brahmins, though to call an Educator a Brahmin is to limit him or her to the socio-political caste system of India, and the abuses that go along with it. "Educator" is a universal term, and it belongs as much to India as to Indiana, to Amritsar as to America: what makes one a given dharma type is one's natural disposition thereto, *not* a cultural or familial milieu. Likewise the other members of India's system—the *kshatriya, vaishya, shudra,* and *mleccha* castes—are regional designations that correspond to but do not define the remaining four dharma types, though the types draw much of their livelihood and original spirit from them.

The dharmic archetypes also differ from the caste systems of India and the world because they are not hierarchical or inherited. The intermixture of people in a modern global society makes it impossible to determine dharma type by heredity, or to class a person above or below another. At one time heredity influenced dharma type; blood succession was important in the Golden and Silver ages when being born to a Warrior assuredly made one a Warrior. However, in the ages that followed, heredity became less and less of an indicator and more of a liability in determining dharma type. These days, with people mixing freely in democratic societies, it is almost absurd to believe that simply being born to a Laborer *has* to make one a Laborer. Bloodlines have "thinned," and what makes one a particular type is more complicated than simply looking at his or her parents. People carry the genetics of many generations, and therefore the possible influence of many dharma types.

The rules that applied to the Golden or Silver ages do not work in the Iron Age. From the Bible to the Vedas, injunctions that applied 5,000 years ago may no longer be relevant today. While the spirit of Natural Law remains the same, its exercise must be modified to fit the times we live in: we have to recognize what is useful and reject what no longer works. The dharma types differ from their correlates in older societies in the following ways:

1. **Nonheritable**

   Your dharma type is set at birth, remains with you for the rest of your life, but is *not* indicated by your parents. It can be deduced from your Vedic Life Map or the Self Tests in the introduction of this book. A person's individual karma is the reason he or she is born a particular type, and in the current age that does not have to match the parental archetype.

2. **Nonhierarchical**

   All dharma types have equal rights as citizens, though each has a unique path to tread in living out its destiny. No restrictions, discrimination, or prejudice with regard to profession, marriage, or religion are consistent with this system—though some types match better in love and business. Enlightenment is available to everyone and joy, life, and happiness are as much birthrights of Educators as Outsiders. No one has a stranglehold on truth, and no one controls the means to self-realization and fulfillment.

Educators are born in slums and in palaces; Laborers can deck the halls of the White House as well as the charnel house.

3. Nontransferable

One cannot, through work alone, become a different dharma type (see number one above). The quality and quantity of your work can determine how well you live out the dharma of your type, but it cannot change it into another. Some of us, especially in America where opportunities abound, think that with enough effort anything is possible. While this may be true, effort must be tempered with wisdom to produce really desirable results. Knowledge of your dharma type is the foremost of such wisdom, as it is self-knowledge. "Know thyself" is the first directive, following which all things can be known.

Karma determines the dharma type—how well we fulfill our destiny depends on free will and personal merit; it is not subject to advantages or disadvantages gained by being a specific archetype. We all start at pole position, at different places on the line. It is how we drive the race that determines our position at the end. It is our inherent talents that dictate who we are, not socio-economic status, birthplace, sex, or race, though all of these color our individual expression. What makes us superior people is the degree to which we have actualized ourselves within the constructs of our dharma type. There are excellent as well as despicable Educators, Merchants, Warriors, Laborers, and Outsiders alike.

This must be true if we are to have any respect for the system—and for it to work today. Prejudice, bigotry, and dominance of one class over another are perversions of ancient wisdom that cannot stand if these archetypes are to be used in their true spirit. In fact, they serve to *eliminate* bigotry by cultivating knowledge and respect for everyone. To fully evolve your type you must understand the others and allow them to evolve themselves. This symbiotic system mirrors the vital operations of Nature, in which one entity feeds another, which feeds the first in turn.

Just as plants nourish us by dying, and we feed them upon our death, and just as we breathe their oxygen while exhaling carbon dioxide for them to breathe, so one type promotes the success of another by its natural operation. It is not a question of *competition,* but of *cooperation.*

The Warrior class rules, protects, and dispenses law and order. Educators give meaning to life, inspiring others with wisdom and good counsel. Merchants enjoy growing society and directing the flow of goods and services, while the Laborer class produces and consumes these goods and services. The Outsider completes the picture as the social misfit and most able commentator on society's ills. Also called rebels, innovators, or revolutionaries, Outsiders are the shadow side of every type and are not bound by rules in the way the other dharma types are. Now let us take a look at each of them in detail as we explore the permutations of what it means to be a dharma type in today's world.

2

Educator

Enlighten Others

Compassion • Wisdom • Self-Control

Famous Educators

(based on birth data and their Vedic Life Map)

Joan Allen

Woody Allen*

Richard Dean Anderson

Alexander Graham Bell

Tony Blair

Michael Bolton

Joseph Campbell*

Jimmy Carter

Julia Child*

David Copperfield

Geena Davis

Robert Dole

---

*Names followed by an asterisk are Outsiders finding their best expression playing another type. More on this appears in chapter 6.

Bob Dylan*

Albert Einstein

T. S. Eliot

Gustave Flaubert

Mohandas Gandhi

Judy Garland

Bill Gates*

Billy Graham*

John Irving

George Lucas*

Marilyn Manson*

Alanis Morissette*

Moses

Barack Obama

Parasurama

Carl Sagan

Martin Sheen

Sir Philip Sidney

Tiger Woods

---

*Names followed by an asterisk are Outsiders finding their best expression playing another type. More on this appears in chapter 6.

Educators, as the name implies, make the best teachers. Whatever their profession they have a natural inclination to transfer information and enrich people with knowledge. It is also their role to give meaning and purpose to life and inspire others with wisdom and good counsel. They do not have to be actual teachers to do so. For example, famous Educators teach the public about their individual causes from the platform of their celebrity. From nonviolent protests to environmental causes and world peace they spread education through their medium, each in their own unique way.

The most intellectually curious of the types, Educators like to read and learn about the world—their curious minds are always at work, and they also delight in games and pastimes to keep them sharp. From Scrabble and Sudoku to crossword puzzles and chess, Educators love games that challenge and occupy their brains.

> **Like the air that gives us life the Educator gives breath to the endeavors of every type by filling them with knowledge and wisdom.**

Educators may also quench their curiosity by learning a little bit about many things. At the root of this desire to learn is a strong interest in self-help, improving their condition as well as the conditions of those around them. Whether investigating Newton's physics or New Age philosophy Educators seek ways to better themselves and their world. Because they are also more sensitive than other types they tend to live for ideals and are driven more by ideas than money, seeking sophistication rather than security. At the root of the word *sophistication* is *sophos,* the Greek word for "to become wise." Ultimately their inner wisdom benefits society as the fruits of their labor eventually come out to serve humanity.

Without meaning life perishes, but with purpose and hope people can survive life's hardships and embrace its blessings. It is the Educator's role to find and share that meaning and inspire hope in others. Although Educators are not physically imposing, their counsel can be a powerful force—Merchants cannot sell, Warriors fight, Laborers work, or Outsiders rebel if they don't know what they are living for, fighting for, working for, or rebelling against. In whatever guise, be it astronomer or philosopher, the Educator's gift is to help others fulfill their dharma. From Carl Sagan, who taught a whole generation to look up and wonder at the mysteries of the cosmos, to Julia Child, who encouraged millions to discover the joy of cooking, like the air that gives us life the Educator gives breath to the endeavors of every type by filling them with knowledge and wisdom.

Every class excels in certain areas, but no type is as well rounded as the Educator. They tend to know a little bit about everything and are the Renaissance men and women of the dharma type family. Educators also represent the civilizing force of society, and their contributions come as much from philosophy as from politics, from science as from science fiction. Their liberality of experience makes them able teachers and provides an ideal model for education.

While no one is better at teaching than the teachers, Educators do not always follow what they preach. They can become poor role models when they fail to walk the walk and do as they say. Perhaps because it is so easy for them to grasp concepts intellectually they do not take the time to master and own them in their core. As a result, they may espouse grand ideals but still be at odds with their animal passions. They may hold others to standards they themselves cannot keep. Here is a case for a priest who, despite great work on the pulpit, succumbs to lust and fornication; a politician whose efforts for peace are tainted by shady deals and bribes; a coach who cannot perform the tasks she asks of her athletes; or a general who cannot stand up to the same standards asked of his soldiers. We see this all too often in media exposés of our stars and senators alike. From Woody Allen to Tiger Woods, Educators often fall from grace because of sexual impropriety. The seemingly reserved Educator holds a powerful sexual center that needs to be properly channeled to remain an exemplar of virtue.

When the Educators we trust to embody high character fail us, they not only disappoint themselves, but the world they are supposed to inspire with purpose and meaning is let down as well. Instead of enlightening people, they darken their own reputations.

A Vedic story expresses this poignantly. When Brahma—creator god and Educator archetype of the Vedic pantheon—created the universe, he marveled at its beauty but was unable to articulate its many wonders. To do so he created the goddess Sarasvati, patron of speech, language, art, and culture. So breathtaking was she that he became infatuated with her beauty, growing heads in every direction in order to constantly behold her. Deeming his lust inappropriate for a patriarch she rebuked him, cursing him as an inadequate object of worship for having succumbed to longing and desire. As a result to this day Brahma has only two temples in all of India, whereas even minor deities enjoy dozens, hundreds, even thousands of shrines! This is a cautionary tale for Educators everywhere, who when they descend into lust lose the respect of those they serve, and their rightful place in society.

In order to learn children must have optimal stimulation through various channels, including kinesthetic (sport), artistic (music, art, theater), linguistic (language), and reasoning (math, science) media. This allows all of the learning channels of the human mind to be tuned to receive universal wisdom. When we shut ourselves down to one or two modes of learning we become as limited and boring as that old television with the rabbit-ear antennae. Education systems that do away with music and art, or sports and leisure, deprive students of the developmental benefits these activities afford. This is particularly true for children under age ten, whose minds are particularly malleable and benefit from a wide range of learning stimuli.

> **Conscience is strong in Educators; they must turn it into consciousness in order to prevent transgressing in the first place.**

Even though children under age ten have the best chance of learning languages and skills that then become second nature, our learning never really stops. Modern research shows that the brain has remarkable abilities to repair itself and continue forging new links analogous with learning well into old age. Therefore it is as vital to form the young in a way that assists them in taking the right first steps in life as it is to show the old how to make their final steps with grace. This can be accomplished through an integrated education that includes every available and effective form of learning, from youth to maturity and well into old age.

Vedic societies developed these methods into their ultimate forms of expression. Sanskrit, the ancient Vedic language, literally means "perfected, polished," and it represents an optimal arrangement of sound and meaning that orders the consciousness of the person who studies it—literally teaching a person to *think*. In much the same way hatha yoga and classical dance arrange the subtle and gross structures of the body for maximal *physical* integration, teaching the body how to move. Ayurveda, sthapatya veda, gandharva veda,* and the many other sciences of the Vedic canon also instruct us how to taste, see, hear, and function in the world by ordering the sense pathways employed in studying them. It is important for any civilized culture to have an educational matrix that fosters well-rounded development. Societies lacking this show low respect for Educators and what they stand for, and ultimately doom themselves to ignorance and rigidity.

INSTANT KARMA

Students cannot learn from someone they do not trust. As priests and counselors of the dharma type family Educators naturally inspire respect in others; people feel they can confide in Educators and see a seriousness in them that makes them trustworthy. They may not be cool or entertaining, but when it comes to matters of importance people turn to Educators for help. This sometimes even escapes Educators themselves, though they would do well not to make light of the trust and esteem with which people hold them. A telling characteristic of Educators is that when they *do* transgress, their karma usually follows instantly. They are likely to suffer the consequences of actions quickly; they will also experience extreme remorse for them. From stepping on a snail to sleeping with another's spouse, many Educators subject themselves to extreme punishment for their missteps, even to the point of suicide. Conscience is strong

---

*The art and science of health (ayurveda); architecture and placement (sthapatya veda); and music (gandharva veda). Sacred cultures around the world teach forms of dance and movement, such as hula (Polynesia) or belly dance (in the Near East), but none are as systemized and developed as in the Vedic traditions.

in Educators; they must turn it into consciousness in order to prevent transgressing in the first place. Being constantly aware of their natures, and of their place in society as the standard-bearers of virtue and trust, they must learn to express their passions appropriately.

> Whether teaching about God or just third-grade math, the Educator must convey Truth by getting out of the way of the message.

Lacking the natural decisiveness of the Warrior type, Educators are meant not to rule over others but to advise and cultivate harmony in themselves and the world. "Give peace a chance" is an Educator mantra, and while they can make excellent leaders in times of need, with great power comes temptation. When Educators co-opt their authority for selfish purposes they lose out in the long run, never attaining the high peaks to which they aspire but instead suffering the pits of infamy and shame for subverting their dharma. The best Educators are those who surrender their own agendas to promote the values for which they stand. Like Gandhi or Moses, who were classic Educators, they are governed by a higher truth so that even when they lead it is not of their own bidding but of a supernal authority that supersedes them. Their role is to set the codes and standards in society, and to live by them as well. They accomplish this by the sincere pursuit of surrender.

SURRENDER

No one understands the value of surrender better than the Educator. Surrender to the creative forces of the universe is a key element for Educators' growth, and the means by which they are able to teach others. From surrender comes a deep level of detachment from material desire. Detachment allows Educators to bear the burdens of karma without the need to fight. Instead their fight is internal, opening up and appealing to the inner Self for help and sustenance. This practice requires sincerity. In the process of going within, Educators are faced with their failings and impure desires, which must be transcended if they are to succeed in becoming models for society.

Educators must surrender their own lives in order to allow Truth to flow through them. Like a vessel that delivers clear water to the thirsty, they must be empty in order to fulfill their purpose. Educators are uniquely equipped to do this. Grade-school teachers surrender their own need for adult company in order to teach when they step through the door of their classroom, living their lives for their pupils. An Educator cannot be a teacher by letting personal priorities, desires, or fixations get in the way of his or her primary purpose, which is to enlighten. Surrender is the means whereby the Educator becomes a vehicle for Natural Law. Whether teaching about God or just third-grade math, the Educator must convey Truth by getting out of the way of the message.

Information contrived by the small self, the individual mind, is inferior to what is inspired from above. The greatest art, science, and knowledge materialize when our petty needs are set aside for a moment. Whether in the shower, in meditation, or at a mountain retreat, those instants when our mind steps away to graciously allow the higher Self to speak are truly divine, and result in betterment for everyone. The same surrender that makes the Educator meek has the potential to inspire armies and change history. The same surrender that allows Educators to do with little can sustain a civilization. Through a fortuitous array of words and notes on paper, a poem or a song can move and inspire millions. In the same way the Educator, though dependent on others for survival, can support the species by feeding it knowledge, truth, and wisdom.

Every type relies on its skills for protection in early life. The Laborer has toughness, the Merchant cleverness, the Warrior strength, the Outsider adaptability. But Educators' usefulness only grows apparent with time. Because they must study in order to teach, a great part of their lives is dedicated to learning. Therefore Educators begin slowly and only mature in the middle and later part of their lives, when learning has led to wisdom, and wisdom begins to emanate from them like charm from Merchants or power from Warriors. In the beginning of life they are fragile, lacking the skills of the other types to protect them. Even when they appear robust and healthy they are usually not so, being sensitive and vulnerable physically, save that knowledge is their power and wisdom their strength. Like the printed word that is quick to perish, Educators' bodies fade with time, but their message can sustain the world for centuries.

Emmet Fox describes the Educator's path of surrender as:

A combination of open-mindedness, faith in God, and the realization that the Will of God for us is always something joyous and interesting and vital, and much better than anything we could think of for ourselves.[1]

This does not mean that all Educators are believers in God. In fact what some call God others term science, justice, humanity, truth—ideals that govern and inspire Educators' lives and never cease to fill them with wonder, appreciation, and the drive to know more. Carl Sagan struggled to understand these ideals by searching the mysteries of outer space. Joseph Campbell, an Outsider playing an Educator, did it by exploring the myths that move our *inner* lives. At their best Educators are uniquely capable of tapping into higher thought and teaching dharma to the masses. Their effort can express itself through any medium and applies to atheists and evangelists alike. Some pursue Truth through science, others through art, still others through social causes, medicine, academia, and so on. Truth has many faces and speaks in many voices.

The key to determine whether we have been successful in surrendering is the effect this has on us—are we able to demonstrate greater compassion and wisdom, or do we just play the part of a meek Educator while harboring petty envy, pride, and anger inside? The circumstances of our lives reveal the answer. Are we better able to relate with our loved ones and contribute more in work? Do we have an undeniably beneficent effect on people and places around us? Do we leave people with more wisdom, compassion, and peace after knowing us than before? If the answer to these questions is "Yes!" then we are indeed on our path as Educators. In every way and in every moment Educators are exemplars of virtue—what virtue we model depends upon our evolution and wisdom.

MONEY

Merchant society does not value wisdom as highly as goods and services. People prefer to be entertained rather than educated; that is why Educators usually earn less than Merchants. Teachers, scientists, and clergy are paid a moiety of what salesmen and business types make. Unless their wisdom is particularly useful to the Merchant society it is not the lot of Educators to be wealthy. The Educator's goal is not *emolument* but *enlightenment*. Educators must be content with what is given to them in a Merchant world without haggling or fighting for it. If they are rewarded with wealth for wisdom, ducats for dharma, that is a blessing they must accept; but money for its own sake is not the best pursuit for Educators.

In fact, Educators often begged for their food in ancient societies. Things are not so different today when we consider that scientists and scholars beg for grants, public radio and television stations hold pledge drives to stay on the air, priests pass the collection plates to feed their ministry, and teachers hold bake sales to raise funds for their projects and field trips. It is natural for Educators to earn their keep by the strength of their wisdom and the charity of the public that it benefits. Their cause earns them their compensation. As the Bible says:

> *Take nothing for the journey except a staff—no bread, no bag, no money in your belts.*
>
> MARK 6:8

This reality has always been the Educator's dharma, and remains so even to this day.

PATH TO DEVOLUTION
Laborer

One of the ways to get the most out of your type is to follow its path of evolution and avoid its path of devolution. This basic relationship outlines the way each archetype harmonizes into the best it can be, as well as how it can self-destruct, and shall be called upon often in this book. Therefore it is important to memorize the evolution/devolution pairs in table 2.1.

For example, Educators do well to take on qualities from the Warrior and to avoid qualities from the Laborer type. Merchants do well to adopt Laborer traits and avoid going down the Warrior's track. Every type evolves into one type and devolves into another. This does not mean they *become* the other type. Instead, points of evolution and devolution show us the path each type must follow for optimal fulfillment. Thus Educators fall apart when they follow the Laborer's road, and Laborers likewise break down when they adopt the Educator's dharma. The same is true of Warriors and Merchants. The Outsider has a special path, which we'll explore in a moment. These designations will become clear as we take a look at how they work.

TABLE 2.1. EVOLUTION AND DEVOLUTION OF THE DHARMA TYPES*

MUTUAL DEVOLUTION	MUTUAL EVOLUTION
Warrior—Merchant	Warrior—Educator
Laborer—Educator	Merchant—Laborer
Outsider—All	Outsider—All

*Though certain dharma types evolve into each other, they never *become* another type. Instead, by taking on qualities of their complementary type, they become the best they can be.

Educators devolve when they become "stuck" in a particular way of being. Fixity and endurance are qualities of the Laborer, and they are good for the malleable Merchant personality that benefits from structure, but when Educators sacrifice their eclectic nature to become dogmatically fixated on anything they devolve, losing inspiration and multiplying frustration. Sitting too long in front of a research paper, a math problem, or a religious conundrum only increases stagnation of the body and mind. By incorporating the Warrior's movement Educators revitalize their minds and energy and return to face their problems with new solutions. Stagnation breaks down the body; movement inspires and heals it.

> **"One's own dharma, even devoid of merit, is preferable to the dharma of another though well-performed. Even death in the performance of your dharma brings blessedness; another's dharma is fraught with anxiety."**
> **BHAGAVAD GITA 3:35**

Educators need to move, play, and be inspired so that they in turn can inspire the world. But sometimes they are forced to get "real" jobs in order to pay the rent and survive in Merchant society, which restricts their ability to move freely. This eventually results in a decline in the ethics by which society itself lives because the people best suited to teach and inspire them are busy doing jobs they were not meant to do. This is not to say that Educators cannot benefit from integrating practical skills into their daily lives, but that preoccupation with nondharmic activity detracts from their basic purpose. And when Educators are deprived of meaningful employment everyone to whom Educators give meaning will also be damaged. In short, when Educators devolve, all society suffers.

When Educators becomes salespeople or day laborers they still benefit by learning from and serving others, but these activities do not represent the full complement of their talents—and their best qualities remain dormant. We must make full use of our inborn faculties or risk short-selling ourselves the success we deserve. Besides, Educators are usually not as good at manual professions as other types. Physical dexterity and endurance are not strong suits of the Educator type, and employers generally do not get what they pay for when they hire Educators for these jobs. In the words of Wayne Dyer, Educators should "get paid by the idea, not by the hour."

Being the Renaissance men or women of the dharma type family, Educators need to learn a little bit about everyone, but when they move too far in the direction of the Laborer personality they begin to lose their objectivity. When Educators localize themselves by education, upbringing, or culture—believing that they are their Ph.D., job position, or ethnicity—they lose creativity and begin to stagnate. When credentials become a source of pride, and accomplishments are subject to monetary reward, Educators can become part of the nine-to-five Merchant machine that seeks only what's best for itself. The true mark of the Educator is her ability not to climb the social ladder, but to elevate the culture of her world and enrich society with knowledge. It is by how much he can help others, not himself, that the Educator is recognized by his peers. The quality of the person, not the paper his or her name is printed on, is what makes an Educator indispensable.

Merchant society has pushed Educators to sell their knowledge in order to survive, and while this has made some Educators fabulously rich and free to pursue their dharma, it has made information itself a commodity subject to the highest bidder. Where this goes wrong is easy to see when we examine the ease with which people can acquire potentially dangerous knowledge, such as how to blow up buildings or hijack airplanes. Knowledge in the wrong hands can lead to disaster. We have seen this even in the subversion of simple spiritual teachings by our major religions: when people do not understand sacred principles, and wisdom fails to erase ignorance, we see the birth of inquisitions and holy wars, ethnic cleansings and the rape of society. A little knowledge is a dangerous thing; it becomes even more so when it is put up for sale.

> **"Science is a wonderful thing if one does not have to earn one's living at it."**
>
> ALBERT EINSTEIN

Traditionally, higher teachings were only imparted to those deemed fit to receive them. Like a weapon, information is dangerous in the hands of those not morally and intellectually equipped to handle it. In older societies every class held its proprietary secrets and passed them on to the next generation of craftsmen, reformers, soldiers, priests, and merchants. This was not so much to hide valuable insights from others but to protect the naive from inflicting harm on themselves and their environment. Today one need only look at the Internet to see examples of inappropriate information commodity.

Another danger of prostituting information is more subtle, but just as pernicious. A preoccupation with marketing and self-promotion in the interest of purveying information leads to attachment and greed and can distract Educators from their purpose—which is not to maintain fiscal solvency, but to increase knowledge and awareness in the world. Galileo was a respected Educator but could barely make ends meet until he invented the telescope. Educators are often forced to create out of their wisdom something valuable to the Merchant culture in order to survive. This is okay as long as it supports their work, but when Educators devote inordinate amounts of time to their own prosperity, they begin to devolve and move away from their purpose.

Educators prefer the ivory tower to the hustle and bustle of the market bazaar. They need alone time in meditation in order to "download" higher information for their society. They may toil in isolation or oblivion for long stretches until the fruits of their efforts see the light of day. Bill Gates opted for his own garage over the lofty Harvard halls when it came to the pursuit of his ideas. Albert Einstein preferred his post at the Swiss patent office to a teaching position, for university life, as he said, would have kept him busy churning out trivial papers and teaching a rigid curriculum that inspired only mechanistic thinking.

This was anathema for the free-spirited thinker for whom ideas were more valuable than grades, and who regularly skipped class in order to pursue his thought experiments.

Einstein detested the regimentation characteristic of schools in Germany, and the tyranny of one system for every student. Such rigid, mindless discipline may appear to be a Warrior quality but is in fact an example of an education model restricted by Laborer mentality. Good teachers know that they must adapt their lessons to the varied learning styles of their students. Thoughtless discipline ignores the needs of people and inspires repression; thoughtful discipline encourages evolution and expression. A mindless adherence to the letter of the law is an example of Educator-Laborer devolution. A vigorous and judicious interpretation of the spirit of a law is an example of Educator-Warrior evolution.

PATH TO EVOLUTION
Warrior

Educators evolve into the Warrior class because the Warrior's self-motivation and pursuit of excellence are qualities Educators do well to emulate. Like Educators, Warriors are not primarily motivated by money—though in many respects Warriors and Educators are also opposites, attracting those traits in each other that balance them and make them better. For example, the Educator's ability to surrender is contrasted by the Warrior's never-say-die attitude; the Educator's compassion is juxtaposed to the Warrior's forcefulness.

Sometimes it is hard for Educators to behave in a way consistent with their own ideals. They know the rules but don't always feel that the rules apply to them. They know better but succumb to depravity nonetheless. Warriors on the other hand have the discipline and character to follow and obey orders, which is why Educators do best to integrate certain core Warrior traits into their personalities—it is easy for them to slip up and succumb to temptation. Money, sex, and power constantly beckon the Educator, whose greatest challenge is to control the senses and overcome the lure of baser instincts. Educators must rise up to take their place as leaders of virtue by example. Their great calling is to inspire the masses—with words and ideas, certainly, but even more than these by their own comportment. Educators' *behaviors* set the standard for society. Those who cannot understand their ideas can see by their actions what needs to be done. Those who cannot hear their words can observe their lives and model their own according to this example. Those who do not have the time to learn an Educator's ideology can nonetheless respect his or her exploits by learning about the individual. Gandhi is one such example. Stories of people living and dying for their principles sometimes inspire more than the principles themselves! Such is the Educator's gift, and it is served by harmonizing with the Warrior type.

Educators can sometimes be too smart for their own good. Because they grasp concepts more quickly than others they can become bored and lazy and never learn the value of work. Being too smart can lead to a poor work ethic wherein Educators learn to rely on their intellect rather than self-effort. They can lose heart quickly when they encounter obstacles, or become heartless toward others. But when Educators integrate the Warrior's courage and self-deterministic attitude, they become idealists *and* effective instruments of virtue.

When Educators become locked into a socially acceptable "good" persona at the cost of denying their sensual impulses they can become polarized—their outward social image may become more and more distant from their inner passions and desires. When their vital energies, including their sexual impulses, are not allowed to properly express they become repressed. Over time, repression turns to perversion. To counter this, involvement in Warrior activities like yoga, dance, sport, and other forms of guided movement allows Educators to express passion without turning it into perversion. Then, the priests and senators of the world become exemplars of virtue rather than polarized personalities who express one persona on the surface while harboring an altogether different character in secret.

In chapter 8 we will learn about the different forms of exercise appropriate for each dharma type. For the Educator exercise is a vital component of a comprehensive approach that integrates movement, leisure, meditation, work, and study. When physical stimulation is taken out of the equation Educators lose out on the inspiration this provides and become stuck in their intellect, fantasy, and ideas. When whites first arrived in Australia the aboriginal people saw them as "walking heads," disengaged from their bodies and disconnected from the earth. This is a lesson for Educators, who need to exercise in order to circulate their vitality and get in touch with their bodies. The rewards they reap are an improved ability to think and a well-grounded energy that allows them to transmit their ideas and effectively relate with others. Movement and exercise promote better self-awareness and can be a blessing indeed for the sometimes clumsy and socially challenged Educators—in fact, so good is the effect on their bodies that some Educators can make their whole lives about sport, becoming coaches, trainers, and even world-class athletes!

Educators also need to continually improve their knowledge. Keeping current with the world around them can take the form of reading the daily paper, listening to news radio, or watching documentaries. Whether searching for political solutions or finding the newest way to teach algebra, the Educator's insight and love of learning is a valuable asset to students and employers alike.

> It is a brutal but patent fact for Educators that earning and learning rarely mix successfully. They need to dedicate themselves to their destiny or succumb to subpar expectations.

In fact, evolved Educators are all about self-improvement. "If you're not getting smarter, you're getting dumber; if you're not learning, you're forgetting" is a mantra for the Educator type. One is either improving or backsliding—there is little room in between. Evolved Educators are constantly engaged in questioning, discovering, and otherwise improving—frequenting the self-help aisles at bookstores and getting up to date on the latest theories in their field. Theirs is the quest for knowledge and the greatest knowledge is self-knowledge. Their obstacle is balancing mundane life with self-improvement aspirations. But earning and learning do not go together; when Educators take on the destiny of the Laborer type and devote their time to just making a living they miss the mark in a couple of ways. First, they deprive others who need to work from opportunities to do so by taking their place in the workforce. Next, they fail to develop their inherent talents, thereby depriving the world of their real gifts.

It is a brutal but patent fact for Educators that earning and learning rarely mix successfully. They need to dedicate themselves to their destiny or succumb to subpar expectations. This is not as hard as it sounds, though it does require an effort of surrender. Effort and surrender may seem like contradictory concepts, but there is enormous willpower that goes into surrendering to our real nature. Fortunately, Educators are uniquely equipped to do this as it entails the use of their inborn faculties and eventually leads them to their highest destiny.

3

Warrior

Protect Others

Courage • Discernment • Strength

Famous Warriors
(based on birth data and their Vedic Life Map)

Arthur Ashe

Fred Astaire

Boris Becker*

John Belushi

Candace Bergen*

Silvio Berlusconi

Chuck Berry*

Joe Biden

Buddha

Richard Burton

George Clooney*

Anderson Cooper

---

*Names followed by an asterisk are Outsiders finding their best expression playing another type. More on this appears in chapter 6.

Michael Crichton

James Dean*

Celine Dion

Robert Downey Jr.

Wayne Gretzky

Justine Henin

Adolf Hitler

Angelina Jolie

Kris Kristofferson*

Matt LeBlanc

Madonna

John McCain

Paul Newman

Rama

Robert Redford

Arnold Schwarzenegger

Robert Shapiro

William Shatner

Sylvester Stallone*

George Washington*

Venus Williams

---

*Names followed by an asterisk are Outsiders finding their best expression playing another type. More on this appears in chapter 6.

Because of their focus, drive, and discipline Warriors can become the most skilled of all the dharma types. They can master practically anything they set their minds to. They are self-starting, self-determining people who believe in making their own fortune in life through struggle and effort. They are fighters, and from Madonna to Arnold Schwarzenegger their decisive leadership instinct inspires others to follow them. Warriors are leaders, often becoming ambitious and relentless in their quest for power, but they may also embody this ethic in surprising ways. From a single mother fighting to feed her children to a human-aid worker fighting for the rights of hungry kids around the world, Warriors' battles take place as much on the global stage as in their own backyards. Whatever their causes evolved Warriors take the side of the innocent, those who cannot fend for themselves. Among celebrities Angelina Jolie does this as a peace ambassador for the U.N. while Robert Redford fights for the rights of independent filmmakers.

The Warrior nature naturally seeks to abide by high ideals and codes of conduct in its search for self-perfection. Warriors like to test themselves and push the boundaries of their endurance. From physical competition to mental and even spiritual challenges, Warriors set and reset the bar on what's possible. Their social role is to protect the weak, the innocent, and the helpless. They are also charged with punishing the guilty—those who willingly flout the codes and standards Warriors embody and enforce. Not surprisingly, modern-day Warriors take to professions in the armed forces, justice administration, law enforcement, and politics. They also make great firefighters, doctors, and athletes. Traditionally leaders and kings came from this class, naturally designed as they were to command and rule in the name of a perfect ideal. However, when Warriors are harnessed to a system designed to promote profit, not perfection, their ideals may become perverted and their talents enslaved to selfish ends rather than the common good. This is spiritual hell for Warriors, whose highest ideals are justice and self-sacrifice, the willingness to give their lives for a greater purpose. Not uncommonly good people entering into law and politics to better society become corrupted by this Merchant system, whence the popular association of lawyers and politicians with sharks and snakes—predatory creatures perceived to have only their own interests in mind. Consequently Warriors may become mercenaries, bought and sold by the highest bidder, rather than self-respecting models of integrity in action. More than any other type they may also become embittered by the ways of the world, succumbing to cynicism and a dog-eat-dog mentality by observing what the world does to those who cannot fend for themselves.

> **For Warriors to excel as leaders they must inspire a palpable team spirit in the people they lead, a sense of common purpose that they not only work for but also embody in everything they do.**

TEAMWORK

It is important for Warriors to have a support system of fellow Warriors and Educators to keep them from descending into cynicism and becoming mercenaries. Warriors gravitate to sports and the armed forces for this reason: there is a camaraderie and cohesiveness generated when like-minded people are subjected to extreme circumstances together. Whether on the basketball court or the battlefield, a special bond is created when Warriors band together for a common cause. This bond is a synergistic force stronger than the sum of its parts; it makes the members collectively greater than they could ever be individually.

Teamwork is evident even when Warriors are leaders or solitary functionaries. A sniper may work alone but he does so within the greater system of a trained unit, and the even greater cause of his fellow citizens and country. A president may be the Commander in Chief, but she cannot enforce policy without a huge support system of trained equals. In fact, for Warriors to excel as leaders they must inspire a palpable team spirit in the people they lead, a sense of common purpose that they not only work for but which they embody in everything they do.

Teamwork invariably helps Warriors to become more than they can ever be alone. Warriors benefit from wisdom and counsel, and the best way to receive this is through interaction with their peers. Michael Jordan was a standout superstar, but he couldn't win a championship until he was paired with a coach and fellow teammates, who provided him a structure through which to achieve greatness. A few championships later Jordan was first to acknowledge that he could not have done it without the special bond they all shared. This drive for personal excellence combined with a teamwork ethic epitomizes the Warrior spirit.

While there may be as many female as male Warrior types in society, the Warrior path has special relevance for men regardless of their individual dharma type because at a primal, biological level all men are Warriors, just as all women are Laborers. From the standpoint of evolutionary biology men express their masculinity as protectors, and women express their femininity as nurturers. Most men thrive on having challenges to overcome and a purpose to fight for, while most women profit from cultivating *shakti,* their feminine energy, which often expresses in the world as nurturing, devotion, and the creation of community. These qualities of Warriors and Laborers represent a basic level of development germane to each gender. Beyond them, of course, lies the higher destiny of the dharma type. Nonetheless, most boys will at some time learn to express their inner Warrior if they are to actualize themselves as men; likewise most girls will cultivate the Laborer's virtues to embody their potential as women. This fundamental reality of biological evolution is an important part of coming-of-age rituals in sacred societies—rituals that have been lost or perverted in modern contexts into shallow and inappropriate displays because Merchant society lacks the traditions necessary to ground and guide them.

Goal-Setting Examples for Warriors

Finances Make coffee at home instead of Starbucks; paint roof white to save on bills; bike to work 2x per week; cut cable bill; wash clothes during off-peak hours

Health Ride bike to work 2x per week; eat at least one salad each day; improve tennis serve

Family Spend one day each week with no yelling at kids; play day with daughter

Romance Do something totally unexpected at least once a week; leave work at work; take a stay-cation twice a month in the city

To find their just cause Warriors must set goals in every area of life, from relationships and health to money, sex, profession, and spirituality. Along with establishing goals, they must write out exactly how these will be achieved. This should be placed somewhere visible and focused upon for at least five minutes a day. Warriors are ruled by the Fire Element, which relates to sight, the Warrior's main instrument. Warriors are visual types, possessing great hand-eye coordination, focus, and intensity. The way to build positive focus for Warriors is to remind them daily of their goals and the path needed to take to achieve them. Repetition is the mother of learning, and Warriors have to see their truth consistently to make it a reality.

THE THREE Cs

First of the three Cs that characterize Warriors is *control*. Because Warriors need to feel in control of themselves, their environment, and their destinies, they can become workaholics in the quest to attain mastery of everything from their finances to their golf swing. There is nothing that gets a Warrior's blood boiling more than the words "You can't!" Warriors also have a natural sense for how to take over a situation in the interest of what they feel is just and right, and to lead and take control of the world around them in order to make it safer for others. They function best in a crisis or when pushed to make decisions, and this quality makes them excellent leaders.

Warriors also *correct* others when their behavior is not up to standard. Their job is to keep people in line, censure and punish wrongdoers, and restore justice in situations from the trivial to the most momentous. Whether in their own family as a single parent or as a world leader, Warriors are a functionaries of law and order acting to enforce it with all their ability.

Warriors also need to hunt and *chase* after or *capture* a goal. When they have nothing to set their minds to they can consume themselves. Like a fire a Warrior's mind needs to be directed into something constructive lest it feed on itself or destroy others. A worthy goal is necessary to channel the Warrior's energy into an attainable outcome. Sport provides such an outlet and Warriors are often, though not always, athletic and capable with their bodies. Sport is about intention: the strength of an athlete's intention overcoming the obstacles that prevent its realization. The more powerful the intention, the greater the athlete—that is why it is important for Warriors to write out worthy goals that remind them of their intentions. Lacking the direction and drive that a powerful intention provides in their lives, Warriors may become lazy, unfocused, and ineffectual—resorting to gambling, drinking, and dissipation in search of challenge and meaning in the world. Robert Downey Jr. is an example of a Warrior once sidetracked by the seduction of drugs and entertainment, as well as the lack of a just cause in his life.

Written goals also serve to focus a Warrior's mind on a just cause, which every Warrior needs to have. By following their just cause Warriors become instruments of dharma. Educators help Warriors find this by steering them in the right direction, akin to the athlete-coach scenario in sports. With a coach's guidance Warriors can scale the peaks of perfection, breaking through records, obstacles, and opponents in the process. The best athletes in the world use coaches to continue improving. Michael Jordan upped his game even after reaching the apex of his sport with coaches who guided practically every aspect of his play—from fitness and health to psychology, nutrition, and recovery. Every martial artist has a sensei, a soldier a captain, a king his minister: Educators are instrumental in guiding Warriors during every step of their lives. Robert Downey Jr. noted that the key to his resurgence to the top of Hollywood's A-list was his continued one-on-one therapy, exemplifying the idea of counseling and guidance to keep Warriors on their path.

A continued respect between Warrior and Educator types exists where each keeps vigilance over the other to prevent regression into their respective failings, particularly pride and lust. Pride is an easy lure for high-achieving Warriors, and Educators help keep them focused on goals rather than achievements, always pushing them to better themselves. On the other hand, from Gandhi to Tiger Woods, lust is a common denominator many Educators must struggle with. Warriors and the Warrior ethic help guide and keep them honest. (Refer to the previous chapter for more on lust and Educators.)

This guidance also comes when Warriors take Educator qualities on themselves—a personal pursuit of wisdom keeps the Warrior's tendency to pride in check through constant self-questioning and introspection. It also keeps Warriors in line with the just cause of their lives. Though the passion to win and conquer is ever within and cannot be turned off by social niceties or political correctness, they can learn to guide their drive and energy into constructive uses by incorporating Educator traits.

PATH TO EVOLUTION
Educator

The evolution of Warriors consists in linking with a just cause, a powerful intention in their lives. Educators help furnish that by teaching Warriors *viveka,* discernment. Ultimately correct discernment is a Warrior's greatest weapon. It is not strength in arms or mental fortitude that make Warriors great, but the ability to judge rightly in any situation. At such a point they know when to speak up and when to shut up, when to fight and when to parlay, when to kill and when to heal. They understand the just cause of their lives and are able to throw the full weight of their considerable talents behind it.

A Warrior without a just cause is like a sports car without a steering wheel—powerful, but without direction, it blindly plows through obstacles and people until it stalls or runs out of gas. Knowing their just cause, Warriors align their lives with their deepest mission, and everything from diet to dating comes out to serve their highest purpose. They drive straight to their destination and reach their goal directly. Finally, when they have achieved a goal, an apt reward is instrumental in keeping them going forward. Positive reinforcement creates better momentum for Warriors than negative feedback. Even small accomplishments should be rewarded, as they promote greater follow-through and the desire to achieve more and more.

> **From reading books to attending seminars or hanging around evolved Educator types, Warriors whet the sword of discernment upon the philosopher's stone of wisdom.**

Educators and Warriors complement each other because one lacks what the other has in abundance. In the Warrior lies the courage, discipline, and drive to which the Educator aspires, and in the Educator the wisdom, tranquility, and just cause that the Warrior longs to possess. Warriors are realists and lean toward cynicism when unbalanced. Educators are idealists and become naive when they lose touch with reality. Warriors keep Educators real and grounded, while Educators inspire Warriors out of their dog-eat-dog mentality with good counsel and motivation.

Just as bygone kings were well advised by their ministers, so modern-day Warriors must perfect themselves through higher counsel and instruction. From reading books to attending seminars or hanging around evolved Educator types, Warriors whet the sword of their discernment upon the philosopher's stone of wisdom.

THE FIGHT FOR DHARMA

In Sanskrit there are three terms that describe the Warrior's evolution: *jnana, dharma,* and *viveka*—knowledge, purpose, and discernment. These can be broken down into three steps:

1. **Jnana:** Obtaining knowledge, the weapon of wisdom.
2. **Dharma:** Having obtained knowledge, donning the armor of the just cause, or life purpose.

3. **Viveka:** Having obtained a purpose, riding out and enacting it with good judgment and without fear in the knowledge that Warriors are protected by the mantle of the just cause they serve.

It is easy for Warriors to follow orders once they know the right path, but first they must arm themselves with enough wisdom to understand themselves and how they are best suited to give their gifts to the world. Knowing this, they must choose a special dharma, or just cause, to devote their lives to. There are infinite levels of dharma, therefore this does not have to be only one thing—for example, a mother has an obligation to her children, her spouse, her own physical, mental, and spiritual well-being, her parents, her society, and so on. Knowing how to live in harmony with Nature and fulfilling these levels of basic dharma is crucial, and Vedic texts like the *Charaka Samhita* and the *Yoga Sutras of Patanjali* have been devoted to getting the most out of our relationships with ourselves and the world. But the special dharma, or just cause, that Warriors must embrace above and beyond these will make their lives truly remarkable. There are no books that detail how to do this, and perhaps that is why the guru-disciple relationship has been so important in Vedic societies through the ages.

> Viveka [is] the ability to tell the difference between what is real and unreal—what serves your highest good and what serves only temporary desire.

Most of our obligations to the world are automatic—being born in a body implies certain duties. Like having a license to drive, having a license to live means abiding by the basic laws of embodied life: exercising proper self-maintenance, fulfilling obligations to family, and learning to live with our environment. But beyond these basic levels of dharma there is a higher purpose to life that must be discovered and embraced to become fully evolved as a Warrior. Once this is found the final step lies in using refined discernment to become an effective weapon of dharma in the world.

Viveka, or discernment, is the ability to relate any decision back to the measuring stick of dharma. For example, let us say that a Warrior has chosen to fight illiteracy at a local school. Knowing this, when requested to teach math at a wealthy school outside that precinct, she or he must ask, "Does doing this serve my fight for literacy?" If the answer is "no" the Warrior must refuse—it is that simple. Knowing your dharma in any area of life you can weigh your decisions and ask yourself, "Does this serve my highest purpose or detract from it?" That is viveka, the ability to tell the difference between what is real and unreal—what serves your highest good and what serves only temporary desire. Viveka comes about from hanging around Educators and cultivating Educator virtues in oneself.

WAR AND WARRIORS

When soldiers fight a righteous battle they are ensured of victory whether they win or lose. But when leaders are corrupted and force soldiers to commit *adharmic* acts (actions that go against dharma), the soldiers must stand up for what is right even if it means going against the grain of the orders they received. This helps to prevent the scourge of post-traumatic stress disorder and other afflictions that haunt soldiers upon returning home (details on how to cope with and understand PTSD are found in chapter 13). Warriors first and foremost fight to protect dharma. Whatever interferes with that must be challenged, even if it is their country, their family, or even their own body and mind. As the Warrior teachings in the New Testament say:

> *If your right hand causes you to sin, cut it off.*
> MATTHEW 5:30

A true Warrior constantly fights the inner fight in order to win justice. This struggle is described in the Bhagavad Gita:

Dharma kshetre kurukshetre
On the battlefield of the world, on the battlefield of dharma.

BHAGAVAD GITA 1:1

Recall from the introduction that the battlefield is both within and without us—it is as much in the spaces of the mind as in the terrains of the wild. In order to fight the fight a Warrior must know what dharma is and how to protect it. Yet the world does not have to be at war for Warriors to be effectual. In fact, most of a Warrior's dharma is enacted during peacetime. Warriors do not lack for causes to fight for at home. They simply need to arm themselves with knowledge, don the protective cloak of their cause, and put their skills and good judgment into action.

When Warriors fail to develop jnana, dharma, and viveka (wisdom, purpose, and discernment) they become distracted, lazy, and addicted to sensations. The restless thrill seeker, the inveterate gambler, the alcoholic—these are some negative patterns of a Warrior lacking a just cause. Devolved Warriors seek artificial stimulation, which is a substitute for the exhilaration they feel when they are aligned with their purpose. By embracing the just fight Warriors are replenished and filled in a way that frivolous activities cannot provide. They become calm, centered, and at peace with themselves while ever in dynamic motion, like the eye of a hurricane that remains tranquil even as violent winds swirl around it.

PATH TO DEVOLUTION

Merchant

When Warriors devolve they become prideful, anger prone, and arrogant. They may still be great fighters, but being a Warrior is not only about fighting—it is about being an agent of justice. To know justice one must have judgment, and that is what is lost when there is a descent into anger and pride. Only by evolving into the Educator does a Warrior acquire judgment. And when the types grow, they begin to look like each other—when Warriors evolve into Educators they become settled, calm, and self-possessed, appearing meek though still tigers inside. In the same way Educators appear athletic, virile, and capable when they evolve into Warriors. Evolved types are easily mistaken for each other, though they never become the other type (as noted in chapter 1).

But when Warriors begin to assign too much value (Merchant) on their strength (Warrior) they devolve into pride and a disdain for weakness. This is deadly because it leads to a loss of those very qualities they cherish most: respect from peers, and ultimately power and authority. Warriors also devolve when they give their lives over to the pursuit of money. In Merchant society, money is power. Because Warriors naturally gravitate to power they can become easy prey to money's lure. The assumption that they can buy security and protection can lead them to the misguided pursuit of financial resources to the exclusion of ethical considerations. But the Warrior's security does not come from wealth. While money facilitates many things it cannot buy perfection and purpose, which is what Warriors truly seek. This is only achieved through self-cultivation. By second-guessing their ideals in the name of profit Warriors fail to honor their basic purpose on Earth and descend into a personal hell.

> Cynicism is as unrealistic as idealism, and more negative for Warriors. . . . But heart and generosity are hallmarks of evolved Warriors. To lose these is to lose oneself.

As a result they can become cynical, resigning themselves to believing that the way of the world is cruel and unforgiving, belonging to those with power. But there is a fine line between realism and cynicism. Realism is the ability to see things as they are. Cynicism is as unrealistic as idealism, and more negative for Warriors, as it can lead them to lose heart and turn bitterly against others. But heart and generosity are hallmarks of evolved Warriors. To lose these is to lose oneself. It is not in harming others but in protecting them that Warriors win acclaim. It is not in anger and resentment that people see nobility, but in even-handedness and humility.

> **When Warriors are seduced by Merchant life their power becomes *anger*, their vitality *lust*, their glory *pride*.**

When Warriors disabled by ignorance mistake petty spoils and treasure for true glory they give away their power and enslave themselves to pride, lust, and greed. We have seen this through the devolution of the ages as Warriors fell from being the upholders of morality in the Silver Age to tyrants and murderers in the Bronze and Iron ages. When Warriors enact brutality upon the weak they suffer a Warrior's hell for the disservice of their gifts for selfish ends. Warriors are entrusted with the protection of their people just as Merchants are made to feed, Laborers to serve, and Educators to teach. When they prostitute their gifts for selfish ends Warriors become no more than mercenaries. Krishna's advice to his friend in the Bhagavad Gita comes to mind:

> *Karmani eva adhikaaras te maa phaleshu kadaachana . . .*
> *Devote yourself to action, never to the fruits thereof . . .*

The Merchant path is not bad for everyone—in fact it is great for Laborer dharma types. However, when Warriors are seduced by Merchant life their power becomes *anger*, their vitality *lust*, their glory *pride*: lust is an attachment to sensuality, pride is a fixation on one's own name and fame, and anger is a loss of judgment. The Merchant life beckons the Warrior into a false sense of glory, one built not on merit and honor, but on power and dominion. It takes a real hero, guided by wisdom and temperance, to wield power and not be a tyrant, to rule but not oppress. Again, no one type or lifestyle is better than another—knowing where you evolve and devolve can help you become the best you can be while avoiding the pitfalls relevant to your dharma type.

4

Merchant

Clothe, Connect, and Animate Others

Personality • Charity • Energy

Famous Merchants

(based on birth data and their Vedic Life Map)

Muhammad Ali

Ammachi

Tori Amos

Warren Beatty

Harry Belafonte

Mike Bloomberg

William F. Buckley Jr.

Charlie Chaplin

Chevy Chase

Bill Clinton

Kurt Cobain

Sean Connery

Miles Davis

Leonardo DiCaprio

Kirk Douglas

Alexandre Dumas

Fabio

Tom Hanks

Hugh Hefner

Paris Hilton

Julio Iglesias

Dwayne Johnson

Jim Jones (cult leader)

Krishna*

Marilyn Monroe

Sean Penn

Michelle Pfeiffer

Brad Pitt*

Elvis Presley

Anthony Quinn

Oskar Schindler

Percy Bysshe Shelley

Frank Sinatra

Britney Spears*

Rick Springfield

John Travolta

Tina Turner

---

*Names followed by an asterisk are Outsiders finding their best expression playing another type. More on this appears in chapter 6.

Merchants are go-getters, scrappers, and make-something-out-of-nothing types. They can talk themselves, and others, into accomplishing anything—which is why they can be great motivational speakers and high achievers or liars and con artists, depending on their level of evolution. Merchants have an entrepreneurial and pioneering streak that typifies the best of the "American spirit," which is why the United States of America is a Merchant nation.*

Merchant types learn from an early age the value of a dollar and never forget it. They put their family's security first—partly because they have felt real hunger at some point in their lives, and partly because they also hunger for the good things in life.† They see others who have, and they work hard to have as well. In the end, as we shall see below, their circle is completed by giving back.

Just as the Educator's goal is to provide spiritual sustenance, the Merchant's natural talents lie in sustaining, sheltering, and providing for the material needs of people. Thus Merchants work well in any profession that caters to the masses—be it in nonessential goods such as fashion and entertainment or day-to-day necessities like food, hospitality, clothing, and drugs. Their natural ability to network and manage material resources also makes them masters of trade, commerce, and banking. Sales is a natural profession for Merchants as they have the ability to evoke and shape strong emotions in others— since most of us are led by our emotions Merchants generate success by attaching their products to the positive feelings people want to have. They are "happiness brokers," and their ability to evoke laughter and joy and to inspire people to live the good life endears them to the world, which is why we live in a Merchant society where everybody is trying to get their piece of the Merchant pie. This ability to inspire is also supremely useful in the entertainment industry, where Merchants excel at creating, performing, and producing popular music, art, and movies. Of all the types Merchants know best how to have a good time!

However, Merchants are not limited to sustaining the masses by

---

*Countries, like people, have personality types, which will be discussed in later sections.
†In regard to bodily functions Merchants relate to digestion and assimilation, what ayurveda terms *samana vayu*. Anatomy and the dharma types are covered in chapter 8.

their profession. In fact most of the time their job is simply about making money, not directly contributing to society. Merchants are the only type with free rein to make money for its own sake, because they can later use this money to benefit society. Engineers (Laborers), doctors (Warriors), teachers (Educators), and inventors (Outsiders) benefit others by the daily operation of their duties. They earn their keep by contributing to society. On the other hand bankers, investors, and speculators benefit only themselves by their professions, which is okay if they are Merchant types because they need to cultivate prosperity in order to give back to the world, as wealth is an instrument for the performance of their dharma. Merchants show us how comfortable life can be. Where Educators teach and Warriors enforce dharma (purposeful living), Merchants are masters of kama (enjoyment) and show us how to live like no other type—in the Las Vegas sense of that word! Ironically they also work harder, putting in more hours, more inspiration, and more cunning than any other type in order to earn their enjoyment.

> **Merchants are the only type with free rein to make money for its own sake.**

Time is money for Merchants. Knowing this, they tend to sleep less and do more in their day than other people, though they can also be extremely lazy when devolved. Whether filling time with entertainment or discovering the newest Internet business strategies, Merchants are always thinking, scheming, and developing ideas. They may not act on all of them, but usually they have enough on their plate to keep them busy twenty-five hours of the day. That is why they are so fierce about their enjoyment: because they take their work *and* play very seriously! In fact, leisure is an important part of Merchants' routine. They become imbalanced if they cannot have some downtime, which usually comes through a form of social ritual.

MERCHANTS AND RITUAL

Merchants love rituals. Social rituals like courtship and parties and spiritual rituals like religious ceremonies have strong appeal for the Merchant archetype. Laborers also enjoy rituals, but more as spectators than performers—they prefer to be the audience while Merchants enjoy being center stage. Merchants are also masters of tension. Building, guiding, and diffusing tension at the appropriate moment for maximal effect is a gift that suits them well in everything from selling cars to selling themselves to an audience when on stage. This mastery of tension makes them captivating storytellers, and from the boardroom to the boardwalk they rarely fail to emotionally hook an audience when they have something to say.

We shall explore in depth the yogic technology of the five bodies in later chapters, but the Merchant's affinity for the Sensate Body, or *manomayakosha,* makes them especially sensitive to the emotional highs and lows of the human experience. Merchants can just as easily become moody as motivated; they can just as easily be depressed as dynamic. They are both susceptible to and masters of the body's emotion cocktail, and they can use it to soar to the heights of ecstasy or bottom out in the depths of despair. One word for emotion in Sanskrit is *rasa,* which also means "juice," or "flavor." Merchants are masters of life's juiciness and they can go to extremes to extract flavor from their experiences, even becoming rasa addicts.

> **Merchants can just as easily become moody as motivated; they can just as easily be depressed as dynamic.**

Don't be afraid of these Sanskrit words, for they stand for things we experience every day but do not have words for in English. In the Vedic worldview, as in chemistry, emotions are material things. Rasa is a physical experience—in our bodies, chemicals and neuropeptides are carriers of emotion and the proof is that we can manipulate them through drugs, diet, and exercise. The Merchant's mastery of these most valuable of material resources, our very feelings and sensations, gives this type an impressive edge when dealing with others. When asked their desires in life most people say they "want to be happy," and as the average person's experience of happiness is tied to his or her emotional state, the Merchant's innate understanding of emotion allows this type to fulfill these needs—and profit *tremendously thereby!*

People can get fired up, inspired, or deeply moved and even carried away by Merchants. They must be careful, however, not to feel let down when the experience is over because there is an inevitable drop after the "Merchant moment" has worn off. This is the buyer's remorse that people experience after dealing with Merchant types. For their part, Merchants need to contain and channel their enthusiasm so they don't misrepresent themselves. In the "Speech" section of chapter 11 we will see how Merchants can get carried away and overstate things, or even blatantly lie, in order to get their point across. They need to rein this in for their own benefit and good health.

Because what we work with becomes who we are, to protect their own reputations and improve their social standing in the long run Merchants need to learn to control their emotions and their speech. In business, in entertainment, and with family and friends, the karma of what we do to others inexorably rubs off on us, which is why karma yoga—compassionate and conscious action and living—is a particularly suitable spiritual path for Merchants.

Warriors live and die by the sword, Educators by the pen. Merchants, who are used to riding an emotional roller coaster, can become worn down by its highs and lows. The process of purveying rasa can drain their own, and as a result they may search out experiences that numb them to the world such as drugs, food, and entertainment. They may also require more and more stimulation to feel pleasure and pain and become willing to push the envelope of accepted social norms to get it. In the fall of Rome we saw a Merchant society taken to debauchery in its search for the extremes of numbness and excitement, stimulation and fulfillment. Rome, a rasa-addicted society, took pleasure in the savage combat spectacles of the Coliseum and the excesses of the marketplace and bathhouse—as well as the exploitation of other cultures through the rape of their people, wealth, and resources. As the history of Rome so aptly illustrates, more abundance and variety of food and luxury cannot satisfy a Merchant society, and its ever-increasing girth, like a person's waistline, expands into ill health and eventually self-destruction.

"The road of excess leads to the palace of wisdom"[1] is a slogan appropriate to the Outsider, not the Merchant, who suffers from the karmic repercussions of too much food, sex, and drugs. Instead of filling up Merchants need to lighten up by shedding excess material, which can take the form of losing extra pounds or cleaning closets and giving away outdated clothes. Charity does for the soul what diet does for the body, and in giving what comes naturally to them Merchants share their gifts with the world while receiving in turn what money can't buy—gratitude.

> **By offering to help, to assist a friend or stranger without thought for reward Merchants grow their network of friends—a network that repays them a thousand times over during their lifetime. . . . Once Merchants learn this basic rule of karma and human relations they are on their way to superstardom in life!**

CHARITY AND SHAKTI

Charity is more than donating things; it is giving your attention and life energy to others. It is offering something, rather than taking it, with no attachment to the outcome. The biblical injunction that it is better to give than to receive is an ironic truth for the Merchant type, for the more they give the more they get. By being attentive and solicitous to others Merchants become indispensable, which in turn increases their value. It is a "no brainer" equation that makes perfect business sense: by offering to help, to assist a friend or stranger without thought for reward, Merchants grow their network of friends—a network that repays them a thousand times over during their lifetime, for it is better to have people owe you than to be in debt to them. Once Merchants learn this basic rule of karma and human relations they are on their way to superstardom in life!

Whether offering a compliment or an article of clothing—especially when they offer these things with no thought of reward—Merchants get back in return the medicine they need most: gratitude. Giving comes naturally to evolved Merchants, and Merchants who wish to grow must learn how to do it effectively. The secret is to begin by giving things that do not diminish you in any way: a piece of fashion advice, the phone number of a business associate, or things you no longer use that someone might find indispensable. Sometimes a smile, a joke, or a heartfelt compliment are enough—these can be invaluable to a person whose spirit needs lifting, and they do not detract from your well-being. In fact they increase your value in the eyes of others by motivating and energizing them.

"Energy" in Sanskrit is called *shakti*. Merchants love to both work with and worship shakti, as it is a way to obtain rasa, the positive emotions they want to feel. In Sanskrit *shakti* is a feminine noun that can mean "energy," "power," or even "money," and like *shekhinah*, a Hebrew word for "God's energy," shakti is associated with the feminine Divine. It is the radiance of divinity, personal charisma, the power of electricity, or even the wave of warm vibes at a concert. Every dharma type possesses its own unique form of shakti, as shown in table 4.1.

TABLE 4.I. SHAKTI OF THE DHARMA TYPES

DHARMA TYPE	SHAKTI	POWER
Educator	Mantra Shakti	The power of good counsel
Warrior	Prabhava Shakti	The power of majesty and strength
Merchant	Utsaha Shakti	The power of effort and desire
Laborer	Prema Shakti	The power of love and devotion
Outsider	Ananda Shakti	The power of bliss and freedom

Shakti is present in every dharma type, though Merchants are the most covetous of it. From performing temple rituals to singing on stage they crave shakti in the form of attention and adulation, but they also best radiate it in the form of charisma and energy. As a result, Merchants tend to be the most famous and remembered people in society. Muhammad Ali made his living by the sting of his wit no less than the fury of his punches. He also revolutionized boxing by making it a big money sport through his gift of gab and self-promotion. In India the great personality Krishna, an Outsider playing the part of a Merchant, was known as Bhagavan (the noun *bhaga* means "fortune" or "wealth"). A bhagavan is one possessed of great glories, including fame, personal magnetism, and prosperity, among others.

> **Merchants are essentially *investors*,
> reaping magnified returns on the investment
> of their time and energy.**

Shakti is also money, the most prominent and material form of it in the world today. Less spiritually inclined Merchants may worship it exclusively because it in turn buys other sources of shakti and rasa such as sex, food, and luxury. In fact, anything that is material and valuable is the purview of the Merchant type.

Merchants are guardians of the most valuable things in life because they know how to attract and keep them. From a beautiful painting to a rare vidya, or body of knowledge, they work hard to earn and hold the treasures of the world. Merchants are often irritated by people they consider to be "freeloaders," who feel entitled to their charisma or prosperity—Merchants work hard to earn what they have, though it may not always appear so. Sometimes a Merchant is born with gifts in abundance—the result, perhaps, of hard work in another life. What people do not understand, though, is that Merchants are willing to put all their shakti on the line in order to generate more. Investors risk their capital for the chance to create exponential returns. Entertainers pour their hearts out on stage for a return of shakti in the form of adoration, applause, money, and fame. Spiritual seekers invest their shakti into a ritual practice in order to culture the mind to such a degree as to earn the blessings of that ritual.

Merchants are essentially *investors,* reaping magnified returns on the investment of their time and energy. As a result they are wary of people who want to reap the fruits of their insight and ingenuity without investing their own. Merchants can grow mistrustful of others, except perhaps Laborers, whom they feel safe around and who are not usually out to get anything from them. Laborers have the simple and unique desire to be with Merchants and to be like Merchants, without the need to leech their energy. Laborers in fact invest energy into Merchants, which is why Merchant types are usually more than glad to reciprocate. Merchants are willing to give their energy to those who give something in exchange. By contrast Educators spread their knowledge to all who want to hear, and Warriors are happy to give their life and breath for someone without expectation of return, but Merchants have to charge money for their gifts.

THE SOCIAL MERCHANT

Keenly aware of social rules and rituals, Merchants are often status-driven creatures who crave the good things in life—as much for their inherent value as for what these things say about them. Merchants buy with an eye for value and luxury, rather than form and function. A typical Merchant appreciates a luxury car more for its cachet than its performance and buys an item because of the status it confers rather than its inherent usefulness. Because of their appreciation for social hierarchies Merchants attempt to "buy" their way up the social ladder using their charm, wit, money, and other talents to get ahead. In the process they set the standards for what is "in" and what is not, what is "cool" and what is passé. Merchants are the mavens of fashion, beauty, and entertainment.

At its finest a Merchant's shakti is incomparable, like the sanguine type in medieval physiology.* Merchants can have bright smiles, alluring energy, and an open, gregarious air. They are able to harness the power of attraction unlike anyone else and are the most popular and likable of the dharma types. Merchants are movers and shakers of energy, creating the rituals and customs of our world from pop music to popular New Age philosophies like that of *The Secret*. They are the artists, entertainers, and media moguls who control what we see, hear, wear, and even think. In doing so they can be outgoing and garish but also quietly controlling, working behind the scenes to create and accumulate shakti in the form of money, power, and influence.

But this desire for attention hides a core emptiness, a sense of inadequacy or of not having enough, that can only be filled when Merchants evolve into the Laborer type. The same emptiness that makes them hate to be alone can drive them to fill their lives with abundance, or it can motivate them to help others by providing resources and opportunities for people, for it is only in giving that Merchant types become ultimately fulfilled. Merchants cannot stand to be alone, and their inner void can become so painful that they search out anything to numb it. But material things are temporary anodynes: money, booze, luxury and entertainment are only sedatives that wear off when their novelty is gone. The permanent cure for their loneliness is charity.

THE GIFT THAT KEEPS ON GIVING

No amount of attention seeking or contrived, paid-for companionship can fill a Merchant's soul to the depths like creating merit through action—karma yoga, which in turn ensures future blessings and continued enjoyment of the good things in life. The goodwill and gratitude created by karma yoga heal a Merchant's loneliness better than any drug

---

Sanguine means "cheerful," "chummy," and also "abundant in blood." Our ancestors thought that having "good blood" made one upbeat and energetic and related this type of person to the Sanguine humor.

can and are freely given by those who have benefited from a Merchant's generosity. The grateful love of a full belly and a warm, sheltered body offer more to the Merchant than any currency can buy.

What happens when Merchants have everything they want? They still feel empty, anxious, and unfulfilled. Having possessions leads to more worry and anxiety. Merchants crave the beautiful things in life, but upon obtaining them enjoyment comes hand in hand with worry over losing them, breaking them, or diminishing their value. A Merchant with a beautiful spouse or a new BMW is more likely to keep a jealous eye out for trouble than someone without these things and may become more anxious and stressed as a result. This stress can force a Merchant to find ways to numb out. But better than winding down after a hard day's work with alcohol, drugs, and mindless entertainment, going to the local homeless shelter and spooning out soup to the hungry, or handing out clothes to the needy, is what a Merchant needs. This is a permanent cure for what ails the Merchant, and the feeling of giving can even become addicting—the sense of wholeness and gratitude can itself become a sort of positive "fix" that healthy Merchants begin to crave!

> **"Ah! what a divine religion might be found out if charity were really made the principle of it instead of faith."**
> **PERCY SHELLEY**

Giving releases Merchants from anxiety. By providing for others they practice letting go, which leads to greater serenity. And the best part for Merchants is that they simply have to apply their natural ingenuity to part with things they no longer need. For example, every year before the Super Bowl T-shirts are printed proclaiming each team Super Bowl champion. Since one team has to lose, half of the shirts become immediately unsellable once the game is over. But to people in developing countries who have little to wear such leftovers are very useful indeed, and a welcome blessing. A company that donates rather than discards what it cannot use becomes both profitable *and* charitable, earning at once material and spiritual merit.

By applying their natural ingenuity Merchants can make the most of what they have and find mutually beneficial ways to help others prosper. As happiness brokers for the world, their dharma is to connect people and things together in a way that enhances their lives and makes them happy. Those who own restaurants, instead of throwing away food, can feed the hungry and poor. Those who have clothing can give clothes, those who have opportunities give opportunity—it is giving that is important, not what is given. Some donate millions to charity, thereby ensuring their long-term success as Merchant types. But giving may mean simply devoting your time and expertise to show others how to prosper. Muhammad Yunus won the Nobel Peace Prize for developing *microlending,* a system that promotes self-sufficiency through business and entrepreneurship by pairing people in Western countries with those in undeveloped parts of the world who receive microloans of twenty to fifty dollars. What is throwaway money for many Westerners can become lifeblood for others—what a Merchant might spend on lunch can be used to feed a family for years when properly channeled. Merchants understand giving in order to receive, whether it is investing in the stock market or investing in their emotional and spiritual prosperity. By caring for the material needs of others they ensure a continued return for their investment in the form of inner peace and serenity.

> As happiness brokers for the world, [Merchants'] dharma is to put people and things together in a way that enhances their lives and makes them happy.

The difference between Merchants and Laborers is that Laborers are completed by family and community, whereas Merchants feed off the gratitude of strangers. It is enough for Laborers to nourish their families—Merchants must nourish the world. They must move beyond the circle of their blood and community to find fulfillment, though this can be difficult to do. Like Laborer types, Merchants value their blood ties. From an early age they are driven to win security for themselves and family. Unfortunately less evolved types do not ever look past this to helping others outside of their inner circle. Because they sometimes mistrust people's motivations, they are especially close to those who have invested energy and resources into them and spend their lives working to prove worthy of this support. In fact one of the hang-ups for Merchants is their sense of worth, and they may go through life trying to prove it by reaching for material objectives—and though the antidote is easily available, it will not be found in these things.

> **"He who sees a need and waits to be asked for help is as unkind as if he had refused it."**
>
> DANTE

Like any skill, giving must be practiced. "It is good to give when you are asked; it is better to give before you are asked" is an injunction from Vedic times that has special relevance for Merchant types, who keep saving and hoping that one day when they are secure enough they will be able to give back. The problem is that day may never come. Anyone can provide for their family; even animals do it. It is another thing to give wholeheartedly to strangers, especially when it is unbidden. This generates a blessing exponentially superior to the value of the thing given, and in a karmic sense it further multiplies the Merchant's wealth and abundance. In essence this is a great deal for Merchant types because they always get back more than they give, and by practicing this skill they are rewarded with further opportunities to do so.

PATH TO EVOLUTION

The Laborer

The Laborer's natural attention to detail, workmanship, and quality offers a model of evolution for the Merchant type. Because Laborers are intimate with how much work goes into crafting something they are less likely to take shortcuts or to step on their fellow workers to achieve their ends, things devolved Merchants may do. Laborers enjoy work; when Merchants tune into the pleasure of the creative process they gain an appreciation for what was made and the hard work that was required. They also learn to value and authentically relate with people.

When Merchants integrate qualities of the Laborer type they gain the serenity characteristic of the Laborer—feeling contented, loved, and connected to their community. Their behavior goes from being attention seeking and overblown to being confident and affable. Their compliments come out of genuine appreciation rather than being surface flattery. They make friends rather than close deals, creating lifelong, ongoing relationships based on caring rather than using people for short-term gain. This produces long-term returns on their investment of time and energy—returns that are infinitely greater than when they treat people as a means to an end.

Laborers teach Merchants gratitude and contentment. Gratitude from others, and their own contentment and gratitude for what they possess, open up Merchants to a wealth of blessings. Laborers also show them how to savor the little things in life and get the most out of their possessions. But even more importantly they teach Merchants the real meaning of community. By learning to expand their definition of "family," Merchants begin to see not just their relatives but also their neighborhood, their city, and eventually the world as their own extended family. Then their potential for good becomes boundless. When Merchants lay down the "what's in it for me?" and take up the "giving feels better than getting" mantra, they enrich not only the world with their talents, but ultimately themselves, earning a wealth of blessings and cheer that is beyond the purveyance of money and goods. It is amazing how a Merchant's inadequacies disappear in the wake of a grateful smile or hug from someone he or she has touched!

This complementary relationship between Laborers and Merchants, characterized by steadiness in character on one side and mercurial dynamism on the other, will balance the Merchant's self-centered attitude, resulting in benefits for each type.

> **Sometimes Merchants have to suffer before they can find a way to help others.**

Chapter 12 will cover myths and the dharma types (the myth embodied by *A Christmas Carol* is a Merchant cautionary tale that demonstrates the importance of family). As mentioned earlier the drive Merchants have to win security begins at home, usually at an early age. Unfortunately once this objective is fulfilled, their inclination to nourishment can turn to greed and overindulgence for lack of anyone with whom to share their bounty. That is, once Merchants have secured their family's needs they seek little beyond their definition of that term. And when their family is no more they may begin to hoard wealth, ignoring the obvious needs of those around them. That was the case of Ebenezer Scrooge, who had no one with whom to share his abundance, or so he thought. However, his epiphany opened him up to a world where he was instrumental not only in benefiting others but in healing himself.

As is the case with many Merchants, Scrooge responded better to fear than to politeness—it can take a traumatic event such as a brush with death to set wayward Merchants on the right path. Sometimes they have to get and beat cancer before realizing that our health care system needs to be reformed. Sometimes they fall upon hard times before realizing the plight of the poor. Sometimes Merchants have to suffer before they can find a way to help others. In part 2 we will discuss the circle of life and the role that Warriors play in keeping Merchants in line so that they abide by their dharma without recourse to such extreme incentives. Merchants need and respect a strong hand that keeps them in line. An everyday example is a Warrior doctor warning a Merchant patient that if a high-stress, no-rest life continues the Merchantwill surely die of a heart attack. The result? A smart Merchant learns to take a vacation or get a massage—and write off the expense!

PATH TO DEVOLUTION
The Warrior

Merchant types like to make noise. If they are the loudest they will get the most attention, or so they believe—and they are usually right. The squeaky wheel does indeed get the grease. The problem is the squeaky wheel makes noise because it is not well, and Merchants act up and make spectacles of themselves because they feel empty inside. They love the energy that attention gives them, and when they get used to getting it attention seeking becomes habitual. However, it does not address the inherent flaw, which is the Merchant's loneliness.

Merchants love to be loved. They enjoy being the center of attention. People are drawn to the sparkling personalities of the Merchant type. When their luster and sparkle are backed by real value they enrich the world with their energy, humor, and vitality. When the glitter is just a surface show, as when the Merchant is on a path of devolution, then it quickly fades to reveal an empty setting—under pressure, the golden sheen peels off to reveal a dull interior. When Merchants harmonize with the Laborer type they gain a level of profundity that only the Laborer can give them. They become solid, dependable, and able to back their words with actions. There is substance to their speech, depth to their dialogue. They are real and approachable. But when they are all talk and no substance they think only of themselves, and cannot be a real friend to anyone. Such a Merchant *competes* with (Warrior) rather than *accepts* people (Laborer).

> From heart surgery to gastric bypass, from valerian to Viagra,
> Merchants believe doctors and drugs are miracle fixes
> that will keep them going.

Merchants do not like to face the consequences of their actions. Unlike Outsiders, who run because they desire freedom, Merchants run away because they desire luxury—the luxury of having their cake and eating it too. The overeater is not concerned about heart disease and diabetes, the binge drinker is not worried about cirrhosis of the liver, and the fornicator does not like to think about child support and alimony. These things are not a good deal for them, and instead of the "buzz kill" of dealing with the effects of their actions directly they try to bargain or even cheat their way around them. At this level Merchants believe they can even cheat death, given the right opportunity.

Instead of diet and exercise they choose the quick fix. From heart surgery to gastric bypass, from valerian to Viagra, Merchants believe doctors and drugs are miracle fixes that will keep them going. Instead of taking more responsibility in relationships, they seek to buy their way out with gifts, threats, flattery, or even rituals, turning religion into a drive-through pit stop to redemption. Instead of looking at the emptiness within, they project their problems on others, eating through people in a stream of empty friendships that leave them worn out and hung over. And when Merchants cannot get what they want with guile and persuasiveness they descend into Warrior tactics of force and intimidation.

> **Merchants are lovers and fighters, but given the chance they prefer the former.**

When they channel their bluster and vivacity into anger Merchants can be noisy and intimidating. But this is not good for them. When Merchants' natural skill for manipulation is channeled into aggression and a lust for power the results are usually disastrous for themselves and the world. Because Merchants do not possess the principled discipline of a Warrior they can take shortcuts to obtain what they want, often at the expense of others—thus going against the basic grain of their type, which is to feed and clothe (provide for) the masses. One of the differences between Merchant and Warrior societies is that Warrior kings of yore proved themselves through extreme trials of fortitude and purity before assuming power. They rode first into battle, dying to defend their people. Such trials were put in place by Educators and Warriors as test and temper of their character. Can you imagine today's political leaders, many of them Merchants posing as Warriors, fighting for their ideals on the battlefield? Would their rhetoric be the same if they had to put their lives on the line to stand behind it? Merchants make great leaders of industry, where their drive and talent make them excel, but they are not meant to lead society.

Merchants are lovers and fighters, but given the choice they prefer the former. Love is a Laborer's game, and death is the Warrior's domain. Merchants do well to stay with their point of evolution and spread love and cheer rather than conflict in the world. Many are given a choice in life between sports and sales, army and entertainment, and most rightly choose sales and entertainment, as these are closer to their point of evolution. Sean Connery, the well-known man's man of the silver screen, dropped out of the Navy because of stomach ulcers. He took up drama, taking acting lessons and learning his craft, and went on to portray his iconic masculinity in roles like James Bond. Merchants do better playing Warriors than being Warriors.

Merchants are volatile and temperamental and sometimes mistake their volatility for violence. But they are not good Warriors because war does not serve their highest good, which is to benefit the body, not destroy it. They also lack the Warrior's ability to follow orders and the judgment to determine who needs to be punished, and when. Therefore Merchants must keep to their own dharma and not get entangled with and destroyed by the Warrior's path.

And though Merchants *can* make their careers in the military or sports, more often than not these Warrior pursuits are cut short for some reason. Merchants may become injured, sick, or otherwise unable to continue their careers, or like Muhammad Ali suffer debilitating consequences later in life. Dwayne "The Rock" Johnson began by playing football before an injury forced him into the World Wrestling Federation and eventually into movies and entertainment. Julio Iglesias was a soccer player before he turned his Merchant skills to serenading the world. WWF wrestling, cinema, and song are more entertainment than competition, and better suited to Merchant personalities, which goes to show that even when we choose to go in one direction fate often chooses otherwise for us—such is the power of dharma!

SAINTS

Sometimes academically inclined Merchants scoff at the possibility that they may be "Merchant types," as if that term were hateful to one for whom the pursuit of knowledge trumped a mercantile instinct, and intelligence is deemed more precious than material possessions. But one need only turn to that famous Indian saint Vivekananda— who at the turn of the last century wowed the Western world with his brilliance, sagacity, and gift for oratory—for an example of a Merchant mind in which intelligence keyed the expression of Merchant dharma.*

Vivekananda means "the bliss of discriminative intelligence," an intelligence that is able to pick out the most valuable things and leave the chaff aside, like the storied swan that separates curds from water in a glass of milk. Merchants have an eye for value, and spiritually minded Merchants can discern what is practical and useful for spiritual advancement, and what is of little service. Merchants place a high value on what can be put into practice to create tangible effects. Accordingly, Vivekananda founded the Ramakrishna Mission to educate, feed, clothe, and uplift the poor and starving millions of India.

---

*Some scholars will scoff at the idea that Vivekananda was a Merchant. However, his Vedic Life Map does show the possibility, along with Educator type. In the author's opinion, a strong case can be made for both.

Because Merchants know what they can achieve with pure effort (utsaha shakti) and what they can't, they also place a high value on grace and blessings. In the *Devi Mahatmya*, a text sacred to worshippers of the feminine divine, a Merchant obtains enlightenment by asking the Divine Mother for that which he could not obtain by his own effort alone: wisdom. His business instinct made him choose the thing of highest value.

Today Ammachi, the "hugging saint" of Kerala, is an example of a Merchant who has inspired an organization that helps hundreds of millions of people from all walks of life. From the creation of hospitals and homes to the building of schools and libraries, her Merchant ability to bless her devotees and organize and galvanize people with her limitless shakti has little equal in either the spiritual or secular worlds.

Merchants are essentially brokers—of people, food, things, and ideas. It is because of Vivekananda that we know the terms *yoga, vedanta,* and *dharma.* Ammachi, with a few of hours of sleep per night and tremendous good cheer, has transmitted the virtues of charity and selfless service to the West in a way never before imagined. Not surprisingly her most cherished exemplars of divine consciousness are Devi/Shakti (the feminine divine) and Krishna (the mischievous Merchant personality of the Vishnu avatar). The dharma types key how we all express our unique gifts—even enlightened sages.

◆ HOMEWORK

As a homework assignment, try to think of other great saints and spiritual personalities according to their dharma type. Consider sages and teachers from the traditions that you know and see how their expression aligns with your dharma type. Later, we will discuss how the types fit together and understand each other according to the languages they speak and the intelligences they use, among other things.

"Caste is good. That is the only natural way of solving life. Men must form themselves into groups, and you cannot get rid of that. Wherever you go there will be caste. But that does not mean that there should be these privileges. They should be knocked on the head. If you teach vedanta to the fisherman, he will say, I am as good a man as you, I am a fisherman, you are a philosopher, but I have the same God in me as you have in you. And that is what we want, no privileges for any one, equal chances for all; let everyone be taught that the Divine is within, and everyone will work out his own salvation."

THE COMPLETE WORKS OF THE SWAMI VIVEKANANDA, III, 246

5

Laborer

Nourish and Serve Others

Devotion • Work • Perseverance

Famous Laborers
(based on birth data and their Vedic Life Map)

Marlon Brando

Maria Callas

Johnny Carson

Saint Catherine

Dick Cheney

Deepak Chopra

Alice Cooper

Kevin Costner

Willem Dafoe

Clint Eastwood

Harrison Ford

Al Gore

MC Hammer

George Harrison

Katharine Hepburn

Benny Hill

Larry King

Rush Limbaugh

Dean Martin

Paul McCartney

Martina Navratilova

Chuck Norris

Shaquille O'Neal

Roy Orbison

Al Pacino

Luciano Pavarotti

Sidney Poitier

Franklin D. Roosevelt

Bruce Springsteen

Mother Teresa

Bruce Willis

Oprah Winfrey

Sometimes people take the test and say, "I hope I'm not a Laborer or an Outsider!" which underscores the hierarchical mind-set and belief that one type is better than another. The truth as we have seen is that all types are equal, with different roads to happiness. But if any type were to be considered fully equipped with the tools to enjoy life, it should be the Laborer. Merchants lack self-esteem and tend to over-compensate for it; Educators are awkward and clumsy and take a long time to develop wisdom; Warriors need guidance and direction; and Outsiders have to play many roles before they find their own unique expression. But Laborers come ready to go from the starting gate. Though they also mature, gaining wisdom and respect with age, they have less of a learning curve than other types and require less reward to feel gratified.

Laborers don't need much from the world to make them happy. The warm touch of a loved one, a place they can call their own, and a way to use their talents to create something worthwhile is enough to make Laborers content. Loving and serving, qualities that come naturally to Laborers, are mainstays of their expression. They express love by creating and growing family, and they serve by giving the gift of their hard work. When Oprah Winfrey or Mother Teresa donate to charity or care for their community, they do so out of a natural sense of service.

Laborers are devotional, grounded, and self-effacing. Ramakrishna Paramahamsa, a Laborer type, embodied the highest states of *samadhi*, spiritual consciousness, but remained ever humble and true to his roots. Another example is Paramahansa Yogananda, also a Laborer type, whose devotion and love for his teachers saturate his seminal book, *Autobiography of a Yogi*.

When Laborers incorporate Merchant qualities, as we'll see below, they become a force of love and nourishment in the world. In fact, when Laborers and Merchants evolve, they begin to look a lot like each other.

Every type receives something by the natural operation of its talents. In protecting others Warriors gain fame and power. From enriching people the Merchant gets money and gratitude. By enlightening the masses Educators earn respect. And by shaking up society Outsiders find their own unique expression. But Laborers have no such agenda. For Laborer types the act of serving is its own reward. They need no gratitude, esteem, power, or soul searching—they already have everything inside them. In that sense they are the most complete type, being able to give of themselves without requiring anything in return. This does not mean, however, that they should work for nothing. In fact, by integrating qualities of the Merchant type they increase their earning power and learn the true value of their work. It also does not mean that they are not insecure. When Laborers slip up, as we all do at times, they doubt their own intelligence and knowledge about the world.

But generally Laborers feel called to service because they have so much of themselves to give without expectation of reward. Subtle remnants of this ethic exist in the service and hospitality industry where waiters and valets work for "tips"—voluntary gifts for service well done. True Laborer types find fulfillment in their work and extra money is an added bonus, not an end in itself—though in Merchant society tipping has become the norm.

Laborers love and feel deeply, though one would be hard pressed to get them to say it. They express love through deeds. They do what they say and say what they do, and they have the strength to stick to their word and follow through with promises. They live by principles that, though simple, are far from simplistic:

Loyalty: Although easy to explain, something especially tough to carry out in practice.

Truthfulness: People are only as good as their word—what they say, they must do.

Work: People earn their bread by the sweat of their brow, and the quality of their work speaks to the quality of who they are.

Love: Difficult to express and hard to feign, and the sum of the previous three. In effect, Laborers show their love by loyalty, plain speaking, and hard work. Where these are present in abundance, there is no need for words.

Laborers enjoy bringing people together and sharing community with others. They love barbecues, powwows, and gatherings centered on food, believing that "the way to the heart is through the stomach" and that it is easier to get to know somebody over a meal and a drink than in hours of stuffy conversation. They are also the most caring of the types and gravitate to industries and professions that succor, nourish, or otherwise tend to the needy, making great social workers, nurses, or therapists. Laborers can often be found working in the trenches, as the first contact with the people they serve.

Laborers also excel at professions of skill and manual dexterity. They are masterful at manipulating material resources and make the best craftspeople, artisans, and engineers. They are usually highly talented in their area of expertise though not necessarily well rounded, and they gravitate to the service and trade industries, again working in the front lines of their field. Thus, while a Merchant type may own a restaurant and work the door, a Laborer would enjoy building, cooking, and serving there. Where the Merchant owns a medical business, the Laborer is the EMT first responder, anesthesiologist, X-ray tech, or nurse who cares for patients.

The Laborer type is a creature of habit and enjoys daily rituals. Routine and simplicity are far more satisfying than the hustle and bustle of busy life. In later years Laborers may yearn for the ways of the past and hearken to a day when "life was more simple." They are also the most superstitious of types, believing things with an ingrained faith that is hard to budge. Getting them to change their beliefs is like pulling teeth. But when they do change they are likely to be as staunch in their new credo as they were in their old, even if it is the opposite of what they used to think!

PATH TO DEVOLUTION
The Educator

When Laborers devolve by taking on Educator qualities, they become literal minded, oversensitive, and dogmatic. They take slight at little things and carry grudges to their graves—sometimes taking offense if people rub them the wrong way and never speaking to them again! When they devolve they tend to overthink things and become stuck in a mental loop from which they cannot get out. They become "fixed," or rooted in a style of thinking or belief. Here is the classic rock junkie who cannot get out of the 1960s, or the televangelist who cannot accept other faiths, or the overpossessive parents who cannot let their children go, meddling in every aspect of their lives. These problems are remedied by the Laborer's evolution into the Merchant type.

Merchants are gregarious while Laborers tend to be closed.

Merchants introduce Laborers to a wide world of sensations, concepts, and new experiences. They are go-getters, while Laborers tend to run on inertia. Laborers are phlegmatic, traditional types who prefer security to extravagance, and when they devolve they tend to fall into animal-realm psychology that is territorial, resentful, and aggressive if challenged. Like junkyard dogs they remain guardians of their private domain without ever venturing to see what lies beyond its borders. They become prisoners of their own knowledge and beliefs, becoming closed in and parochial. They may also misuse knowledge to the point of becoming obsessed with an idea. Obsession means possession, and Laborers can become fixated on a person, place, or thing to the point of being unable to see anything else.

When Laborer types take on Educator values they begin to assume they know it all, which can lead to fundamentalism that tries to convert others to its cause. There is a narrowness of vision in Laborers that doesn't work well with issues that require a broad perspective and the willingness to see different sides of a story. Because they also tend to mix emotion with reason, and sentimentality with logic, they may come to conclusions that feel right but often have no objective value. For this reason politics, law, religion, and philosophy are areas where Laborers are disadvantaged. Ironically, when they devolve they become interested in just such topics. And while the result is that they convert many to their cause by their tireless work and good intentions, the cause itself will be diminished in the long run for their lack of liberality.

Laborers are heart-based, feeling deeply whatever they believe. When a devolved Laborer misconstrues fact and feeling the result can be catastrophic for the world, as in oppressive political ideologies, fundamentalist religious sects, and petty, bigoted philosophies. By nature Laborers tend to be conservative, in the sense that they have a deep appreciation for past traditions. William F. Buckley Jr., one of the pioneers of modern conservatism, defined conservatism as the "tacit acknowledgment that all that is finally important in human experience is behind us."[1]

When this love of the past embraces life-affirming traditions it preserves the best of civilization. When it indiscriminately clings to the past over progress it risks embarrassing the Laborer with wrongheaded thinking.

Progress is the hallmark of a liberal mind-set. Webster's defines liberalism as "a political philosophy based on belief in progress, the essential goodness of man, and the autonomy of the individual and standing for the protection of political and civil liberties." While not every Educator is liberal, and not every Laborer is conservative, these strains of progress (Educator) and tradition (Laborer) tend to run strong in these two types. In the final analysis they both need each other, as new ideas cannot be built without the foundation of the past. Tradition cannot be maintained without embracing the progress that allows for improvement of our daily lives, be it through indoor plumbing or the recognition of the civil rights of all races, genders, ages, and physical abilities. Both inclinations, both types, need to recognize the value of the other. But when they devolve they both become stuck, unable to move from their positions.

Laborers think they *know;* Educators think they *can.* This is another mantra for these types when they devolve. On the one hand Laborers believe that they are sufficiently informed to be righteous and dogmatic about a cause. On the other, Educators think they have the skill to create and maintain projects that require manual dexterity, endurance, and perseverance. In fact the Educator has none of these in sufficient quantities, nor does the Laborer possess the quality of information to make judgments on matters of political, philosophical, or religious relevance. The problem with the devolved type is that it believes it has enough of another's attributes to be successful in its work. Reality, however, does not bear this out. The Educator's work quality, and even body, suffers from the stress of disintegration, while Laborers' accumulation of fact and feeling suffices to build a box that closes in around and chokes them.

> **It is hard enough to do what you were born to do; why complicate it by trying to be someone else?**

The Vedic view of personal dharma is simple: it is hard enough to do what you were born to do; why complicate it by trying to be someone else? Why take away another's livelihood when it is so difficult to find and follow your own? This is the gist of the evolution and devolution points. One path leads us to our dharma, the other away from it. These observations are not value judgments, or imprecations on the intelligence, decency, or moral character of the types. We find PhD candidates among Laborers just as we find craftsmen among Educators. In fact, it is not the quantity but the quality and specificity of intelligence that is at question here.* The point is that, all factors being equal, Educators are bound to possess a liberality and worldliness that Laborer types lack. For specialists like accountants or rocket scientists these may not be considerations, and Laborers are qualified to perform these professions. Where laser-like focus and specificity is required the Laborer is advantaged; where wide-ranging knowledge of language, customs, and policies is required, as in, say, diplomacy, the Laborer is disadvantaged. In much the same way the Educator is at a deficit when it comes to the cleverness and application of manual skill and mundane duties. While the Educator may know the perfect recipe in theory, it will not taste as good as the Laborer's creation because of the latter's indelible instinct for its real-life preparation, seasoning, and presentation.

INFERIORITY

Other instances of the Laborer's devolution are feelings of inferiority and being overwhelmed when confronted with too much information. Laborers can become anxious and closed down if they feel that they are

---

*Refer to chapter 11 for more on the intelligence specific to each type.

not smart enough in a given situation, beginning to doubt themselves even to the point of not trusting what has worked for them for years. Oprah Winfrey, an evolved Laborer type, has commented on her diffidence in front of certain audiences that make her doubt her own wisdom. A famous story illustrates the concept:

Once there was a Tibetan farmer who was visited by a young itinerant monk. The farmer welcomed the monk with great reverence and sincerity, offering him shelter, food, and, of course, butter tea. Impressed with this genuine display of devotion, the monk asked the farmer about his spiritual practice. The farmer smiled sheepishly and said that he only knew one mantra, but that he practiced it faithfully every day while he was tilling the fields. Curious, the monk asked to hear it.

As the farmer began to recite, a peaceful smile washed across his face, the sun came out from behind the clouds, rainbows appeared in the sky, and birds in the valley began to sing. Impressed, the monk said to the farmer, "You have done well, but you are mispronouncing it." With this, he instructed the grateful farmer on the mantra's proper usage and, thanking him for his food and board, left to pursue his journey.

A year passed, and the monk happened again through that valley, but now it appeared dark and desolate, a shadow of its former self. When he came across the farmer he asked, "What happened? This field was once so green and full of life!" The farmer bowed respectfully and said, "Ever since I changed the mantra, my life has been falling apart: there are no crops, no animals, and no food in the valley."

Incredulous, the monk asked, "Then why didn't you change back to the way you used to recite it?" Shaking his head, the farmer replied, "I could not, for fear that I would displease you, God, and the holy order of monks. But it's okay, maybe God intends for me to suffer this karma for my highest good."

Saying this, he smiled resignedly and turned to go. The monk now realized his mistake and, embarrassed by his own hubris, begged the farmer to resume his mantra the old way, whereupon the valley re-blossomed with abundance and cheer.

> For [Laborers] the essence of a rose is always more important than its name, and confusion sets in when they try to replace pure experience with its linguistic counterpart.

Laborers possess a natural devotion and humility that is beyond the artifice of superficial information. For them the essence of a rose is always more important than its name, and confusion sets in when they try to replace pure experience with its linguistic counterpart. That is not to say that they should not learn or study, but that information should be subordinate to experience. Pavarotti could not read or write music, but oh, could he sing! An experience is always more than the sum of its parts; the chemical constituents of a flower cannot explain how it makes you feel to smell and see it, and notes on a page are nothing until they have been amplified by the tenor's heart and soul. The linguistic is the realm of the Educator, while the experiential belongs to the earthy Laborer type. When one tries to take over the function of the other, confusion and misunderstanding ensue.

> Pavarotti could not read or write music, but oh, could he sing!

PATH TO EVOLUTION
The Merchant

By taking on qualities of the Merchant type Laborers begin to see boundaries not as borders but as meeting places—not a way to keep people out, but a place to welcome and communicate with neighbors. By incorporating movement and music in their lives they stir the depths of their soul to new levels of expression and emotion. Music is important to Laborers, who feel it more deeply than perhaps any other type. Musical styles like blues, country, R&B, and traditional are staples in their lives. (Different styles of music and their relationship with the dharma types are discussed in chapter 12).

Kinesthetic sense is also strong in Laborers, and they need to touch and be touched to connect to their emotions. Carbohydrate-rich food is optimal for them. Unlike Warriors, who do better on higher protein and moderate carbohydrate diets, Laborers love carbs, which pack their muscles with energy for long bouts of physical movement. Perhaps more importantly carbohydrates also release serotonin in the brain—encouraging e-motion, the expression of feelings. This is vital for Laborers, who tend to shut down and get stuck when they devolve. There is no emotion *without* motion, and anything that keeps a Laborer type moving is good. From ballroom dancing to hiking and gardening, exercise is great for Laborers, especially outdoors in the natural world. Laborers think and feel deeply, and they can become depressed if they begin to obsess on negative thoughts. Distracting themselves with music, massage, and movement is a way to reframe their thinking.

Evolutionary integration between Merchants and Laborers occurs when each adopts qualities of the other. As a Laborer type Johnny Carson tapped into his down-home, Midwest sensibilities to reach and appeal to huge masses of people on his way to super popularity. The entertainment industry is a Merchant business and well suited to Laborers who can break out of their shells and relate to the public. Laborer types are storytellers, but not in the same animated way as Merchants. They love to tell jokes and anecdotes and to share their values with the community—when they integrate the Merchant's natural volubility and social ease they can move audiences to tears of joy and sorrow.

Whether keeping alive the stories of their ancestors or their nation they also make natural historians, antiquarians, and archaeologists— the latter especially for their connection to the Earth Element. Using Merchant savvy Laborers popularized dusty professions like Egyptology by connecting the mysteries of the earth with people's natural desire to discover and learn. Laborers enjoy digging for mysteries, and combined with their one-track mind and dogged persistence they can unravel practically any detective story—even those told by hieroglyphs in stone.

For optimal evolution Laborer types need to think like Merchants to receive their due in society. They need to learn the value of their work, and Merchant society has done much to benefit them in this respect—agriculture, landscape, construction, and other skilled Laborer professions these days are highly remunerated. Laborers also make great engineers, accountants, builders, and carpenters because their hands are golden. They can take a piece of metal and make it work in the service of mankind, like a plumbing pipe that brings clean water to a city or an automobile that drives us to and fro. They can take a piece of wood and make it serviceable to their needs as art, like a statue, or as a work of utility, like a dresser drawer. Laborers are gifted with their hands and possess practical skill in just about any trade they choose to tackle. Being close to the earth, they prefer to live on ground floors rather than loft apartments. The heights are not for them—another reason they devolve into the Educator, who prefers a high tower to the common halls.

Music and touch, along with good food and sensual enjoyment, tend to keep Laborers happy, allowing them to express love, which is their highest purpose. This is not the mushy sentimentalism we associate with the word today but the tough and ever so practical love of a Mother Teresa who takes other's problems on her strong and steady shoulders. While Merchants may provide the *means* of support, Laborers are the *way*. That is, they are on the front line of care for those who most need it. Merchant types are responsible for providing capital and resources to build an infrastructure, but Laborer types are the ones who actually work to make it operable. Their work and service are love in action, called *seva* in Sanskrit, and the spiritual path that best fits the Laborer's disposition.

Merchants and Laborers, capital and labor, have always complemented each other, for one has what the other one needs. One example is the relationship between the United States and Mexico. A Merchant nation, the United States contains well over 10 percent of Mexico's population, which comes to trade its labor for increased financial opportunities. On the other hand many Americans willingly trade their capital for the dream of a relaxed, worry-free life—portrayed by tourist hubs like Cabo San Lucas and Cancún—in search of the simple pleasure of margaritas and the beach. In fact, Merchant types in America have made Mexican exports like beer and tequila staples of American weekend rituals. This is one of many examples illustrating the mutual evolution between these types, an evolution that goes beyond just personal growth into the nature of relationships, government, and even spiritual realization—themes explored in the chapters that follow.

6

Outsider

Innovate, Rebel, and Free Others

Empathy • Freedom • New Advances

Famous Outsiders

(based on birth data and their Vedic Life Map)

Antonio Banderas

Brigitte Bardot

Roseanne Barr

David Beckham

Halle Berry

Bjork

David Blaine

Richard Branson

Yul Brynner

Tim Burton

George W. Bush

Albert Camus

George Carlin

Johnny Cash

Jesus Christ

Joe Cocker

Salvador Dali

Johnny Depp

Lady Diana

Jane Fonda

Redd Foxx

Greta Garbo

Jimi Hendrix

Jacqueline Kennedy Onassis

Martin Luther King Jr.

Evel Knievel

Jeddu Krishnamurti

John Lennon

Ian McKellan

Liza Minnelli

Osho/Rajneesh

Vincent Price

Ravana (Rama's enemy)

Chris Rock

Martin Scorsese

Sting

Jesse Ventura

Denzel Washington

Foxes have holes and the birds of the air have nests, but the son of Man has no place to lay his head.

LUKE 9:58

Such is the fate of the Outsider—a traveler, a searcher on a quest, blending in everywhere, fitting in nowhere. Rebels, radicals, enigmas even to themselves—while most people have well-outlined dharmas Outsiders' destinies are loosely sketched and mostly masterpieces of their own creation. Their role is that they have no role; the purpose of their lives is to find their purpose. Theirs is the double-edged sword of freedom and confusion, equally as comfortable in the clubhouse as in the slaughterhouse.

Nothing new comes into existence without the Outsider's touch. There is no innovation or revolution without the Outsider's instigation—anything that requires radical rethinking, leaps of imagination, and creative synthesis of many elements is the Outsider's purview. Ruled by the Space Element, Outsiders have no "where" they cannot travel, just as there is no experience they cannot have. From the highest of the high to the lowest of the low, Outsiders trek the terrains of the wild and the inner spaces of the soul, reaching to depths and heights where no one else dares to follow. Laws and morals hold little power to obstruct their need for experience, and Outsiders are most creative in their interpretation of social strictures. As a result they can just as easily fall into depravity as soar to the heights of purity—such is the razor's edge that defines the Outsider's path. However, just as it is easy to fall off track, it is also simple for Outsiders to get back on, for they are never far removed from redemption, though it may not seem that way to them. Examples of criminals turned saints abound in sacred literature, illustrating the Outsider's roller-coaster journey from truth to error—and back again.

Outsiders often feel alone, as if they are the only ones of their kind in the universe. Unlike Merchants, whose emptiness is inside, for Outsiders the void appears all around them, making it difficult to know their place in the world and how to relate with others. They are everyone and no one. Although they have good reason to feel this way, it is ultimately not true—there is a community out there for even the most estranged of Outsiders, and part of their purpose is to find it. The journey may take them to places far and away but the end is well worth the pains. In fact, Outsiders are the most populous of all the types in the Iron Age—from breatharians living on nothing but sunlight to trekkies who live on sci-fi reruns, it is far easier to find solidarity with fellow Outsiders in the modern age of the Internet.

Because they are searching for themselves Outsiders are quick to identify with anything that personifies something they believe. From Egypt and her mysteries to Vedic devotional chanting Outsiders espouse ideologies that reflect Truth for them, the truth of their real identities. As a matter of rebellion, they often embody exotic or different beliefs in order to assert their independence from "normal" people. They are masters of change, and when one identity no longer suits them it is quickly shed for a new and better fit. From Rastafarian chic to business casual they change fashions with the seasons, all with the passion of their quest for unique self-expression.

Outsiders may spend most of their lives searching for purpose and meaning in the world, but when they find it they are potent forces for change. And where they go during this quest for self-fulfillment none can follow. Society awaits what they bring back, for though Outsiders leave, they must eventually return to their culture with the treasures of their journey, be they rare jewels or jewels of rare wisdom. This is how they earn their place and value in the world while changing and redefining it thereby.

Outsiders have the unique ability to blend disparate entities and make a wholly new creation from their union. This is the cook who combines Asian and Western recipes to create fusion cuisine. It is the country singer who mixes gospel and blues to create rock 'n' roll. It is Martin Luther King Jr. bringing Gandhi and Indian philosophy to bear upon the American social scene. This is the yogi who melds yoga and fitness to create a marketable new workout craze.

In fact, in traveling West the Vedic Vidya herself* has entered into an Outsider life cycle, a period of time characterized by great change and contact with new elements. Her exposure here lends itself to all sorts of new creations, some more successful than others. Innovations that remain rooted in the authentic soil of Vedic wisdom prosper; those

---

*The feminine personification of a body of knowledge—generally, the Vedic culture.

that cut themselves off from the source of their life wither and die.

This is a lesson for Outsiders, who must never lose sight of the original society that forms the backdrop to their lives. The only way to earn true freedom is to come back to the place that made you. Prophets are never prophets in their own hometown, but the best Outsiders, like Jesus, return from their journeys to face the music and give people the unique insights of their inner and outer explorations.

> **"Society is like a stew. If you don't keep it stirred up you get a lot of scum on the top."**
> EDWARD ABBEY

Of course, this return is sure to disrupt the status quo because new ideas are always unsettling. There is always upheaval in the wake of the Outsider's interactions. People are left with a new awareness, a positive or negative change in their mental state. From Salvador Dali to Bhagavan Rajneesh, Outsiders are a slap in the face of conformity. The hippie movement is an example of such values taking over the world in an Outsider cycle that spanned the 1960s and 1970s. It was countercultural and experimental, and it blended influences from other cultures into its own—an example of how, just as people can travel through life cycles, countries and cultures also move through different periods in their evolution. And just as the free-love hippie revolution inspired change it also highlighted Outsiders' glaring shortcomings, most notably their lack of self-responsibility.

WHO'S TO BLAME?

Outsiders are the "accusers" and whistleblowers of society. When evolved they find what's wrong and bring it to our attention. When devolved they are blamers, lacking self-awareness and making others responsible for their shortcomings. The Space Element that rules Outsiders can cause confusion—with no direction or point of focus it is easy to become disoriented by such limitless freedom. Space, or the element ether as it was once known, can cause confusion, delusion, and outright unconsciousness. But Space is also perfectly clear, allowing Outsiders to see things with unmatched perspicacity if they have proper orientation. Not even Educators, whose Air Element is a filter to perfect sight, can see with the same clarity.

The Laborer is blinded by Earth (physicality), the Merchant by Water (emotionality), the Warrior by Fire (ambition), and the Educator by Air (ideology), whereas Outsiders are unfettered—free to see things as they are, provided they have a permanent fixed star by which to get their bearings. Ultimately, for the most evolved Outsiders that fixed star becomes a spiritual referent, for everything in the physical world is perishable— that is why so many of the earth's saviors and prophets are Outsiders. In Judeo-Christian terms, Jesus and Satan form bookends of the Outsider model. Satan (literally "the accuser") stands on one end as utter darkness, like the darkness of space. Jesus stands on the other, as the embodiment of light (Messiah, radiantly "anointed"). Thus the Outsider embodies both colors, black and white—colors, incidentally, that Outsiders favor in both personal fashion and outer design!

Which Outsider you become depends upon your orientation. Do you have an anchor, like the dharma type, to keep you grounded in reality? Do you have a technology and a system to keep you in check, to help you find your way when you stray? Below we will consider the paths to evolution, and the slippery slopes that spill us down into utter distress. Good Outsiders know when to upheave society and when to fly under the radar. But devolved Outsiders are lawless reprobates who feel justified in destruction, unwilling to implement conscious awareness in the process.

Between these extremes, of course, lies the more common group of Outsiders—anxiety ridden, flowing with society but never really fitting in or knowing themselves, unable to understand how to optimize their considerable talents for self-fulfillment. By using the three steps to integration that we shall see in table 6.2 (page 120) and learning how to include the best aspects of every type into their own, Outsiders can ultimately achieve this otherwise elusive sense of fulfillment.

The Laborer is blinded by Earth (physicality), the Merchant by Water (emotionality), the Warrior by Fire (ambition), and the Educator by Air (ideology), whereas Outsiders are unfettered—free to see things as they are, provided they have a permanent fixed star by which to get their bearings.

PATH TO EVOLUTION

All—The Rebel with a Cause

Like hermit crabs moving from shell to shell Outsiders can trade identities from time to time. Outsiders may go through a Warrior "phase," during which they delight in Warrior-type activities, or may immerse themselves in a Laborer period, taking on the Laborer personality and assuming its evolution and devolution points. These phases may be brief, lasting a few months, or lengthy, lasting decades, depending on their life cycles and other circumstances. And while this is true to a degree for everyone, the other dharma types never really lose themselves in a life cycle like the Outsider does. No one is as good at blending in as the malleable Outsider, which is ironic, since no one is as good at sticking out when they want to as Outsiders!

There are three ways in which Outsiders assume their identities (see table 6.1 on page 119). They may play one of the four types and stick to that identity all their lives. They may opt to remain simply Outsiders, without taking on any other roles. They may opt to change roles according to the season of their life cycles. This is the most common. Here are examples of each type:

As an Outsider, John was always athletic. His family moved from India to England when he was very young and he quickly fell in love with soccer. Over the years he distinguished himself with his skill and competitiveness, and he went on to play semi-pro before entering law school and becoming an immigration lawyer, helping qualified foreigners obtain legal status.

This story illustrates one of the prerequisites for being an Outsider. More often than not Outsiders are either born different or experience great change when they are young, such as moving from one continent, religion, or culture into another. This does not always have to be the case but is often true for Outsiders, who do not feel "at home" in their place of birth. They may travel widely, or simply embrace foreign customs. Madonna, a Warrior type, moved to England and embraced Kabbalah during her Outsider life cycle. In this case, John is a real Outsider whose greatest fulfillment came through playing a Warrior due to his natural talents and genetic disposition. Throughout his whole life he enjoyed competition and other Warrior pursuits, eventually settling into law as his profession. Let's take a look at another example:

Fernando grew up on the mean streets of South Central L.A. to Hispanic parents in a Latino neighborhood. He resented authority and got into scuffles with his teachers, elders, and eventually the police. From tagging buildings and highways to breaking into homes he felt justified in taking from the "rich" because they had opportunities he didn't. To his mind, they didn't understand what it was like growing up in a place where every day is about survival—and they never would.

In this example Fernando is an Outsider who has chosen not to take on another role. He remains a true Outsider. While this particular portrayal is a negative example, true Outsiders can be as benefic to society as others are destructive—the example is not a judgment of good or bad, but an illustration of how, like John above, Outsiders can emulate any type or none of them at all.

Sara is a free bird that flies with the wind. When she was young her parents brought her from South Africa to America, where she grew up feeling different from other girls. While her parents were wealthy, she never really fit in with their crowd. She went to college to study medicine but dropped out three years later to pursue Thai massage. She married, had children, and settled into the quiet life of a dutiful housewife. When she divorced a few years later she decided to open a Thai massage studio and soon became financially independent. Embracing East/West concepts she grew attached to the plight of Tibetans living abroad, and began contributing to their cause by donating money, clothes, and shelter. Finally, she challenged herself to actively campaign for their rights by organizing Free Tibet protests in her city and working full-time for their cause.

Here is an example of an Outsider who goes where her life cycles take her. From Merchant ideas of business and prosperity to Warrior values of protecting and fighting for the rights of others, she embraces the roles her cycles give her, sometimes going back and forth between them. In this case she went from studying medicine (Warrior), to practicing massage and raising a family (Laborer), to owning a business and contributing to her community (Merchant), and finally back to Warrior by becoming a civil rights advocate. Life cycles can and do repeat. Sometimes people see just one or two cycles, while others experience all five over and over again across the span of their lives. These will be discussed in the final chapter.

TABLE 6.1. THE OUTSIDER'S THREE ROLES

ONE FIXED IDENTITY	NO CHANGE OF IDENTITY	CHANGES IDENTITY
Warrior, Educator, Laborer, or Merchant	Remains an Outsider	Adopts multiple dharma types over life cycle

Outsiders make the best actors because they can blend seamlessly into any role. Thus some play many, while other Outsiders play one dominant role during their lives. They remain Warriors if that is their dominant personality, or Educators if that best reflects their life purpose, taking on evolution and devolution points of each.

Such Outsiders would look, talk, and act like Educators, though on closer inspection their Outsider qualities would inevitably show through. They might teach foreign subjects or study arcane lore. They may be interested in Sufi dance while living in Minnesota. They may study and speak the Inuit languages, though hailing from the deserts of Arizona. Joseph Campbell is an example of an Outsider firmly fixed into an Educator role. A self-proclaimed maverick, he revolutionized the study of myth and culture through his synthesis of world traditions. In Sara's example above, Outsider qualities were always present regardless of what role she played. As a young girl she felt different from her peers, while as a mature woman she embraced foreign ideas from Thai massage to the cause of Tibetan liberation. Whatever identity she adopted, she retained some of her Outsider uniqueness.

KEYS TO SELF-REALIZATION

Because Outsiders are unique, free-flowing creatures they must remain ever vigilant and self-aware so as to not fall into self-deceit, blaming others for their problems. Self-awareness is their most important tool for staying honest with themselves and present to the circumstances in their lives—and it is their first step in integration. The second step lies in finding their unique expression. Finally, they must return and share their unique expression with the world. Table 6.2 shows what these three steps look like, as well as their obstacles.

TABLE 6.2. INTEGRATION OF THE OUTSIDER

THE OUTSIDER'S THREE STEPS TO INTEGRATION	THE OUTSIDER'S THREE OBSTACLES TO INTEGRATION
Self-awareness	Self-deceit/blaming others
Finding unique expression	Getting lost in confused thinking
Returning and sharing unique expression	Fear/anxiety about being accepted/understood

Standing in the way of the ability Outsiders have to be self-aware is the propensity to lie to themselves, blame others, and not take responsibility for their circumstances. Standing in the way of their ability to find their unique gift is their confusion about who they are and how they are supposed to live. Finally, fear of being rejected and misunderstood keeps them from sharing their gifts with the world. When they can overcome these obstacles Outsiders become incomparable jewels, invaluable and rare.

For many Outsiders this may mean changing roles over their lifetime and learning the dharma of every type before understanding their own. Like a bee hopping from flower to flower they may need to imbibe the nectar of each dharma type in order to obtain its most authentic essence, and with inner alchemy create the honey of their own unique expression. Having to do this makes being an Outsider more difficult, but it also gives them the freedom to express themselves in ways other types can only dream of.

> Like a bee hopping from flower to flower Outsiders may need to imbibe the nectar of each dharma type in order to obtain its most authentic essence, and with inner alchemy create the honey of their own unique expression.

This change of roles is often not a conscious choice but is a result of their growth as human beings. Being an Educator might suit them for a while, but they may later need to become Warriors. As discussed above, though, some Outsiders never change roles. They remain in the costume of one type, or no type at all—being simply Outsiders. Whatever the case, Outsiders get to enjoy the dharmas of the other types as no one else can. They get to make their own road to happiness and create their own purpose. This freedom is paid for by the work they do to understand every one of the other types and their destinies.

RESPONSIBILITY AND TRUE FREEDOM

Outsiders have a special gift, a unique expression to share with others. There is something that they can do differently and better than anyone else in the world. Finding it, Outsiders arrive at their unique expression, or at least one of them, for they may have many unique talents. These first two steps to integration, self-awareness and finding a unique expression, are instrumental to the Outsider's liberation. The final step is returning to society.

Outsiders must remember that they are only Outsiders in relation to something—therefore they must not abandon the society that defines them even if it defines them by not recognizing them. The ultimate freedom for the Outsider type is to return from time to time to the normal world, bringing new gifts and awareness to it while recharging, resting, and preparing for another adventure into the unknown.

Outsiders cannot be honest with themselves if they leech off people and then turn around and decry them behind their backs, the way of criminals and thieves, the worst Outsiders.

However, the best Outsiders receive knowledge from Educators, skill from Warriors, wealth and shelter from Merchants, and food and craft from Laborers, and they are fed by their community. What they give in return are new perspectives on their own paths. From their explorations they bring new philosophies, weapons, currencies, and recipes for the other types to enjoy.

The Outsider's path to evolution lies in accepting that no embodied being can be completely independent. Since we all require food to eat, air to breathe, and clothes to wear, we are tied to the environment that provides these for us. We cannot totally destroy the society that gives us sustenance, no matter how wicked or depraved it may be. Few of us can live naked in the wilderness and none of us can do it alone—no one can survive without the support of Nature, for we are all embodied beings in bondage to the exigencies of food, water, shelter, sleep, and sex. In sharing these with all humanity lies the connection between Outsiders and the rest of the world.

True freedom for Outsiders comes when they acknowledge and accept their dependence on the world. They can do nothing without the favor of Nature, society, and the other dharma types. When they realize this they understand that there is nothing to run from, and nowhere to run. Wherever you go, there you are—Outsiders bring their inner demons with them wherever they turn. It is in facing and owning these that they can free themselves *from* themselves, and move on to fulfill their highest destiny. Running away is a form of self-deception, a way to refuse and deny what you don't want to look at. Outsiders' progress begins when they look at their inner lies and boldly own up to them. Let us look at this first step of self-awareness in greater detail.

SELF-AWARENESS
Overcoming Deceit

Outsiders have a looser concept of right and wrong than any other type. Their reality is fluid, changeable, and hard to define. They are for the spirit of the law, rather than its letter. As a result Outsiders can be perceived as being untruthful, unreliable, or even masters of deceit. At their worst they lie to themselves, unaware of their own self-deception, refusing to apply the same critical eye to themselves that they cast on the world. Unlike Educators, who feel great remorse when they fail to walk the walk, Outsiders are often ignorant of having done any wrong because they believe that the laws that apply to others don't apply to them. When they overcome this blindness and see themselves with the same eye with which they see the world, they can become masters of Truth. Very few Outsiders have the responsibility, ruth, and respect it takes to accomplish this; accordingly, few Outsiders live up to the unlimited potential of their type.

Therein lies the great mystery of the Outsider gift: no matter how mottled their past, they are always an inch away from grace!

1. **Responsibility:** Being true to yourself means taking responsibility for everything in your life, including things beyond your control. For John, who came to England as a young boy from India, though it was not in his power to change it, it meant owning his past and making the most of it. For Fernando, it was taking responsibility for his crimes and the effects they had on his community. Responsibility is refusing to lie to yourself and others. This is the most difficult step, and it involves delving deep into your inner demons and confessing them truthfully. Good counsel is a must at this stage, and it is important to have trustworthy people to confide in.

2. **Ruth:** In confession there is a profound contrition that goes along with having revealed your darkest secrets. That is why responsibility and ruth go hand in hand. At this stage Outsiders resolve to fight self-deception and blame and to never repeat their wrongs—a deeply cleansing process. With ruth also comes the resolution to do something positive with your talents, a desire to achieve a goal and change the world. As Outsiders begin to work their resolutions an abiding respect begins to well up from inside their being: respect for others, but mostly respect for *themselves.* In turn, this self-respect is reflected back on them by others. People begin to sit up and take notice of the person who has walked through the valley of the shadow of death—and survived. They become eager to hear what you have learned.

3. **Respect:** Outsiders' responsibility and ruth naturally lead others to respect them. People see the power and strength it takes to own your life, and respect is their gift. Outsiders feel a deep pride in having overcome their demons, and self-respect is the natural outcome. It glows from evolved Outsiders and is unmis-

takable to any with whom they come into contact. This is the level at which Outsiders can create monumental changes in the world.

A story from the New Testament sketches out this process. As Jesus lies on the cross, two criminals beside him also paying for their crimes, we witness one Outsider's redemption and another's damnation. The first robber turns to Jesus and cries, "If you are the Christ, save yourself and us!" Here is the blamer, who cannot convict himself for his own fate but imputes responsibility to others. Immediately, from the other side, his fellow criminal pipes up, "Hey, do you not fear God? You who are yourself on the cross, do you even rail at the innocent? You and I are executed for our deserts, but this man has done no harm!" Here is the ruth of the noble Outsider. He owns up to his crimes and accepts his punishment. Taking responsibility for his soul, he entreats Jesus, "Lord, remember me in your kingdom." As a result, he is forgiven immediately and given his respect and absolution as Jesus replies, "Even now, you are blessed with me!"

TABLE 6.3. THE OUTSIDER'S THREE STEPS TO SELF-AWARENESS

Self-awareness begins with: 1) Responsibility: Telling the truth to yourself. 2) Ruth: Resolving what you want to do with your life, and what you will never repeat. 3) Respect: Developing self-respect that leads to respect from society.

Unique Expression begins with: Self-awareness and searching for your unique gift to the world. Finding your unique expression may mean blending many other things or inventing something totally new. Every Outsider has a unique expression—find yours!

Return to Society begins with: Sharing your unique expression with the world. Returning does not mean you ever left society; it means sharing the gifts of your nature with it.

And therein lies the great mystery of the Outsider gift: no matter how mottled their past they are always an inch away from grace—

and this redemption is not just a religious concept. The graffiti artist who gets to paint city hall, the mugger turned respected self-defense teacher, the check defrauder teaching the FBI how to spot bad checks—all examples of everyday redemption that mean not just paying for misdeeds, but turning them around into respect when given the chance.

> **"Improvement makes straight roads, but the crooked roads are roads of genius."**
> **WILLIAM BLAKE**

The Outsider's is not the straight path but the path of mystery. As far as Outsiders may seem from redemption, a shortcut can take them there in no time. Consider the stories of vagabond saints through history who spent their lives in thievery, lust, and murder—like the Vedic story of Valmiki, author of the great Vedic epic Ramayana, and in the Christian tradition Paul (or Saul as he was then known), who was a fervent persecutor of early Christians before a beneficent vision turned his life around.

On a more prosaic level, consider the modern Freedom Writers, whose story was made popular by a movie of the same name. These were inner-city kids who were never given a chance until a momentous encounter with teacher Erin Gruwell changed their lives, eventually turning them into college graduates and contributors to the community.[1]

Being a moment away from redemption does not mean Outsiders do not have to pay the consequences for their deeds; it simply preempts further suffering, bringing Outsiders closer to realizing their inner self—which is always free, always full of respect. Karma is ineluctable; even the most reformed Outsider has to pay karmic debts. Valmiki, whose name means "anthill," is so named because of the power and duration of his austerities, remaining locked in meditation for so long that ants are said to have built a fortress around him. One may have to go to great lengths to pay one's debts, but redemption cannot be bought. It is free for Outsiders who take the steps to responsibility, ruth, and respect—and these in turn eventually lead to their freedom.

> **By earning their own freedom Outsiders also free others. . . . Only the Outsider's Space Element exists within and without, everywhere and nowhere, unbounded and free. Like the Space Element, Outsiders represent the freedom potential in each of us.**

Freedom is all-important to Outsiders, and the three steps summarized in table 6.3 (page 125) are how they ensure it for themselves and their community. By earning their own freedom Outsiders also free others—by demanding their own rights, they ensure the rights of everyone like them. Educators enlighten, bringing wisdom and understanding to the world through their professions. Warriors protect the environment, people, animals, objects, and ideas. Merchants enliven the world and make people happy. Laborers nourish by feeding, raising, and caring for others. Outsiders, for their part, are ultimately responsible for *freeing* others—from physical, mental, emotional, and spiritual concepts and restrictions. Even the Educator's Air Element is restricted to obey certain laws. Only the Outsider's Space Element exists within and without, everywhere and nowhere, unbounded and free. Like the Space Element, Outsiders represent the freedom potential in each of us.

Consider Krishna's description of the spirit in chapter 13 of the Bhagavad Gita:

> *It exists without and within all beings, and constitutes the animate and inanimate creation as well. And by reason of its subtlety, it is incomprehensible; it is close at hand and stands afar too.*
>
> BHAGAVAD GITA 13:15

Or his outreach to the most estranged Outsider:

Even if the vilest sinner worships me with exclusive devotion, he should be accounted a saint, for he has rightly resolved.

BHAGAVAD GITA 9:30

Following the three steps to integration over and over, Outsiders refine their being and ability to refresh society to such a degree that they become indispensable to it. Repeating this three-step process is in fact crucial to the ongoing success of the Outsider type: it does not suffice to go through it once but must be done over and over again until your expression and sharing become second nature, ensuring that you never slip back into self-destruction.

PATH TO DEVOLUTION
All—To Hell with the World

Outsiders pride themselves on being unique, one-of-a-kind creatures. When they devolve, they use their uniqueness to justify acting out in the belief that no one understands them. But when they do this Outsiders prove themselves quite predictable, blaming others for their plight and fleeing from problems and the hard reality of their present moment. They evade, deceive, and run—mostly from themselves.

Evolution for Outsiders is predicated upon honesty—telling the truth to themselves *about* themselves. Outsiders can lie and cheat others, and the greatest lies they tell to themselves. But understanding karma, that all-important leg of the Vedic tripod (dharma, duhkha, and karma*), allows Outsiders to make peace with their past, accept their present, and act decisively to create their future. Karma is universal justice—it relates to actions of the past that have created the present, and actions of the present that create the future.

Let's take a look at how this works. It is Outsiders' past karmas

---

*Dharma, duhkha, and karma correspond to purpose, suffering, and justice, as discussed in the introduction.

(fate) that give them the current life situations they must deal with; it is their own present karma (free will) that determines the results they reap from these situations. Outsiders are the authors of their destinies, and they must realize that instead of blaming others for their woeful story they can take up the pen and write it themselves. This is the Vedic view of universal justice, and for Outsiders to have justice in their lives they must first own up to their present situation.

> **When we own our grief and suffering, rebellion comes out to serve, not punish, society.**

Awareness of your karma leads to responsibility. Taking responsibility for your situation means that you acknowledge your present circumstances as a product of your actions, a result of your own behavior. Thus there is no one to else to blame or point the finger at. When we own our grief and suffering, rebellion comes out to serve, not punish, society. The best Outsiders have this orientation and are backed by the Universe in their nonconformity. They come to be revered by the very society they decry. Chess players cannot blame others for playing poorly; likewise we are responsible for the chessboard that is our life, and the Vedas say that we have to embrace, own, and change our karma if we are to enjoy our time on this planet. Just as fate gets us into this life in the first place, our own free will gets us out!

Western-minded Outsiders who are not as quick to embrace karmic philosophy can find other systems emphasizing responsibility, ruth, and respect, the three steps to self-awareness. These principles permeate many self-help methods, from Christianity and other religions to Neuro-Linguistic Programming, hypnosis, the Enneagram, and other empowering techniques.

In the Vedic view karma is the root of all creation and the efficient cause of the five dharma types. Being born an Outsider is the direct result of your own activities in previous incarnations. Far from using this as an excuse, the Vedic view squarely says that you have to own what you are because you got yourself there in the first place. Cultivated awareness is the answer to karma's proper diagnosis, integration, and discharge. Indeed, karma is the ultimate philosophy of responsibility and self-respect. Arthur Ashe summed this up in his three-volume history of black athletes, *A Hard Road to Glory,* when he said:

> At some point, each individual is responsible for his or her fate. At some point, one cannot blame history. Does the legacy of slavery explain why Mr. Jones eased into class ten minutes late this morning?[2]

For Outsiders the path to destruction lies in seeing themselves as victims of the world, thus stopping their own progress and growth. As victims they feel justified in acting out because of having received a raw deal in life, and because the world deserves their wrath. In this case it is not the destruction they cause that is the tragedy—because in truth Outsiders sometimes *do* get a raw deal—but the attenuation of the growth process inherent in that attitude. For Outsiders to evolve they must be honest with themselves, which is not possible when their mind is wrapped up in lamenting its sorry situation.

Sometimes Outsiders are physically different from others. Illness, disability, and other afflictions may segregate them from society. Other not-so-apparent factors may also alienate Outsiders from others. These include sexual orientation, chemical imbalances, environmental sensitivities, political or social policies, and other influences. This does not mean, however, that all gays or disabled people are Outsiders. It means that all factors being equal they experience a different reality from the average person. Blacks and other minorities have been treated historically as Outsiders in Western society, and this persists into today. As a group African-Americans have collectively been in a long Outsider period, regardless of their individual types. However, while social distinctions weigh on the dharma type, it is ultimately your fixed, inherent makeup that determines who you are, not Jim Crow laws or the fashions of justice. It is individual karma, not social situation, that makes a particular dharma type. That is why black Warriors, Educators, Merchants, Laborers, and Outsiders will all express themselves differently given the opportunity in a free society.

> **In survival mode we revert to more basic archetypes: men become Warriors, women Laborers . . . regardless of [our] original dharma type.**

Unfortunately, in many societies men and women are not given the chance to be more than just pure survivors. In countries where slavery, oppression, war, famine, or other tragic situations exist people are not given a chance to actuate their destinies and must search instead to eke out a limited existence. In survival mode we revert to more basic archetypes: men become Warriors, women Laborers. This is a deeper wiring in us that we experience in emergency situations. Whether killing a bug that has strayed into the house or fending off home invaders, a man kicks into Warrior mode when his hard-wired response is activated. Women for their part transform into nurturers, workers, and supporters—they become Laborers, regardless of their original dharma type.

Instead of trying to be like others Outsiders must embrace their uniqueness. Instead of resenting "normal" people they must contribute their distinctive talents to the world. They not only will be valued by their peers but will realize that they do not want to be normal at all, for so-called normal people are bound by the very rules that make them normal! Remember that Outsiders' foremost desire is freedom. They can never have it by living someone else's life. They must be grateful for the life they have, for all of its unique paths and crooked roads. Evolved Outsiders cherish their uniqueness, not as a point of rebellion but as a valuable contributing identity to the social order. It is, in fact, cool to be who you are.

The other dharma types have a path, a boundary. Outsiders have no boundaries and can truly make and define their own road. Because of that, however, many get lost, convincing themselves that they are right and the world is wrong. But those who refuse to lie to themselves become geniuses of society. Jesus was such an Outsider, scourging himself with scrutiny and penance before subjecting others to it, clearing the road within before imposing revolution without. Outsiders can take the best and worst qualities of every type, and he took the Warrior's penance, the Educator's wisdom, the Laborer's love, and the Merchant's charity and made them hallmarks of his ministry.

> **"We must become
> the change we desire."**
> **GANDHI**

In order to grow Outsiders must have an inner revolution before imposing external change: inner evolution before outer revolution. They must kill their own deceit before destroying the faults of others. These values run deep in the teachings of Christ, as evidenced in the following quotes:

> *First remove the plank from your own eye, and then you will see clearly to remove the speck from your brother's eye.*

> *Whoever desires to come after me, let him deny himself, and take up his cross, and follow Me . . .*

Those Outsiders who do not take up their crosses to bear the burden of their karma cannot wholly share their gifts with the world. Even Martin Luther King Jr.'s revolution of values was hampered by his philandering. Those Outsiders who do not purify themselves within will never know purity without, and they will ultimately fail to become the change they desire. These are Christian examples, but purification practices are common in every spiritual tradition.

OVERCOMING ANXIETY

Outsiders tend to run anxious and at extremes can be paranoid or even schizophrenic. Perhaps they have higher anxiety levels than other types because as Outsiders they fear the judgment or verdict of others, as they have always been stigmatized by society (hence the name "Outsider"). To combat this they must remember that they are now the most populous type and have more in common with others than they suspect. Their uneasiness is more of a genetic, physiological remnant of bygone ages than an accurate response to real stress. Therefore, relaxation techniques and self-acceptance are important for the Outsider's evolution.

Having high anxiety levels also leads Outsiders to blame others for their misfortunes—they will swerve into a lane and then scream at another driver for cutting them off; they get themselves into trouble and imprecate others when they suffer the consequences. When they are poorly integrated, Outsiders implicate the world in their problems; when evolved, they identify the problem and implicate themselves in fixing it. Being the troubleshooters of society they can quickly see what's wrong—and when evolved work to find solutions. To his enduring credit Martin Luther King Jr., in addressing the issue of equality, offered real solutions to achieve it. Evolved Outsiders not only identify what isn't working but also work to fix it. Take a look at the list of rebels and dissenters in your life and you will see a lineup of evolved and devolved Outsiders: those who create change to better the world, and those who disrupt the world so they don't have to change themselves.

STEREOTYPES AND SOCIAL HIERARCHIES

In conclusion let us look at what some of the negative stereotypes associated with Outsiders really mean. The degradation of caste systems and social hierarchies led to Outsiders being vilified with slurs like unclean, unreliable, thief, liar, vagabond, and deviant. Here is another way to look at these characterizations through the lens of the dharma type.

> Take a look at the list of rebels and dissenters in your life and you will see a lineup of evolved and devolved Outsiders: those who create change to better the world, and those who disrupt the world so they don't have to change themselves.

Unclean

Outsiders have their own, unique views on hygiene. Their tendency to extremes can lead them to become neat freaks or slobs. Whatever their orientation, Outsiders do not place as high a value on superficial cleanliness as they do on inner purity, such as they define it. More precisely, Outsiders keep pure what they value and let go what isn't important to them. Their lesson is to find balance between the two extremes.

A Harley biker might polish his chrome to a bright shine but defile his mouth with obscenities. The Rasta environmentalist might have pure thoughts about cleaning the environment but may not shower for weeks, or may pollute her inner environment with daily pot smoking. Outsiders make their own roads and redefine cultural practices, including personal hygiene. As Outsider Jesus cried to those who sacrificed inner purity for superficial appearance:

> *Blind Pharisee, first cleanse the inside of the cup and dish,*
> *that the outside may be clean also!*
> MATTHEW 23:26

Thief

Because Outsiders empathize well they can become anyone they desire. This can be misconstrued as copying or stealing another's identity. On another level, Outsiders who are often underprivileged may be forced to steal resources in order to survive. Coupled with their looser views of right and wrong, this sets up Outsiders to be fall guys in society. But if Outsiders were not marginalized and had been allowed the same economic, health, and political rights as other citizens they would not need to resort to crime. Consider the overwhelming statistics that blacks face in America. Though supposedly living in a post-racial society they are more than twice as likely to be poor, imprisoned, and marginalized than whites. Such is the Outsider legacy they still face. Let every minority and oppressed group heed the Outsider recommendations in this chapter in order to loosen the bonds of their oppression and transcend the petty customs that keep them in check. All Outsiders must learn the three steps in order to free themselves and change the world around them.

Deviant

Outsiders have looser definitions of sexual propriety, and as a rule they require more frequent as well as more varied sex than other types. When they do not get it, they are more likely to masturbate and seek to self-gratify, being less inhibited about sexual expression. People who find themselves in an Outsider period will often experience a sexual "awakening" of sorts that may lead them to explore depths of their sexuality hitherto untapped. Deviancy truly occurs only when natural sexual impulses are repressed over time and inappropriately expressed when they finally come out. Repression can be imposed by society, religion, family, or one's own ideologies. In any case, Outsiders need to learn the fine line between repression and expression, deviancy and self-control. Like anything else in their lives, they walk the razor's edge that separates healthy sexual attitudes from perversion and self-destruction.

7
Summary of Part One

SUMMARY OF EACH DHARMA TYPE

Educators

Strongly idealistic, but not necessarily practical

Noted for intelligence and grasp of abstruse concepts

Generally not forceful; physically less resilient than other types

Good counselors, but unable to follow their own counsel

Motivated by truth rather than money, but prone to indiscretions like anger, lust, or greed due to a lack of control over their senses

Sanskrit terms: jnana, dayaa, kshanti—wisdom, compassion, forbearance

Outsiders

Culture, beliefs, race, physicality, and other traits make them different from their immediate environment

Travel to or live in foreign lands and different or unusual places

Absorb and adopt foreign ideologies and concepts

Incredibly adaptive; able to blend in and wear many hats

Resent establishment and the "normal" life of others

Keenly aware of injustices in society, be they economic, educational, or political

Value personal freedom over other things

Sanskrit terms: ananda, kaivalya, svatantriya—bliss, isolation/independence, freedom

Warriors

Motivated by challenge to improve self and others

Interested in protecting those who cannot protect themselves

Respond to defiance and competition

Value knowledge, wisdom, and innocence in others

Sanskrit terms: yukti, virya, viveka—skill, strength, judgment

Merchants

Strongly motivated to secure personal and family interests

Need to be around others; feel lonely or empty without company

Smooth talkers: likable, glib, socially active, and highly entertaining

Feel best when giving, at first to family, then to community and eventually the world

Understand how the Merchant society functions and are good at taking advantage of it

Sanskrit terms: shakti, rasa, danam—energy, juiciness, charity

Laborers

Strong likes and dislikes

Deep sense of community and belonging

Emotional ties and loyalty to their own things: family, country, job, home team

Good physical strength and endurance, and a powerful work ethic

Capable of great service and self-sacrifice

Strong intuition and specific intelligence, but not well rounded

Sanskrit terms: bhakti, seva, dhriti—devotion/love, service, solidity/endurance

TABLE 7.1. ATTRIBUTES OF EACH DHARMA TYPE

DHARMA TYPE	SKILLS	STRENGTHS	WEAKNESSES
Warriors	Both gross and fine motor skills; usually a combination of the two that allows for the achievement of a goal (i.e., a soccer player).	Generous and self-sacrificing. Can achieve anything in the name of a good cause.	Pessimistic, cynical, materialistic. Do not believe in saving grace, and become prone to a dog-eat-dog mentality.
Merchants	Fine motor skills. Less goal-oriented, more focused on refinement (i.e., a violinist).	Inspirational and charitable. Entertaining and funny. Can motivate people.	Insecurity. Need constant validation from others to believe own worthiness.
Educators	Mental skills. Possess less motor skills than other types; often clumsy or uncoordinated.	High minded, pure, and noble. Sources of wisdom and purpose to others.	Wishy-washy, feckless, no backbone. Schism between ideals and reality, especially as pertains to base emotions like lust.
Laborers	Gross motor skills, usually applied for self-sustenance as in a trade or hobby.	Loyal and devoted. Hardworking and unaffected. The backbone of functional society.	Intense jealousy. Attachment to people, things, or ideas to the point of irrationality.
Outsiders	Can mimic any of the types. Usually have affinity with Laborer types.	Born to free other beings. Instigate revolution, progress, and positive change.	Blame, self-deceit. Refuse to accept responsibility for their own actions; blame the world for their problems. Cannot see their own faults and shortcomings.

TABLE 7.2. COMMON EMOTIONS
FOR EACH DHARMA TYPE

DHARMA TYPE	NEGATIVE EMOTION	POSITIVE EMOTION
Outsider	Deception, anxiety	Empathy, wonder
Educator	Lust	Compassion
Laborer	Sloth, jealousy	Love, loyalty
Warrior	Anger, pride	Generosity
Merchant	Greed	Conviviality, enthusiasm

 HOMEWORK

Take a moment now to determine your type, and if you're ambitious find the types of friends and family too. Try to understand the individual points of evolution and devolution and see if you can judge how to implement these in your life. Do you remember times when you went against the grain of your nature and later suffered for it? Or have there been times when you pushed yourself to develop and integrate skills that ended up benefiting you immensely, so much so that you cannot see yourself living without them now? Try to learn three things about each type; this will benefit you as we build on them in the following chapters, showing you how to implement dharma type strategies in everyday life situations. Even memorizing each type's Sanskrit terms from pages 136–37 can be invaluable to unlocking their meaning. But don't worry if you do not understand everything at once. The five types and their qualities will be developed throughout this book, by the end of which you will be able to confidently use your knowledge of them in practically any situation you should encounter.

Educators

The pen is mightier than the sword and the Educator's weapon is the modern version, the laptop. But as an Educator you will obtain more inspiration and better ideas by moving your energy and cultivating the Warrior's gifts of discipline, action, and strength than by sitting motionless in front of a computer screen all day. Therefore, take some time to discover a new form of exercise this week. From yoga to horseback riding, take a class or hit the trails to find newfound growth and inspiration in your life.

Warriors

Warriors evolve by learning and envisioning their just cause. This week, Warrior, take some time to study deeply about an issue that is important to you. Do some research, expand your mind—you just may find that you were wrong about something you held as certain. Next, write down your goals on a sheet of paper and how you might achieve them, as solutions present themselves. Do this for each aspect of your life—family, profession, sex, spirituality. Nothing is as useful to Warriors as seeing their truth. Post this somewhere visible, and make it the object of your daily focus for at least six weeks.

Merchants

Merchants need to feel needed. There is no more useful way to fill up on pure energy than by giving to others. This week, find something you can do to benefit your community. Volunteer at a soup kitchen, donate your old clothes or appliances, or teach others new skills. Take little steps; you do not need to give away the farm. Become a part of the community that supports you, and you will find an ever-renewing source of vitality and health.

Laborers

Laborers love their routines. This week, take a new spin on your daily routines by doing them differently. From brushing your teeth with the non-dominant hand to taking in new restaurants, movies, or even a vacation, try something new, dear Laborer type, and let yourself be inspired and distracted by the ever-changing world around you.

Being natural detectives, Laborers love Easter egg hunts and fact-finding missions. They are also thrifty and naturally economical. One way to keep your routine lively while stimulating these skills is to go to a new place to eat, shop, or hang out each week using the coupons from your daily paper or mailbox. Many Laborers also prefer to take stay-cations, leisurely vacations where they live, discovering interesting places while staying close to home—saving money on hotels, gas, and even food. Take a look at your surroundings and see if you can discover new and exciting things to do around you.

Outsiders

Out of fear or frustration Outsiders often fail to deliver their truth to others. This week, Outsider, find a way to be relevant and share your truth with the world. In between the blank stares you might also get a few minds to light up and open to your unusual wisdom. Also, ask people who know you about your best and worst qualities. Ask them what you could do to become a better, more authentic person. The responses you get might surprise you! You do not have to do everything they say—use this exercise as a form of reflection and self-inquiry. It is often hard to see the truth about ourselves, but when reflected back on us by others it can be a revelation.

PART TWO

Authentically Living Your Dharma Type

8

Five Paths to Wellness

The following chapters detail the mundane matters governed by the dharma types in an organic, sequential order. This means that although chapters on subjects like health, entertainment, and profession are discrete entities the reader is better served by reading from beginning to end, rather than skipping through. Where the meaning of a particular topic is not outlined for Outsiders, it is implied that they are following one of the four other paths. Not every type is given equal treatment in every section, and some are emphasized in different parts. For example Warriors get major billing in the government section, though less press in the anatomy section, and so on with the other types. Over the course of the next several chapters, however, every type is fleshed out and explained fully in different sections according to context.

ANATOMY

In the *Rig-Veda* it is said, "The Educator sprang from the mouth of God, the Warrior from His arms, the Merchant from His legs, the Laborer from His feet." To this can be added the Outsider, who is the skin that connects them all. To eliminate even one of these renders the whole being ineffective. You can no more subjugate one class than cut off your hands or feet—each is essential to the survival of the organism as a whole; each plays a unique role without which the entire being suffers. That is why when one class usurps power and seeks to skew the natural order, all society pays, as the following anatomy description illustrates.

TABLE 8.I. DHARMA TYPE ANATOMY

DHARMA TYPE	GROSS ANATOMY	SUBTLE ANATOMY
Outsider	Skin	Bliss Body
Educator	Head, face	Wisdom Body
Merchant	Digestion, legs	Sensate Body
Warrior	Heart, blood, arms, prana, muscles	Vital/Breath/ Energy Body
Laborer	Reproduction, bones, feet	Food/Flesh Body

In yogic philosophy there are five bodies that also correspond to the five types: the Food or Flesh Body, the Vital or Breath Body, the Sensate Body, the Wisdom Body, and the Bliss Body. Each of these bodies, or sheaths, has a special intelligence and relationship to its corresponding dharma type (see table 8.1). The yoga bodies and their intelligences are covered in later sections; for now, let us consider gross anatomy by examining which organs the different types use the most. For example, Educators use their brains more than any other part of their bodies. Warriors, who value physical competition and battle, need strong hearts to circulate blood and courage to the muscles. Laborer types have strong bones and reproductive organs, while Merchants have an affinity with the digestive tract. Let's take a look at these below.

Outsiders

Outsiders represent the skin. They live outside the body of society, though remaining intimately connected to it. New ideas and discoveries are their specialty—they experience new sensations first and carry them inside to be interpreted by the brain (Educator) and integrated or rejected by the body. They may tattoo or pierce their skin to set themselves apart, and though such voluntary decorations are characteristic of Outsiders, stretch marks, acne, and other skin afflictions may also distinguish them from their fellow dharma types. Skin is also the largest organ, and Outsiders are the largest population in the world. There are more Outsiders than any other type in the Iron Age, though evolved Outsiders are as rare as evolved Educators, Warriors, Laborers, or Merchants.

That is to say that Outsiders who have cultivated self-awareness, have found their unique expression, share their gifts with the world, and continue to repeat this three-step process are few and far between. Most Outsiders stop at the first or second step, or go through the process once and stop there—they find something they're good at, share it with the world, and become content to sit on their laurels. But Outsiders need to continuously expand their horizons, like the Space Element that rules them and the skin that is constantly shedding, renewing, and regenerating. Evolution is an ever-turning wheel, and these steps need to be repeated to keep that wheel turning. Constant expansion ensures freedom; stagnation ensures bondage.

Some Outsiders may seek destructive ways to expand their awareness using intravenous drugs, pain, or other means of overcoming the structures that bind them. But short-term fixes only end up limiting their freedom by creating addictions, legal entanglements, and economic burdens that keep Outsiders from evolving into the people they can be.

In chapter 6 we saw that Outsider categories come in threes. Like the layers of skin (epidermis, dermis, hypodermis) there are also three types of Outsiders—those who face away from society and the body; those who look both ways and are intermediary between society and the fringe; and those who look in, staying in society most of the time. Each type has slightly different functions. Outsiders who stay completely away from society are like the epidermis. They are the ascetics, gypsies, criminals, and off-the-grid types who prefer to have as little to do with society as possible. Like the epidermis, which is nourished by diffusion from the capillaries, they are not fed directly by the body of society.

The second level, like the dermis, mediates between civilization and the wild—these Outsiders go back and forth, sharing their gifts with the world but also taking time to retreat from it. Tattoo ink is held in the dermis, and these second-level Outsiders sometimes get tattoos to distinguish themselves from others.

Finally, the third level is the hypodermis, which is intimately connected to the body and rarely if ever leaves society. These Outsiders look the most like anyone else and assimilate better than others—like Halle Berry, Barbara Streisand, and David Beckham, Outsiders intimately benefited by their society and tied to it by their identities and professions. Because the hypodermis is 50 percent fat this level of Outsider is also usually well insulated: well-to-do and comfortable in the world. These Outsiders do not often connect to the outside fringe, though like domesticated animals they retain a bit of the wild within.

Another way to view the three layers is as successive degrees of integration. The first-level Outsiders are the most ordinary: they are numb to their own nature, have little connection to the society that feeds them, and are callused, insensitive, and disconnected. They do not look within but only see what is wrong with others, fleeing society instead of integrating. The second are the Outsiders who have found their gifts and returned to share them with the world. Finally, the third level of Outsiders have mastered themselves to such a degree that outside and inside have no more meaning—they are as comfortable in the world as without it.

Educators

Educators are the brains of the outfit. They rely on the rest of the body to support and feed them while processing higher information and guiding the organism. They interpret Natural Law for the benefit of the body of society. From looking both ways before crossing the street to making world-changing decisions, Educators, like the brain, steer society in the direction of its highest destiny. They may do this through science, religion, politics, health, or any number of disciplines, but their basic role remains the same—to teach and inspire society toward its highest good.

The size and function of our brains sets us apart from lower animals. Educators likewise make the difference between an animal existence and a meaningful life by providing purpose and dharma to people. A body without a head lacks intelligence, but a head without a body is also a useless lump of matter. Therefore Educators have to remember their place in the social order and learn humility. The brain uses up a large amount of the body's resources, and a brain that does not know how to make itself useful simply becomes a drain on the system. Also, by itself a brain is helpless; it needs the rest of the body to implement its ideas. It needs the skin and bones to protect it, legs to carry it where it needs to go, and arms to bring desirable objects to it while keeping the undesirable away. The lesson is that the body serves the brain, and the brain in turn serves the body. A teacher without students cannot teach; a coach without players cannot win; a pastor without parishioners cannot save. Educators must remember that without the body of their students, pupils, or followers, they are useless.

> **"The central nervous system . . . requires more energy than any other tissue of the body, including muscle. . . . In fact, every day our brains require the equivalent of a quarter-pound of sugar to be converted into the chemical form of energy, ATP."**
> **DR. BENJAMIN V. TREADWELL**

There is also a special relationship between the organs that illustrates dharma type evolution and devolution. For example, the heart pumps blood to the brain, and the brain reciprocates by regulating the heart's function. This illustrates how, from anatomy to zoology, dharma type relationships influence our lives at the most personal and mundane levels, whether we're aware of them or not.

Laborers and Merchants benefit each other through the reproductive and digestive systems, respectively. It takes proper digestion and assimilation of nutrients to feed the reproductive system, while healthy sexual activity exercises the organs and stimulates digestion. Each organ benefits its neighbors by its normal operation, and without the function of one, the whole body suffers. Like the dharma types, it is a question not of competition, but of cooperation. Our individual parts, like the dharma types, have a symbiotic relationship that prospers the whole body when they do their jobs.

Laborers

Laborers are the feet of the cosmic person. We tread the earth with our feet and rely on them to carry out our dharma. Consider the consequences if everyone on Earth sprained their ankle for a day. What would happen if you could not walk to the store for food or go to work to earn money? Society would likely grind to a halt, a helpless, hobbled thing. Without feet to ground us we could not realize the full meaning of our material existence.

Laborers also rule the generative organs. These are linked to the human creative impulse, both in the material sense of creating children as well as in artistic creativity. Laborers like to build something out of nothing. In previous ages they were the proletariat whose job was to propagate the species. Though today Outsiders are the most populous type, Laborers' instinct to raise children and cohere family, community, and country is still supremely powerful. They are the glue that holds society together, and in the body that glue is represented by the reproductive impulse.

There is a correlation between sex and vitality, and sexual organs are also sources of vitality and vigor. The ancient healing traditions of the Orient state that the stronger one's reproductive function, the stronger one's constitution, because for the reproductive organs to be optimally nourished nutrition must pass through the rest of the body's tissues first. Having the most endurance and lasting power both physically and sexually, Laborers are the longest lived of the dharma types and are usually spry well into old age. This endurance differs, however, from the Warrior's energy. Warriors are associated with ATP and the cell mechanisms that turn sugar fuel into quick-burning energy for the muscles. But Laborers are connected to the bones, the solid structures in the body that confer structural integrity and thereby longevity. Warriors are good for quick bursts of strength, while Laborers are better suited to longer bouts of exertion. Warriors tend to burn out, while the Laborer flame is long and steady.

Warriors

Because of their association with blood Warriors have good circulation, and sometimes even a ruddy complexion that marks them as the action heroes of the dharma type family. Being the heart of the cosmic person, they also represent courage and energy. While under stress Laborers may get broken bones, stressed Warriors usually get broken hearts, problems with bleeding or circulation, even heart attacks.

Just as Educators rule the brain and nervous system, Warriors are the electricity that runs along the nervous system, carrying out the brain's orders. One executes the commands of the other in an instantaneous dance of cause and effect. Warriors are the chi, prana, or life force that courses through the body. As in the Merchant-Laborer dynamic above, the Warrior-Educator relationship is based on reciprocity, much like the heart and brain working together to coordinate the actions of the body, each giving life to the other through an orchestrated interplay of purpose and energy.

> **Without movement of food through the intestines and the colon, there is no movement in the body.**

Merchants

Merchants rule the digestive organs. It is their role to digest experience in the world. From thrills and excitement to food and drink, Merchants are the hedonists of the dharma type family. This is rightly so, and why

Merchants are given a remarkable ability to recover from binge drinking, eating, and other excesses. Educators, Warriors, and Laborers cannot endure the party hardiness of the Merchant type, and the emotional roller coaster that sometimes characterizes their life experience. Merchants are in constant pursuit of rasa, life's juiciness, and the digestive organs offer a perfect metaphor by taking in, digesting, and assimilating experience.

Merchants and Laborers complement each other because it takes food to nourish the reproductive impulse. And, like the digestive process, Merchants are responsible for moving resources/rasa in society. Without movement of goods and capital, society stagnates. Without movement of food through the intestines and colon, there is no movement in the body. Although the colon is actually a Laborer organ, it is part of the digestive system, a fact that illustrates the inseparability of Merchant and Laborer types. This story details the colon's importance to the body:

Once, all the organs convened to determine who was the most important. Of course the major players, the heart and brain, had their say, and their claims received much bluster and applause. Other organs spoke out as well, like the lungs and liver, each making its eloquent claim for supremacy. Finally, after everyone had had a turn, a tremulous voice piped up from the rear, "What about me?" It was the colon.

As the organs turned back to look, a round of laughter boomed through the body: "What will you do that is greater than the heart?" said the heart. "What can you do that is greater than the brain?" asked the brain.

"Nothing," replied the colon, and he turned to leave. "I will do nothing." And true to his word, he quit working. After a couple of days, things began to get a bit uncomfortable in the body, and after a week, all the organs were feeling sluggish from the backup of morbid elements. Finally, after two weeks, they lined up each and every one to beg the colon to resume his duties, whereupon the body gradually returned to optimal function. The very happy organs then unanimously accorded him the honorary title of Mr. Most Important!

In ayurveda health and immunity are centered in the colon. Even modern medicine recognizes that up to 70 percent of the body's immunity is located in the gut. By keeping a clean and healthy digestive system, by stoking *agni* (digestive fire) and feeding the body rasa in the form of nourishing food and positive, sweet experiences, there is nothing that it cannot digest and no pathogens it cannot fend off. But when we abuse our digestive system, when we overeat, drink, or take inappropriate food combinations, our internal Merchant system suffers and we become sluggish and sick. And like a sick society, a sick body suffers and can eventually break down and become overrun by its enemies. Therefore, Merchants must take special care not to abuse their digestive organs and to learn proper diet, food combining, and supplementation.

THE BRAIN

Working with the dharma types lends itself to endless creative applications. Just as some animals can be subclassified according to the dharma type of their breed, the function of some organs in the body can be similarly broken down. For example, dogs are Warrior animals—but even within their species there are some breeds that are Educators, like golden retrievers, while others are Laborer types, like bulldogs, and still others are Merchants, like Chihuahuas. In the same way, though the brain is an Educator organ, its functions can be insightfully stratified according to dharma type.

In his book *Change Your Brain, Change Your Life* Dr. Daniel Amen* describes five brain systems that remarkably mirror the function of the dharma types and their evolution and devolution points. Reading these descriptions through the lens of the dharma type lends itself to a deeper understanding of the brain and how it influences behavior. A summary of these brain systems and their relationship to the dharma types follows.

---

*For more information on these systems and hyperactivity, and for suggestions for dealing with problems of the basal ganglia, visit www.amenclinics.com.

Merchant: The Deep Limbic System

The deep limbic system is the emotional center of the brain, most closely associated with the Merchant type. It is implicated in our ability to bond socially with others. Desire, passion, and libido are also strongly connected here. As discussed in previous chapters, Merchants are masters of the emotion cocktail that makes us tick, and they derive their inspiration from the thoughts they have and the emotions these create. A Sanskrit phrase puts it succinctly: *yato bhaavas tato rasa*— "whatever your state, that's your experience," or "where the mind goes, emotion follows." Managing their internal state is the most important lesson Merchants can learn. Neuro-Linguistic Programming (NLP) and other techniques, such as those popularized by Anthony Robbins, work wonders for Merchant types. According to Robbins there are no good or bad people, only resourceful and unresourceful *states*. This can be a revelation for Merchants—when negative thoughts can be eliminated by positive states, one can escape the depression, moodiness, and unreliability common among devolved Merchants.

Prescriptions for Merchant types are similar to those for the deep limbic system. St. John's wort, valerian, and other herbal remedies help to keep them emotionally steady, relaxed, and able to sleep at night. Merchants also grow when they take on qualities of the Laborer type, who is steady, loyal, and heart-based. When Merchants take the time to form deep, lasting bonds with others their deep limbic system tends to normalize. On the other hand, when they make only casual or superficial friends their limbic system becomes overactive, and their inner void expands.

When Merchants relate authentically they form lasting relationships that fill their void, conferring on them a durable fulfillment that they cannot get through superficial contacts. Research consistently shows that marriage, especially sex with a life partner, is more deeply satisfying than fly-by-night liaisons with many partners because there is not enough time for the deep limbic system to form emotional bonds during a one-night stand. This lack of connection eventually wears on

Merchants, driving them to look for more and more experiences while gaining less and less satisfaction in the process.

> **"Perfect valor is to behave, without witnesses, as one would act were all the world watching."**
> FRANÇOIS VI, DUC DE LA ROCHEFOUCAULD

Warrior: The Prefrontal Cortex

The prefrontal cortex is the executive part of the brain that supervises, directs, and focuses our behavior. It is responsible for goal setting and follow-through, for planning as well as completion of tasks, which are Warrior functions. The prefrontal cortex is also responsible for critical thinking and judgment (viveka), vital skills for Warrior types (see chapter 3). When it is working properly it promotes thoughtfulness, learning from mistakes, and applying the lessons of the past to the present. When it is out of order it leads people to repeat mistakes and to have poor attention, focus, and follow-through. Attention Defecit Disorder (ADD) is a result of dysfunction in the prefrontal cortex. The prefrontal cortex influences self-control and the ability to act in consistent, thoughtful ways. Like well-trained martial artists who know when to act and when to step back, it confers the ability to think through and understand the consequences of actions.

Interestingly, the prefrontal cortex has many connections to the limbic system, the Merchant part of the brain, sending inhibitory messages to help keep emotions under control. In the next chapter we will see this expressed explicitly in the circle of life as the Warrior's duty to patrol and govern the Merchant type. Form follows function, and the beauty of the social relationships between the archetypes is mirrored in their physiological interactions—different parts of the brain interact like the dharma types. As a result our martial artists are able to control primal emotions and make the right decisions in a crisis, which in turn earns them respect and a place of leadership in their community—the evolved Warrior's natural function.

Generally, Warriors and the prefrontal cortex do well on higher-protein diets, with more fruits and vegetables as carbohydrate sources than grains and simple sugars. Other recommendations consist basically of the Warrior's harmonization into the Educator type: using *praise* rather than *pressure*, and incorporating Educator values of coaching and positive reinforcement. The mark of an evolved Warrior is relaxation and self-control, not hyperactivity and impulsivity. Educator techniques that promote relaxation, like guided meditation, are excellent. Devolved Warriors, like people with ADD, tend to be in constant turmoil with people around them. They seek conflict and distraction as a form of self-stimulation. While searching out distraction is okay for Merchant types, it is not for Warriors, whose hallmark is focus and intensity. When they evolve they naturally regain focus, good judgment, and control over their brain's limbic system.

Laborer: The Cingulate Gyrus

The cingulate gyrus is the gears system of the brain. When it is out of balance people cannot shift into new modes of thinking and become cognitively inflexible. They only eat certain foods, do things a particular way, and are unwilling to try anything new. They keep their space a certain way, make love a certain way, and become upset if things are changed on them. This is how devolved Laborer types function. They become stuck in what Buddhist psychology calls an "animal realm" that makes them territorial, confrontational, and unable to relate to people using natural, healthy boundaries.* They tend to suffer from obsessive-compulsive disorder and other related problems such as body-dysmorphic and eating disorders, autism, compulsive behavior, chronic pain, gambling, excessive and senseless worrying, and other addictions. These all stem from negative repetitive thoughts that they cannot shift in their brains. The answer lies in the Laborer's evolution into the Merchant type.

Merchants are constantly on the go, and movement is key for

---

*For more on Buddhist psychology please refer to Lar Short and Martin Lowenthal's excellent book, *Opening the Heart of Compassion* (Charles E. Tuttle Company, Inc., 1993).

Laborer types. Physical movement such as exercise, as well as emotional and mental stimulation, keeps Laborers from getting stuck in one mode of thinking. Distraction, the Merchant's forte, is essential in redirecting negative thinking.

In a difficult work environment it helps to sing a song as you work to make the day go easier. Stories and tales also serve that function, and Laborer types make excellent storytellers. Prayer and mantra also help to reprogram negative thought patterns into positive states. Rosary beads, which could have been invented for Laborer types, serve to keep their thoughts focused on resourceful vibrations. And just as they serve the Merchant's deep limbic system, NLP and other state change exercises, as well as 5-HTP and natural supplements that help optimize dopamine and serotonin levels, may also be useful for Laborers.

Outsider: The Basal Ganglia

The basal ganglia are associated with the body's anxiety levels, controlling both ecstasy and paranoia, extremes that typify the Outsider personality. Outsiders often feel the world is against them and read the worst into otherwise neutral situations. George W. Bush, an Outsider type playing a Merchant, spearheaded a campaign called the "War on Terror," which is ironic since fighting fear with fear only builds more fear and makes it impossible to sever its vicious cycle. This politics of paranoia is a hallmark of the devolved Outsider. Evolved Outsiders, however, can soar to the heights of ecstasy, like Martin Luther King Jr. and his revolution of values. The ability Outsiders have to refresh society depends upon their personal evolution, and whether or not they are grounded in the three-pronged approach of responsibility, ruth, and respect. Outsiders earn respect when they have been honest with themselves and the people around them and have expressed ruth for their past misdeeds. This is also a healing strategy for the basal ganglia because fear cannot exist where awareness lives. Taking responsibility for our actions focuses awareness into every area of our lives, and vowing not to repeat mistakes brings mindfulness and meditation to our activities.

Fear cannot exist where awareness lives. Taking responsibility for our actions focuses awareness into every area of our lives, and vowing not to repeat mistakes brings mindfulness and meditation to our activities.

Problems with the basal ganglia express in negative Outsider traits: irrational anxiety, nervousness or fear, panic attacks, a tendency to think the worst, tremors, tics, low motivation, and even Tourette's syndrome. Outsiders are the most likely type to turn to drugs, particularly consciousness-altering substances, to deal with their reality. From marijuana and peyote to LSD and ecstasy, Outsiders are the psychonauts of the dharma type family, their Space Element driving them to explore the inner and outer reaches of consciousness. Ultimately, however, they must find a balance between mundane and extraordinary reality, because as many Outsider spiritual traditions relate: the truth is where you are, here and now.* Escapism and drugs eventually corrupt an Outsider's soul. Learning to be grounded in reality while using natural, sustainable strategies for dealing with anxiety is an individual and lifelong journey for the Outsider.

Educator: The Temporal Lobes

The temporal lobes are intimately involved with understanding and processing language, complex memories, and visual and auditory recognition. Language is what sets humans apart from other animals. Reading, speech, and understanding language are higher human functions that correspond to the Educator type. Educators rely on their memory power to recite complex information, which is strongly connected to the dominant (usually left) temporal lobe. Reading facial expressions and appreciating music are connected to the nondominant (usually right) temporal lobe. Interpreting and giving meaning to information, conviction, great insight, and the sense of truth are also attributed to the temporal lobes.

---

*Outsider spiritual traditions include Tantrism and Taoism.

Memory is responsible for learning. We cannot learn if we cannot remember. Memory also reminds us of who we were as a family, culture, or species. Educators are wisdom keepers who connect us to our ancient roots. They write books, do research, and teach in order to keep alive the lore of our ancestors. When there are problems in this part of the brain, there can be memory impairment as well as violent thoughts, anger, and susceptibility to slights. Educators often internally entertain strong base emotions like lust, anger, and greed. Their ability to control these is what makes them great teachers and peacemakers—they understand the inner struggle and work hard to resolve it. When they fail to do so and act out, they may become so guilt-ridden as to even resort to suicide. Whatever the case, Educators are always sorry when they give in to these base emotions and usually suffer the consequences of such behavior quickly. As the moral exemplars of the dharma type family, their karma is instant when they fail to live up to the high standard of their type.

The temporal lobes are also active during spiritual experiences, and Educators, the priests and philosophers of the dharma type family, serve as mediators of the spirit for the masses. Head injuries to this area of the brain can sometimes spontaneously produce such experiences, or do quite the opposite, making it impossible for an Educator to handle temper and rage. Natural substances that help the brain like gotu kola, brahmi, and saraswati are useful for Educators.

BODY TYPE

While body types vary by genetics, race, and geography, and there is no distinctive mark that sets one dharma type from another, there are general characteristics inherent to different physiques that give us a clue to their dharma type.

Educators

Although they can be tall and burly, Educators are not usually blessed with imposing physiques and powerful personalities. Those things are reserved for athletes and salesmen and do not endear Educators to the masses. In describing Jesus, Gary Wills writes:

> Hurt people are not drawn to the aggressively healthy, to the televangelist's plumy voice, the fire hose gush of bonhomie.[1]

This is true of Educators. A sensitive, truth-seeking nature essentially breeds a sensitive physical nature, as the spiritual person shies away from violent displays of strength and domination. Accordingly, as Educators get older their physiology shrinks from the lack of attention, just as their psychology commensurately grows. Stephen Hawking provides a striking example of someone who has had to surrender the function of his body even while cultivating the function of the mind.

> **[Educators] should rely not on their strength of arms to get them through life, but on their strength of wisdom.**

Although Educators are archetypally gentle there is a contingency among the priestly class that is also large, forceful, and even imposing (at least at first glance), with a robust body and a demeanor to match. After all, Educators evolve into Warriors, and it makes sense that they should develop those traits natural to the Warrior personality—force of will and power. These types carry a certain authority and swagger that serve them on the pulpit as well as in the classroom. They are strong, articulate, and outgoing, though ultimately fraught with contradictions, as their strength is more like the Hindenburg airship: impressive at a glance, but structurally vulnerable to calamity, disease, and physical degeneration.

Why is this?

In the material world you cannot have it all. This is particularly true of Educators, who have to surrender some portion of their lives in order to fully evolve. Some give up sex, some money, and still others fame and power. Whatever their sacrifice, Educators are the most willing to surrender to life's demands. "Do not lay up for yourselves treasures on earth, but lay up for yourselves treasures in Heaven." These exhortations from the Beatitudes are Educator sentiments.

Embodied life is about giving one thing up for another. This is celebrated in spiritual institutions like marriage, where we give up lust for the many for the love of one, and in traditions like fasting, where we abstain from food in order to feast on good health and spiritual blessings. Material life is a constant tradeoff—we can never have every desire fulfilled and we must learn to make do with what we have, to surrender to what is. One of the ways Educators learn this is through their bodies. Experiencing the limitations of physicality, through debilitation, pain, and suffering, breeds in them compassion and the desire to help other beings.

It is the Educator's job to mentor and minister to the general welfare of society. A solitary scientist may labor away in the laboratory with the burning desire to cure cancer because of witnessing its ravages firsthand. A foreign aid worker may pledge to tirelessly end hunger because he has hungered or witnessed people die for want of food. An astronomer may plunge into the lake of stars to bring back pearls that inspire humanity with knowledge and wonder because she too wondered and wanted to know. Whatever their profession, Educators have an obligation to every type—the scientist has an obligation to science as well as society; the priest belongs to the people as much as to God, with one foot in the world and one foot beyond it.

Therefore Educators may become too distracted to care for their own health and appearance, whereby the Laborer and Outsider types are called in to support them in their daily duty (see the discussion of the circle of life in the next chapter). It is sincerity, not good looks, that makes them attractive. It is the light of truth burning in their eyes that shines forth and calls people to their side, not the ripple of muscles or the glimmer of jewels. In short, that which is neglected fades away—and Educators' bodies fade with time, just as their presence and authority grow, for that which is fed by attention becomes powerful. Einstein was great for his ideas, not his stature, nor was he disliked but beloved of all for being physically unassuming.

Educators are more fragile and less dynamic than the other types, except when in the full train of their dharma—when teaching, researching, or preaching they take on a magnitude greater than their everyday demeanor. Like Moses in the face of Pharaoh, Educators are irresistible when they have tapped into the full force of their dharma.

Yet it is often true that you can't have brains *and* brawn. Though they would like both, on average life makes Educators surrender and choose brains, while for their part Warriors select brawn, as these best represent their individual dharma. But that does not mean that Educators should give up on physical cultivation—only that they should give up attachment to the results thereof. Educators must release any attachment to strength and force because violence does not become them. They should rely not on their strength of arms to get them through life, but on their strength of wisdom.

One of the lessons for practitioners of jyotisha (Vedic astrology) is learning to live with the effects of Saturn. In a horoscope the planet Saturn denotes those things that are difficult to change, what we in the West naively call "karma." Taking Saturn's lessons and transforming undesirable karma is one of the most difficult things for anyone to do because Saturn teaches us what we are not keen to learn: humility and obeisance. These qualities are present in Laborer types, as Saturn is a Laborer planet. However, Saturn also teaches surrender, a quality especially important to Educators.

Warriors

Where the Educator's body is vulnerable, the Warrior's physique is made for the rough and tumble. It is resilient, self-healing, and able to withstand the shock and stress that the Warrior personality imposes on it. After all, it is Warriors' primary tool in the service of their mission. Their mission is the vehicle of their purpose, and with judgment and wisdom they use it to protect others from harm while putting themselves in harm's way.

Where Educators' eyes shine with truth and compassion, Warriors' blaze with stored power—the force of will to burn through anything to achieve their ends. The lesson Warriors learn from physicality is not *surrender* but *sacrifice,* and they learn to push through hardships and pain to achieve their goals. Accordingly, physicality presents a challenge to them, not a limitation. Their strength of character gives them the drive to break through physical barriers and triumph where others fail. As a result, they are not interested in empathizing with others but in energizing them.

Warriors offer themselves as examples of what *can* be done. They charge people with energy and inspiration. Educators inspire the soul, Warriors the body. Educators empathize, Warriors galvanize. Both have their place, and neither approach works for all situations, which is why the dharma types complement rather than compete with each other—they all have different gifts to share with the world. Where the Educator is understanding the Warrior is demanding; one says, "Let it be," the other, "Let me see."

> **Educators inspire the soul, Warriors the body.**
> **Educators empathize, Warriors galvanize.**

Warriors have a palpable presence that makes them seem larger than life, regardless of their physical stature. They exude a readiness for action that makes others take notice and tread lightly in their presence. They menace not only physically but intellectually as well, for violence can also take the form of words and ideas. Anyone confronting them may as well be ready to battle, in a court of law or on the tennis court, for in either arena they come to win.

That is not to say that Warriors are always about competition, for they can have gentle demeanors when evolved. Even so, the stored potential for violence that marks Warrior personalities is always present, no matter how peaceful they may appear. This is usually reflected in them as an athletic or capable physique, though they are not always "fit." Their ability to generate and express energy—be it kinetic, psychic, or spiritual—is second to none, and what sets Warriors apart from the other types. This affinity for expressing chi, or prana, is discussed in chapter 11 when we return to look in greater detail at the yogic system of the five bodies.

Laborers

If Warriors have an affinity with the Vital/Energy (prana) Body, the Laborer type is associated with the physical or Food/Flesh Body. The Laborer body is built for work. It may be short and stocky or long and lean—depending on genetics, racial heritage, and other factors—but its pervasive quality is a well-knit toughness that gives it ample strength and good stamina for long bouts of physical work. Because of their proclivity for family and community, Laborer type women may have wider hips or a stronger reproductive system for giving birth, and Laborer men have bones that are generally stronger and bigger as required to provide for a large family. And, consistent with the Earth Element, Laborers tend to be hardheaded and thick-skinned. Whether these metaphoric descriptions have an actual physical correlation is a matter for medical research, but they nevertheless describe the toughness of the Laborer body.

That does not mean that Laborer types do not get sick. Laborers endure pain and suffering like anyone else, but this is usually because they overwork and do not invest enough attention into self-care. Because they are hardy Laborers often ignore their own needs, later suffering the effects of bad diet, stress, and poor habits. Ideally they must pair up with a Merchant partner who can teach them the value of working smarter, not harder, or another Laborer as a spouse who will at least nurture them and take care of their needs. Laborers match up best with Merchant partners, just as Educators do with Warriors.

Merchants

Merchants' physiques are the most malleable of all the types. Just as their emotions fluctuate from extremes of loneliness to conviviality, the

Merchant's body can also be fit and athletic or morbidly obese. There is a kind of "smoothness" to a Merchant's physique, however, that sets it apart—Muhammad Ali had a fluidity and looseness that separated him from his Warrior or Laborer type opponents. Merchant types are go-getters and self-made people, and when physicality is their profession they will care for their bodies like business owners care for their business. But when it is not, it has a low priority. Britney Spears, an Outsider playing a Merchant, may have done hundreds of sit-ups on her way to the top, but that fell away when it was no longer necessary to maintain her popularity.

A side note about Merchants and fitness is that because they devolve into Warriors, they do not have a natural sense for discipline and training. Merchants often follow routines and diets that are less than scientific, and even dangerous. Popular books and trendy magazines are more inspiring to Merchants than real training expertise. As a result they may do thousands of crunches per day where a few well-executed Dragon Flags would work wonders.* They may fast on celery and soup where a nutrition program based on their body type would serve them better. Or they may resort to plastic surgery where proper diet and exercise are more natural and less expensive. But of all the types they are the one allowed to experiment with beauty and fashion, and they benefit more than anyone else from nips and tucks and other enhancements when done in moderation.

Outsiders

Outsider bodies come in all shapes and sizes. Aside from obvious decorations, like tattoos or extreme hairstyles, they do not have telltale characteristics that set them apart from others. It is precisely because of this that they sometimes seek to match their unique internal states with the aforementioned external decorations along with piercings, garish outfits,

---

*Popularized by Bruce Lee, and more recently by Russian dynamo Pavel Tsatsouline, Dragon Flags are one of the most difficult but effective abdominal exercises. More information on hard-core ab training and fitness is available from www.dragondoor.com.

or other unusual apparel. But most Outsiders just blend in nicely with everyone else, particularly the types they are emulating. Boris Becker and Sly Stallone look like typical Warriors, but they are Outsiders. Farrah Fawcett and Halle Berry appear mignon Merchant types, though they are both Outsiders. Joseph Campbell and Steven Spielberg may look like Educators, but they too are Outsiders. When their integration is smooth there are no problems, but when their ability to emulate others is disturbed there can be considerable fallout. Such was the case of Britney Spears when she sought to regain her Outsider identity, going to great lengths to show the world more than her manufactured Merchant pop persona, even to the point of cutting off all her hair.

As a counterculture statement Outsiders may also adopt uniforms to mock the uniformed conformity of others. Ironically, these can create structures subject to the same conformity as the other classes: a nun and a Goth, or a soldier and a Hell's Angel, share the same attachment to their uniforms. Evolved Outsiders seek freedom from all labels while learning to abide and live within them, which is true independence.

DIET, EXERCISE, AND FITNESS

Exercise

In matters of health and exercise dharma type philosophy defers to its sister sciences ayurveda and yoga, the first for diet and lifestyle and the second for specific exercise recommendations. While yoga is considered the perfect form of exercise in the Vedic tradition, it must be practiced along with a deep knowledge of ayurveda and your individual *dosha,* or mind/body constitution.* Different yoga *asanas* (postures) and even different forms of yoga conform to each of the mind/body types and should be learned from a qualified professional.

---

*Determine your predominant dosha (*vata, pitta,* or *kapha*) with a free mind/body type evaluation at www.lifespa.com, where you will also find excellent information on ayurveda, diet, fitness, and holistic living. For more on ayurveda, or to consult with an AyurYoga professional, visit the Ayurvedic Institute at www.ayurveda.com.

Western exercises can also be adapted to your constitution once you understand that each dosha has a muscular region where it collects and needs to be discharged from for the body to function optimally. Vata collects most in the largest muscles: the legs and buttocks. Vatas are *ectomorphs,* thin and small-boned people characterized by constant movement and coldness in their extremities. Vatas find it difficult to sit still, especially when imbalanced, and therefore need to ground themselves to the earth.

Massage, especially of the thighs and buttocks, is helpful for vata types, as are squats. Properly executed squats work wonders for vatas by promoting blood flow to the legs and massaging the colon and organs of the inner abdomen. Legs are the roots of the body tree, extending down to connect us with the earth below. By squatting in slow, deliberate, and weighted repetitions vata individuals connect to the heaviness of their bodies and the density of the earth while building strength and size in their legs, the part of their bodies most prone to vata accumulation, which can take shape in any number of ways. Vata is dry and cold, qualities that promote muscle loss and adhesions in the fibers. Adhesions are deleterious "knots" in muscle tissue that reduce strength, impede muscle function, and cause pain by tying up microscopic muscle fibers into ineffective traffic jams. These jams are best relieved by warm massage, self-myofascial release, and proper exercise, the most important of which is squatting. It is important to build from no weight up to heavy weight when doing squats, while avoiding excessive joint loading and strain. The advice of a well-qualified personal trainer is necessary before embarking on any training program.*

> **Push-ups are metaphorically related to pushing things away—like the dessert plate—a skill kaphas would do especially well to cultivate!**

---

*Qualified personal trainers can be found through the National Academy of Sports Medicine, the American College of Sports Medicine, and other quality sports certifying bodies.

The exercise best suited to kapha types is the chest press, whose most common form is the simple push-up used to train the chest and abdomen, two areas where kapha accumulates most. Kaphas are *endomorphs,* big-boned, heavy, and naturally muscular. They are the most prone to fat accumulation, especially in the kapha areas of the chest and stomach. Therefore vigorous exercise, like push-ups, helps bring blood flow to these areas and stimulates the kapha type into action. Metaphorically the pressing motion is also related to pushing things away, like the dessert plate, a skill kaphas would do especially well to cultivate! Kaphas benefit from learning to exercise restraint and say "no," to themselves and others, who sometimes abuse the kapha's easygoing nature.

Mesomorph pittas benefit from a complex exercise called the "snatch." This is a one- or two-handed version of an Olympic lift characterized by explosiveness, control, and total body integration. It requires the coordination of practically every muscle in the body working together as a team. Teamwork is something solitary pittas particularly benefit from learning. The one-handed kettlebell or dumbbell snatch entails lifting a weight from below one's knees to above one's head in a single fluid acceleration. This exercise targets the muscles where pitta accumulates most—the back, neck, and trapezius—muscles pittas also do well to have released. Also, by extending rather than flexing the body and the hips, pittas practice opening their chest and their hearts to the world. This is the opposite of what doing push-ups achieves—the closing up and pushing away of the world to establish proper boundaries, which is good for kaphas. Pittas already have well-established boundaries and need to learn to relate more with other types.

The properly performed one-handed dumbbell—or better yet, kettlebell—snatch is a complex skill suitable for pitta types who like the challenge of mastering difficult tasks. It keeps their sharp and busy minds yoked to the drill's proper execution while pumping enormous amounts of blood throughout the body. Proper circulation is vital for pittas, whose blood tends to stagnate and become "dirty," slowing down liver function and contributing to the infamous pitta temper.*

Fitness

Fitness is optimum vitality that allows for a full experience of life with health and longevity. Fitness is achieved through movement, and every dharma type prefers a specific kind of movement intimately reflected by the five yoga bodies described in the anatomy section earlier in this chapter.

Laborers

Being tied to the Earth Element and the Food/Flesh Body (or sheath), Laborer types thrive on physical movement. Their muscles and bones must flex and move if they are to feel healthy and happy. Movement for Laborers can take many forms, though it should serve a practical or functional purpose and help support Laborer types financially if they are to adhere to it. Exercise for its own sake is low on the Laborer's list of priorities. Because Laborers are fed and nourished by the physical body they must also feed and nourish it in turn with good food, massage, stretching, and self-myofascial release. Relaxation using warm heat, like saunas or hot tubs, works wonders to revitalize a sore and aching Laborer body.

Laborers can access subtler realms of existence like spirituality, psychology, and morality directly through the body. This is also true of other types, but nowhere as intensely as for the Laborer. For Laborers, a thing has to be here and now to be real, and nothing makes them present to immediate feedback like their own body. Laborers have to feel something in their gut to really get it. Consider that half of the body's nerve cells are located in the enteric nervous system (the gut), and that the brain and gut originate from one clump of tissue during embryo-

---

*For information and videos demonstrating proper execution of the one-handed snatch visit www.dragondoor.com.

genesis. The brain and the gut are the two thinking centers in the body, and Laborers are expert at using the gut's intelligence.

> Competition is the test and temper of energy mastery, as it demonstrates the degree of control and skill Warriors have over themselves.

Warriors

To keep fit the Warrior requires movement of breath and energy. From chi to electricity, energy is the intelligent movement of intention through the body. Electricity carries messages from the brain to the muscles to make them work—if harnessed sufficiently it can cause them to contract with such power as to snap the bones that support them! Such is the potential strength in every human being. However, most of us can't access that strength, as the body has built-in fail-safes to keep energy in check. It is Warriors' dharma to challenge these fail-safes, to develop and ride the body's natural energy systems in the service of their just cause. This is accomplished by practice and study, what in yoga is called *abhyasa* and *vairagya*. In Sanskrit *yoga* is the meaningful linking of two elements such as the hand and the eye, the foot and the ball, or matter and spirit. Another Sanskrit term for this is *yukti*: skill. It takes great skill to achieve mastery. Thus, yoga is said to be skillfulness in action.*

When a person wants to accomplish any skilled task the brain directs the muscles to fire sequentially and intelligently to achieve it. In yogic terms prana is the carrier of intention and energy, and Warriors are best suited to harness and direct their prana for a specific purpose. That is why in a boxing ring or a courtroom, even disadvantaged Warriors can take out a better-equipped Educator or Merchant, for they have the ability to channel their energy directly onto opponents' weakness and destroy them.

Thus goal-oriented activities like sports, law, or debate that

---

*"Yogah karmasu kaushalam" (Bhagavad Gita 2:50).

stimulate the need to compete and exercise the Energy Body are preferred by Warriors. Competition is the test and temper of energy mastery, as it demonstrates the degree of control and skill Warriors have over themselves. To keep fit Warriors must also exert their lungs in order to exchange oxygen and refresh their systems. Warriors need to run, play, or perform yogic exercises called *pranayama* to keep their Breath Body functioning. Experienced yogis and chi gung practitioners are famous for demonstrating the capabilities of the Energy Body through unbelievable exploits.

> **"I can resist anything—except temptation."**
> **OSCAR WILDE**

Merchants

Just as it is more difficult to control one's energy than one's body, it is even harder to master the mind and its senses. This is a task set to Merchant types. Earlier we said that Merchants are masters of indulgence—drinking, gambling, sex, and spending. However, Merchants have a natural sense of what is acceptable indulgence and what oversteps their ability to recover. Warriors, by contrast, whether because of overconfidence or pride, put themselves into unwarranted risk in these areas, which is why Warriors are traditionally prohibited from preoccupying themselves with drinking, gambling, dissipation, and wealth. Notice here that they are prohibited not from engaging in sex or making money, but from undue preoccupation with the same, for these activities lead away from the just cause of their lives and into dissolution. It is supremely difficult to master addictions to gambling, sex, and alcohol, especially for Warriors. This, in effect, is their Achilles' heel. Famous examples of virtuous Warriors or Educators who have succumbed to pride and lost themselves through intemperance abound in the world's sacred scriptures. Yuddhisthira is a hero famous for losing his kingdom, brothers, wife, and even himself in a game of dice in the Vedic epic of the Mahabharata.

That is why Merchant activities like gambling and drinking should be left to Merchants, who can enjoy sense stimulation without letting it overwhelm their personalities. Merchants require movement of the senses and emotions; they *need* to be stimulated and inspired by something. This is what leads them to try new foods, music, and other enjoyments. They become connoisseurs of culture, media, and entertainment.

What does this have to do with fitness, you say? Nothing. That's the point—Merchants need to be coaxed out of their normal routines of sense gratification and taught to experience the sense enjoyment of a fit and healthy body. Looking good is one motivator. In fact, Merchants are largely responsible for the fads and standards in fitness and fashion. If a six-pack abdomen is what's in, that's enough motivation for Merchants to get started. But because they are not primarily creatures of the Earth (physical) or Fire (energetic) elements, exercise does not have for them the natural hold that it does for Laborer and Warrior types. As a result they need constant support and encouragement in order to keep on track, such as one gets from fitness coaches, dietitians, or other self-help gurus.

Lacking these, Merchants may turn to doctors and plastic surgeons to "fix" them without having to expend the effort. The truth is, Merchants are so busy with other things that exercise, diet, and wellness are just not at the top of their agenda—unless of course their careers require it, as for movie stars, models, or athletes. Eventually, however, Merchants do come to a point of balance and learn to maintain health without any help from the outside. But that process can take a long time, which is why until then they need the positive reinforcement of a health and wellness professional by their side.

> [For Merchants] walking on a treadmill is boring; walking on the beach in Hawai'i is much better. Doing endless push-ups on the dirty gym floor is loathsome; doing push-ups on top of your lover is exciting.

Merchants work as hard as any type. They can perform physical labor and become great athletes if this leads to fortune and glory. As long as their first priority of financial security is met, Merchants are willing to dedicate themselves to any pursuit. Some of our greatest sports heroes are Merchant types who decided to earn money with their bodies. The difference between Merchant and Warrior athletes is that the former are flashier and have a greater flair for self-promotion. Their gift for gab and ability to handle the media make their personalities bigger than the stage they play on, and often lead to fame and notoriety.

Fitness for Merchants must be associated with pleasure. It must be interesting, sensually stimulating, and fun if it is to grab their attention. Walking on a treadmill is boring; walking on the beach in Hawai'i is much better. Doing endless push-ups on the dirty gym floor is loathsome; doing push-ups on top of your lover is exciting. Merchants and their trainers need to change up their routines and find stimulation in everything they do in order to accommodate their short attention spans. Ultimately Merchants stick to a wellness program when they see real value in it. Their motivation may be hope for gain or fear of loss—they may be scared straight by their doctor, or they may have to learn the financial setbacks of illness in order to understand that health is a commodity as precious as anything else in life. Then they can give it due attention without feeling that they are wasting their time.

Educators

Movement of ideas is the primary "exercise" of the priestly class. Playing chess and solving puzzles, as well as solving real problems with their minds, constitutes mental fitness for Educators. Walking, hiking, and light activity is also good—but only insofar as it stimulates mental health. Their bodies are not made to withstand the rigors of heavy exercise and will break down if overworked. Instead, their minds are capable of intense activity analogous to the efforts that Laborers or Warriors put forth with their bodies. Notwithstanding this caution against excessive strain, Educators must have adequate movement of their physical, energetic, and emotional systems if they are to really stimulate the intellect and be considered evolved persons.

According to the yogic classification of human constitution, each body depends on the one beneath it for optimal well-being—thus, while the Laborer is mainly concerned with physical being, Warriors must train their physical body and energy systems to be optimally functional. The Merchant, in turn, must have adequate physical activity (work), proper intent and goal orientation (Energy Body), and leisure entertainment (emotional movement) in order to achieve optimal fitness and obtain satisfaction in life. Remember, there is no e-motion without motion.

The Educator needs to have physical, energetic, emotional, and intellectual development to ensure happiness. That is why Educators are often called the Renaissance men and women of the dharma types. They must master, or at least become conversant with, the ways of the Laborer, Merchant, and Warrior types to be useful Educators. Teachers must know their students to be good teachers—this means they must become students for a large part of their lives if they are to learn the ways and attitudes of the world. It is only by learning from others and understanding the Flesh, Energy, Sensate, and Wisdom bodies that Educators become truly useful. When they fail to do so, they may become ineffectual, distracted, or lazy.

A balance of light activity, skill development, emotional variety, and intellectual stimulation is necessary in order for Educators to experience proper fitness. This is why Educators are often perceived as finicky, for they have special needs that must be met for them to function optimally. Remember that fitness is optimum vitality allowing for a full experience of life with health and longevity—Educators' fitness is predicated upon movement of ideas, and ideas only move when they have well-developed physical, energetic, and emotional pathways to travel upon.

Outsiders

If mastering four bodies makes the Educator well rounded, what are we to say of Outsider types, whose ownership of the Bliss Body is contingent on mastery of five sheaths? They would be the real Renaissance men and women if they subscribed to social systems that make such distinctions. But Outsiders are usually happier without restrictive labels. They value freedom above everything else—freedom to think, say, and do what they feel. The founders of the Americas were Outsiders (though in practice the United States is a Merchant country).

The *ananda maya kosha* (Bliss Body) is the least defined and most tenuous of the five sheaths. We can feel the flesh, the breath, and our emotions—and even measure intelligence—but there is no measure to the Bliss Body. This is the most conceptual of the five sheaths, and consequently it is up to Outsiders to define their own fitness strategy according to personal experience. In doing so Outsiders must follow the guidelines and avoid the pitfalls for their type as described in part 1. Outsiders must be allowed to roam and explore the world with their Food, Energy, Sensate, and Wisdom bodies in order to obtain the *ananda,* bliss and freedom, promised by their own.

Practically, fitness for Outsiders consists of exercises they piece together from their explorations. They are more or less successful based on how well they understand the other four bodies and their requirements. Outsiders are true experimenters and are often themselves the vessel for the experiment. Like the alchemists of yore they combine and recombine, add and subtract, different elements from different disciplines to come up with something that fits their life—something that ends up being a totally new creation in the world. From Tae-Bo to Botox, Outsider inventions are different, weird, and, when they work, sometimes revolutionary!

Diet and Health

There are no specific diets related to the dharma types since nourishment from food is limited mostly to the Food/Flesh Body, which is tied to our ancestry, culture, and environment more than any other identity factor. Nonetheless, long bouts of work require carbohydrates, while short bouts of strength and intensity are anaerobic and need protein for large muscles. Thus Laborers generally prefer carbohydrate-rich diets that are also good for the cingulate gyrus system, while Warriors do well on a high-protein regimen to fuel their muscles and the prefrontal cortex. Educators do well on vegan, vegetarian, or other specialized diets, while Merchants and Outsiders can eat anything—Merchants because they love pleasure, and Outsiders because they love the unknown.

We can see the different effects of diet on the Food/Flesh Body simply by looking at Olympic track athletes. Those who require intense, short-lived energy such as the 100- to 400-meter sprinters are always larger and more muscular than those who need sustained, longer-lasting energy like marathoners. In the Middle Ages feudal lords knew this well and used it to control the masses, feeding their laborers high-carbohydrate/low-protein diets while reserving a high-protein meat diet for their armies and themselves. This went so far as the outlawing of hunting and the punishing of poachers with death, thus ensuring the compliance of serotonin-drunk vassals who suffered the perils of severely low protein intake like poor health, lack of motivation, and a short life span.

Things may not be much different today. Though good food and protein are abundant, much of our fast food is high-carb/low-quality processed fare made to satisfy the palate but not the soul. It is stuff that lulls the population into a drone-like existence, ensuring little resistance to longer working days and less time for self-reflection. After all, self-reflection nurtures rebellion, and for this reason it is not a high priority in a Merchant-run society. Self-reflection is a quality pertinent more to the "thinking" duo of Educator and Warrior types, whereas Merchants and Laborers are the "feeling" duo who rely more on experience than abstract concepts. As a result these two camps suffer different types of stress, as illustrated in table 8.2 (page 176).

Laborers tend to suffer long-term chronic disorders, typically as a result of failing to take care of themselves while preferring to care for others. They can be lazy in their diet and self-care regimens and as a result suffer from nutritionally related illnesses such as diabetes and heart disease, or work-related stresses like joint pain, arthritis, and exhaustion. Because Laborer types are hardy they will not see the effects of bad diet and health choices until later in life, which makes such afflictions more difficult to treat. Consequently, Laborers along with Merchants are most likely to take prescription drugs for illnesses that have been entrenched in the body for a long time.

Warriors prefer to feel pain than to feel subpar.

TABLE 8.2. DHARMA TYPES AND STRESS

DHARMA TYPE	RULED BY	TYPE OF STRESS	NATURE	EXAMPLES
Laborer	Feeling	Long-term emotional	Chronic	Worry, low-level anxiety
Merchant	Feeling	Short-term emotional	Acute	Anxiety, panic attacks
Warrior	Thinking	Short-term mental	Acute	Post-traumatic stress*
Educator	Thinking	Long-term mental	Chronic	Spaciness, dementia

*Post-traumatic stress disorder is further detailed in chapter 13.

Warriors and Educators lean less heavily on drugs than do Merchants and Laborers, as drugs are inventions of the Merchant type. Warriors especially hate taking drugs like antibiotics and pain medications unless it is a life-or-death situation. There are three reasons for this. First, as a matter of competitive pride, they prefer to fight their symptoms on their own—and win. Second, their Energy Body is wired like a finely tuned machine—introducing clumsy drugs can dull their senses and make them perform at less than 100 percent. As a result, Warriors prefer to feel pain than to feel subpar. Finally, drugs are an invention of the Merchant, who represents the devolution point of the Warrior.

Essentially drugs work well on the body, but they have side effects that Educators and Warriors are less willing to accept. Laborers are more ready to deal with side effects if their medications are effective. While they don't mind pain, they mind not being able to work and will do anything to keep from being useless, which is hell for a Laborer type. Merchants for their part hate pain and rely on painkillers, antidepressants, alcohol, and recreational drugs like marijuana to keep them emotionally level and relieve tensions.

Laborer	Long-term prescription drugs
Merchant	Short-term prescription drugs
Educator	Long-term alternative medicine
Warrior	Short-term alternative medicine

It is no sin to use drugs to treat disorders of the Kali Yuga, at least as an adjunct with lifestyle modifications. The ultimate goal is to attune to the natural rhythms of Nature and the body so that we do not have to use drugs to stave off disease. Ayurveda is a healing science that teaches how to do this most elegantly, for laypersons and health professionals alike.

Ultimately the cure is present in the disease: we must remedy the ills of the Iron Age with the tools of the Iron Age. It is not wrong to employ science to understand Nature so long as we place our understanding in the greater context of dharma and sacred history. "Use what you have" is the mantra of Kali Yuga—and "use it wisely" is its implicit corollary.

Maintaining Balance

Laborers

Laborers and Warriors possess the most vitality of the dharma types (see table 8.3). Laborers in particular are less concerned with their physical bodies, being well knit and built to withstand enormous workloads. Aside from the normal aches and pains of work, Laborers suffer little in the way of physical damage save for self-neglect. However, like Merchants, they can be emotionally vulnerable, though unlike Merchants their stress results from long-term worry rather than short-term anxiety. They worry about their sons and daughters, about their parents, and about the state of the world. Little concerned for their own health, they make it a point to involve themselves in the affairs of others because of their selfless sense of community.

TABLE 8.3. HARDINESS OF THE DHARMA TYPES

ORDER OF PHYSICAL HARDINESS	ORDER OF MENTAL HARDINESS
1. Laborer	1. Educator
2. Warrior	2. Warrior
3. Merchant	3. Laborer
4. Educator	4. Merchant

Their antidote is simply to *love*. Worry is low-level fear, while love is the opposite of fear. To love and serve, and to be a constant source of devotion for friends and relatives, ensures that the Laborer will be taken care of by the world. When Laborers feel the need to react, correct, or otherwise involve themselves with the affairs of others as critics rather than nurturers, they get in trouble. Instead they should let go and allow people to make their own mistakes, while still supporting and nurturing them. That means not that they have to endorse an action they deem unfitting, but that they should love others despite their failings and ill choices. The Laborer's mantra in this case is "I hate what you do, but I still love you."

Laborers get health complications when they complicate their lives by involving themselves in politics, intrigues, plots, and schemes that block their natural ability to love. A simple life is simply marvelous. Untangling from their need to change others is the miracle that heals Laborers. Miraculously, by doing nothing they accomplish everything. This is the principle of "Not my will, Lord, but thine be done!" Laborers are healed when they open up their hearts and share their natural loving ability with the world.

Because of their physical and emotional endurance Laborers make great parents. Their abundant patience, devotion, and love naturally make them family patriarchs and matriarchs and earn them the respect of their community. Patience and endurance have a strong physical component, as anyone knows who has raised a child. Likewise, caring for a community takes a Herculean mental and physical effort that only Laborer types are ready to give. Furthermore, because Laborers evolve into Merchants there is a certain skill and craftiness they bring to bear to get things done. Mother Teresa was not above wheeling and dealing when it came to promoting her causes. As long as their cause is based on love, devotion, and nurturing others, the world supports Laborers. When love is present Laborers are advantaged in all their dealings with the world and become a true force of Nature! Love in action is service. While Laborers may be the last to admit that they are "loving," their actions, not words, express this sentiment. Service, or seva, is compassion in motion.

Love in action is service.

Merchants

In contrast to the Laborer's susceptibility to long-term stress and chronic illness, Merchant types suffer from acute, short-term disease—as a result their highly wound nervous system responds particularly well to stress management. Merchants, whose instincts drive them to self-medicate, often go about this haphazardly by shopping, relaxing at the spa, taking pills, or using recreational drugs. However, real health begins when they incorporate wisdom in their approach and learn lifestyle adaptations from health professionals—be they practitioners of ayurveda or allopathic medicine.

There are a number of ways for Merchants to improve their lifestyles. First, they must eliminate multitasking as much as possible. While this is a lofty goal for those with the on-the-go Merchant personality, it will improve their productivity and ability to enjoy life by keeping them healthy and stress-free. You cannot truly enjoy something unless you give it full attention: eating and watching television while talking on the phone does not translate into an enjoyable meal, movie, or conversation. By taking the time to focus on their activities Merchants actually get more out of life than when they rush through things.

There is little you can accomplish when you're sick and strapped to a hospital bed. But because Merchants have obligations that require their energy and attention, they allow themselves little time to relax and de-stress—even though this is exactly what they need. Even if they have to take the phone off the hook, all Merchants deserve a little break. The reward will be increased mental focus, productivity, and immunity.

The second thing Merchants can do is to ensure they are protected. Insurance is a Merchant invention—life, home, and auto insurance is a must for Merchant types who worry about their health, property, and possessions. The more things you own, the greater your commitment to securing their safety. If you have beautiful objects, the stress associated with owning them can detract from the pleasure they give. Such are the paradoxes of embodied life: more wealth requires more care, which creates stress and anxiety. Perhaps this is why Jesus lamented, "It is easier for a camel to pass through the eye of a needle, than for a rich man to enter into the kingdom of God." Of course Merchants can divest of unnecessary things in order to reduce stress, but they will always be drawn to the precious and beautiful in life, for you can never escape your dharma.

Ultimately, the highest form of security is spiritual certainty. Our prophets tell us not to lay up treasures for ourselves on the earth but to secure our treasures in Heaven, which is the highest form of Self-realization. In such a state we obtain fullness from within and do not require sustenance from without. To get there, baby steps can be taken whereby Merchants can learn to be happy with fewer material things and more spiritual attainments. In fact, the savvy Merchant can make rapid gains to self-realization by understanding that the tradeoff value of material to spiritual things will always favor the spiritual.

Here's an example from the *Devi Mahatmyam*,* a Sanskrit text sacred to worshippers of the feminine divine (paraphrased).

Once, a Warrior king was overthrown and exiled to a forest, where he happened upon the ashram of a holy saint. There, he met a Merchant who was also homeless and alone, having been plundered of his possessions by his greedy family. Upon meeting the sage, the king and the Merchant were introduced to the story of the Divine Mother and her mysterious power, and each assigned their own mystical practices to invoke her. After three years of successful tapas, or spiritual austerity, the king and the Merchant finally received a boon from the Divine Mother. The king asked her for restoration of his kingship, and a very long rule. The Merchant, instead, asked for wisdom. His business instinct made him choose the most valuable prize, for more valuable than money or power is that which cannot be obtained by human effort alone. They both got what they wanted.

The point to the tale is that even power to reign over the earth is nothing when compared to the wisdom of Heaven. In the end the

---

*Like the Bhagavad Gita, the *Devi Mahatmyam* is part of a larger work. Also called the *Chandi Path*, it forms the thirteenth chapter of the Markandeya Purana.

Merchant was enlightened while the king remained trapped in the cycle of worldly suffering for ages to come. When Merchants understand the value of karmic merit, compassion, and spiritual attainment, they can apply their work ethic and ingenuity to receive it in record time. This in turn reduces their stress and leads to greater health, wealth, and happiness in this world and the next.

9

The Social Conscience
of the Dharma Types

CIRCLE OF DUTY

The circle of duty, also called the circle of life, is the most important tool for understanding the social function of the dharma types. Every type has a duty to another in the daily course of its existence. It is pictured in figure 9.1 in a counterclockwise direction. For example, the Educator's duty is to teach and form those of the Warrior class so they can better enforce the rules and principles of society. It is the Warrior's duty in turn to attend to the Merchant, who needs the Warrior's enforcement of those rules for the well-oiled function of the economic machine. Merchants then give their duty to Laborers and Outsiders, who share the same functions in the circle of life and are the primary consumers in society. These in turn care for Educators, who pay only selective attention to really caring for themselves.

Priority, on the other hand, flows in the opposite direction. In times of need or crisis, the Educator's priority is to care for the Laborer and Outsider classes. Embattled Outsiders and Laborers turn to the open-minded Educator to redress momentous problems such as issues with law, religion, or education. Because Educators are well rounded and well read they offer solutions the other types cannot—for example, immigrant workers entering the United States need Educators to translate, teach, and advocate for them to maintain their legal status. Once this is done Educators and Laborers revert to their normal duties. Only in times of need is one type given priority; at other times duty takes precedence, informing the everyday functions of the dharma types.

The Warrior's priority is to the Educator, who may need the Warrior's protection in times of extreme stress. During war or conflict it is the Warrior's obligation to protect the Educator, who represents the founding principles of society. Bodyguards "taking a bullet" for a prime minister, or diplomats granted immunity by law enforcement officials, illustrate priority being given to Educators by Warriors. In their daily duty, however, Warriors are more concerned with keeping the Merchant in line and maintaining the smooth operation of civil life.

Priority is always to a higher, usually more acute purpose; duty is to a lower and more quotidian function.

The Merchant's duty is to Laborers and Outsiders—to employ, pay, and shelter them, the largest constituent of society. Because Laborers and Outsiders are the most populous of the dharma types and present the largest consumer base, it is the Merchant's daily obligation to create opportunities for them and service their needs. The Merchant must also keep an eye out for the Warrior class, who take priority in times of need and crisis and may require shelter and resources in emergencies. To this day vestiges of feudal societies where Warriors ruled unilaterally remain, namely in how government retains basic rights over citizens and their land, especially in times of extreme need. Police power and eminent domain, the right to seize and condemn property, are examples of such rights. Temporary confiscation of personal or real property is a dramatic illustration of the priority given to the Warrior by Merchants. Warriors may need to take over a building in a hostage situation or commandeer a vehicle in pursuit of criminals, and they can always find shelter with Merchants, who respect and fear them. In turn, Warriors give their lives as part of their duty to protect Merchants and other classes. This is the real meaning of the Warrior's "line of duty."

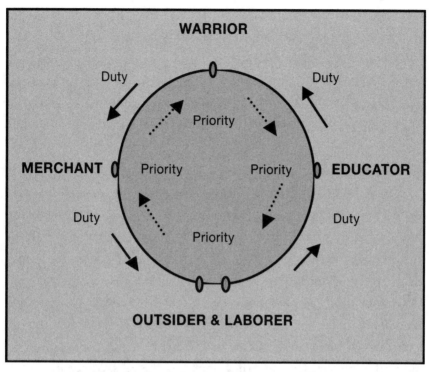

Figure 9.1 The circles of duty and priority.
Duty connotes the oversight, obligation, persuasion, discipline,
punishment, vigilance, and lessons one type gives to another.
Priority connotes the exigency, intervention, and protection that
one type gives to another.

Merchants will stop what they're doing to acknowledge a Warrior, though they know their bread and butter is the Laborer type. Like gazelles in the presence of a lion, Merchants react to Warriors as to a nearby predator. This is their natural sense of priority, an instinctual reaction that may not be evident on the outside but one that sharpens their inner senses and makes them ready to do what needs to be done in order to survive. This fight-or-flight dynamic is hardwired into the sympathetic nervous system, which is controlled by the hypothalamus in the brain. The hypothalamus is part of the deep limbic system, the part of the brain most closely associated with Merchant types. Thus Merchants are most susceptible to these instincts, though the instincts are hardwired in all of us. Anytime we feel stage fright or butterflies in our stomachs, we are connecting to the Merchant part of ourselves. Some Merchants thrive off these feelings, gravitating to performance and entertainment—and the emotional high that is the payoff for anxiety and fear. Interestingly enough, the parasympathetic nervous system, responsible for relaxation, is also governed by the hypothalamus; thus our bodies show the potential to display calm and integration as well as stressed-out devolved qualities of the Merchant type.

The Laborers' priority is to the Merchant, their material benefactor; Merchants are more directly responsible for Laborers' well-being than any other type. Laborers instinctively feel it is more important to work and pay their bills than to finish their next homework assignment, except where education is directly useful for their advancement. Merchants' realities hold more clout than Educators' concepts for Laborers, who are more concerned with practical knowledge like the trades, which Merchant types are better suited to give them. Grammar and philosophy are fine, but they don't pay the bills. Merchants teach Laborers how to make money and feed their families—the number one concern for Laborer types. In return, they receive the Laborer's gratitude and priority.

Thus, every type has a duty and priority to its neighbors. What one does, all must do. What one receives, all receive—there is no question of high or low, of one type above another. Every type must swallow its pride and abide its neighbors in the daily course of its duties. This does not mean, however, spending inordinate amounts of time with them. Warriors do not need to interact with Merchants in order to maintain the law and order that directly benefits them. Merchants do not need to be around the Laborers and Outsiders to whom they provide shelter, work, and inspiration. Educators do not need to look over the Warrior's shoulder to make sure that their precepts are followed. And for their part, Laborers and Outsiders are required not to attend to Educators' every whim, but simply to provide them with what they need to survive.

> **Who teaches the teachers? It is the Laborer and Outsider classes that demonstrate the real-world applications of the Educators' dreams and ideals.**

Tithing is a practical example of a duty that has been practiced for millennia in Judeo-Christian circles, in this case the Laborer's duty to the Educator. Mosaic law required farmers and workers of the land to give one grain in ten, or one sheep in ten, to priests of the church who owned no land and raised no animals. What Laborers have in abundance—nourishment and material goods—they must share with those who need it the most. In turn Educators care for Laborers and Outsiders in their own way, giving them priority in times of great need while teaching in their daily duty the Warrior class, who then share their natural gifts with Merchants, and so on down the line in a well-run society.

Another way to picture the circle of duty and priority is to substitute duty for what each type has to teach another, and priority for how each type protects another.

Educators teach Warriors the principles and ideals necessary for them to live dharmic lives. Warriors teach Merchants discipline and how to walk the straight and narrow with honor and respect. Merchants then teach Laborers and Outsiders how to prosper themselves, how to increase their work yield, and how to be happy. Finally, Laborers and Outsiders teach Educators the practical morality Educators need. Who teaches the teachers? It is the Laborer and Outsider classes that demonstrate the real-world applications of the Educators' dreams and ideals.

Going in the reverse direction, priority equates to protection. Warriors protect Educators from physical harm, while Educators protect Laborers and Outsiders from forces beyond their control—such as legal, political, and social issues. Laborers and Outsiders then protect the Merchant class, while Merchants in turn protect the Warrior by providing shelter, resources, and exclusive access to them when necessary.

> **Relationships . . . are the machine steered by the wheel of duty and priority.**

Discipline and Persuasion

The direction of duty also gives us an idea of the best persuasion tactics to employ with each type and indicates which types are best suited to discipline others. This can be invaluable to parents, sales professionals, corporations, and even governments. From dealing with employees to relating with your children, knowing how to guide and discipline others is key to getting the most out of your personal and professional relationships, which are the machine steered by the wheel of duty and priority. Let's take a look at how it works.

Merchants respond to fear and intimidation, the strong hand of the Warrior. At their best Warriors do not need to say or do anything at all; their inner strength and potential for action are enough to keep even the rowdiest of Merchants in line. This is not cruel or harsh, for Merchants actually appreciate a firm hand—Merchant personalities have little respect for people they can just run over with the bluster of their words and the charm of their wit. They appreciate a strong guiding presence to keep them in line, just as children respect parents who are firm but loving, though they may whine and complain to test the limits of that firmness and love. When Warriors prove that they are strong, just, and equitable, like good parents they earn the Merchant type's respect and enjoy a profitable and mutually beneficial relationship.

However, if Warriors succumb to excessive force, anger, and other out-of-control behavior they become unfit to guide the Merchant type, just as parents who behave this way are unfit to discipline their children. Anger and violence are actually weaknesses that demonstrate the Warrior's lack of self-control. Warriors not in control of themselves cannot hope to control others, which is why they need to be disciplined by the Educator type. Educators in their duty are best at disciplining and persuading Warriors.

Just as Merchants respond to strength and seriousness, Warriors respond best to praise and encouragement. Educators can appear stern on the outside, but in the final analysis they are the mildest types. Warriors are already competitive by nature and need not a mentor who gets down on them but one who lifts them up. Educators in their natural duty to the Warrior do this best, and they appeal to the Warrior's gentle side. Thus, while an iron fist works wonders for Merchants, it is misplaced when dealing with Warriors. Taking away privileges, punishing, or otherwise berating Warriors will only motivate them for a short while—and even then in a negative way. Instead, giving them goals to accomplish or a prize to win is a better strategy.

For their part Educators respond to persuasion and discipline by Laborer and Outsider types. Educators have a soft spot for the ingenuousness of the Laborer and the mystery of the Outsider. Finally, Laborers and Outsiders are best disciplined by Merchants. Laborers instinctively respond to Merchant tactics of seduction, incentive, and the promise of pleasure. Merchants are also great at the takeaway—refusing incentive rather than offering it. Here's an example:

"You couldn't have this even if you *did* your homework."
"*Why?*"
"Because your teacher said you're falling behind in class."
"I'll do it all and get an A, I promise. Just let me have it!"

Merchants are masters of the takeaway, of temptation, and of the promise of reward. They also steer the changing fashions in society. They dictate what's in and what's out, and since their greatest consumers are Laborers and Outsiders they get people to do what they want by associating themselves with what's cool and making others want what they have. Thus, to get a Laborer or Outsider to toe the line, it is best to call in a Merchant type or to use Merchant tactics.

Priority

A type tends to be softer on its point of priority and harder on its point of duty. Warriors will tend to go easy on Educators while being rough on Merchants. Educators will lend a kind ear to the Laborer class while holding Warriors to more rigorous standards. Even though Educators are encouraging to Warriors, they also expect more of them. Not so with Laborer and Outsider types, who have their priority. You can sometimes see this dynamic in the way parents interact with their children. Laborer children may be treated differently than their Warrior siblings, especially by Educator parents. This does not mean that one is loved any more or less than another; it simply shows that for Educator parents the natural priority is to the Laborer child, though their committed duty is to the Warrior. The Bible also provides examples of this. While Jesus forgave others their debt, he held his own disciples to stricter standards and made them accountable for their actions: "Anyone who does not take up his cross and tread in my footsteps does not deserve me" (Matthew 23). Such attitudes are typical of Educators in relation to Warriors because Warriors represent the Educators' point of duty.

> There is karmic merit to playing your role in the circle of life, and each type grows tremendously as a result of following its dharma. The Warrior, Laborer, Merchant, Outsider, and Educator learn things they could never learn otherwise—and mature emotionally, socially, and spiritually.

On the other hand, Educators do not expect Laborer and Outsider types to undergo the same arduous training and give them instant attention in times of need. Warriors, being groomed for the just fight, are subject to greater penance and their training can take years of tutelage. In much the same way Merchants treat Laborers and Outsiders with less delicacy than they display toward the Warrior type, just as Laborers tend to be more direct toward Educators while being more ingratiating and softer to the Merchant class. This bluntness and directness is perhaps why a type can persuade and even punish its point of duty better than anyone else.

Priority is not always pleasant for Educators, who devolve into the Laborer type, but it ultimately benefits them, as it does every type who gives priority to its neighbor. There is karmic merit to playing your role in the circle of life, and each type grows tremendously as a result of following its dharma. The Warrior, Laborer, Merchant, Outsider, and Educator learn things they could never learn otherwise—and mature emotionally, socially, and spiritually.

These examples of persuasion and priority are only some of the ways that the circle of duty can be used. Since duty connotes the idea of vigilance and obligation it is useful in practical applications like conflict resolution. In an argument a Merchant is better equipped to handle a Laborer than is an Educator. Likewise, Warriors prevail over Merchants better than do Outsiders. If a Laborer is being difficult, send in a Merchant to calm him down. If an Educator is complaining, send in the Laborer to soothe her. This reflects the natural order of duties.

However, in more intense situations that require emergency intervention, the opposite is true and priority takes precedence. Because of this it takes a hero to stop a rogue Educator from destroying the world—comic books and movies are full of similar scenarios. Educators gone wrong are beaten only by the courage of Warriors engaged in their priority. Likewise, the greed of the Merchant class is overcome by revolt from the working classes, whether by strikes or revolutions. Finally, Warriors gone berserk are best handled by the Merchant's cleverness. While Educators and the other types are no match for rogue Warriors, Merchants know how to outwit them and find their weak points. A historical example is found in the Roman Empire's destruction of its Germanic enemies by burning the forests and fields that provided food and shelter for them. Although inferior in hand-to-hand combat, the Merchant Roman culture nevertheless understood how to defeat its foes by attrition, deceit, and other tactics that avoided direct conflict.

There are numerous ways to use these principles, and sacred societies naturally practice the circle of life—though it may be called different things in different places. In India, for example, it is common to feed a *brahmana,* an itinerant Educator type. Educators, who often toil in anonymity for long stretches in their search for Truth, may have little concern for mundane matters like where their food will come from or how they will dress themselves. Here Laborers become especially important in helping Educators remain healthy by keeping them well cared for and nourished. While other types may also lend a helping hand, such duties bubble forth naturally in Laborer types, who have the love and stamina to nurture others. The devotion present in them finds an outlet in the hapless Educators, who need the practical sense so pregnant in Laborers and often so barren in themselves. In return, Educators solve the problems Laborers cannot resolve themselves. Ultimately it is a sacrilege to see people who work for Truth suffer for want, and a sacred society actively practices the circle of duty to promote the welfare of all its members.

AVATARS

A Story from the Circle of Life

All *avatars** (incarnations of God) are Outsiders and as such can play any role. Thus Krishna behaved as a Merchant, Christ as an Educator, and Rama as a Warrior. The Buddha was born into a Warrior family and functionally played the part of a Warrior. Upon obtaining enlightenment, he resolved that people were not ready to hear his message because of the difficulties inherent in achieving freedom from samsara, the cycle of suffering. However, even the Buddha could not ignore his physical karma and the circle of duty it followed, so his first and last lessons were given to Merchant types.

Reportedly, as he was strolling one day through the forest the marks

---

*In Sanskrit *avatar* means someone who "crosses over" down to earth.

of his enlightenment—the glory emanating from him—betrayed him to two Merchant travelers whose cart was trapped in a muddy road nearby. These evolved Merchants immediately realized that something special was afoot and took it upon themselves to discover what.

They sought him out, and understanding their Merchant dharma, they offered him food and gifts in order to earn his blessing. As the story goes, the Buddha then gave his first words of wisdom not to ascetics and Warriors, as is commonly believed, but to the Merchants who fed him. "Always feed a yogi," he said, "and you will have luck in commerce, and you will thrive and prosper." This, of course, is the essence of the Merchant's path to merit. He also gave them a mantra to keep their travels free of trouble. Since then Buddhism and business have been bosom buddies, and the Buddha is considered to be lucky by hopeful shopkeepers who rub his belly and keep his statue near at hand.

The Buddha understood his duty to oversee the Merchant class. Over the course of his life he gave extensive discourses and advice on practical matters such as proper business practices and fiscal management. Of course, moving in the other direction, he also attended to his priority by gathering his yogi comrades and giving the first official sermon to these Educators who sought him out for the more serious task of enlightenment. Thus even though he was born a Warrior prince, and though his sermons were perceived by the brahmanical religion of his time as Outsider teachings (avatars always rock the boat), Buddhism to this day carries great appeal for evolved Merchant types, who intuitively understand the idea of karmic merit and practice compassion in action to accumulate it.

In part 1 we saw how devolved Merchants run away from karma. They try to avoid the bad deal that is the negative consequence of their actions—be it overeating, overworking, or fornication. Devolved Merchants seek to buy their way out of trouble with gifts, flattery, even force. However, evolved Merchants, who understand that there is no free lunch and are keenly aware of the laws of cause and effect, seek to tip the karmic scales in their favor through right action and compassionate livelihood, which comprise part of the Noble Eight-fold Path of the Buddhist tradition.

Ojas (splendor), chi (vital essence), and mystical powers accrue for the spiritual practitioner just as money, fame, and security accrue for the worldly seeker. It is simply a matter of penance and time. The worldly person obtains merit by rising early and working late, by treating others with compassion, and by sharing wealth with the poor. The spiritual individual does it by observing vows, performing rituals and mantras, and practicing charity. There is no secret to getting the things we desire from life—we must simply be willing to do what it takes. Well aware of this, evolved Merchants place a high price on everything that is created out of their own effort—as a result they never trade anything unless it is for equal or greater value. A savvy Merchant may trade gifts and food for blessings, for gifts and food are easy to get, but real blessings are rare.

GOVERNMENT

The roles of the dharma types in government flow from their natural abilities. Warriors and those in Warrior life cycles are best suited for executive, leadership positions; Educators and those in Educator periods serve as diplomats and legislators, writing laws and counseling leaders; while Merchants and those in Merchant periods are best suited to trade and commerce. Like their role in the body, where they assimilate and partition nutrients, Merchants are accorded the function of guiding the benevolent expansion of society through managing and overseeing its resources via food distribution, urban development, transportation, and utilities. In this function they work most closely with Laborer types, whose service as engineers, accountants, builders, laborers, and agrarians make manifest the Merchants' plans. Laborers, who balance Merchants' visions of grandeur with real-life know-how, are the dollars-and-cents reality behind the dream. Laborers' practical ingenuity and specialization allow them to get the most out of limited resources and to make everything work. The ultimate beneficiary of an industrialized society, Laborers know what is needed to hold it together and are the key to keeping cities working and functional.

Finally, Outsiders find their wanderlust and adaptive nature well suited to foreign relations, spy services, export/import, and other government positions that require secrecy, adaptability, and foreign contact. Outsiders forge a link to the outside that keeps society relevant and tests its usefulness on a global scale. Outsiders are also troubleshooters, useful for finding what doesn't work and offering solutions for how to fix it. The movement toward using renewable resources and environmental cleanup, and the awareness behind it, is spurred by Outsiders and people in Outsider periods. A case in point is Al Gore, a Laborer type whose concern with the environment did not reach fever pitch until he entered into an Outsider phase, during which he won the Nobel Peace Prize for his work in bringing to the world's attention the dangers of global warming.

The circle of duty gives us another insight into the roles of the dharma types in government. In its duty each type is responsible for overseeing the actions of its fellow types—Educators oversee Warriors, Warriors keep check on Merchants, Merchants oversee Laborers and Outsiders, and Outsiders and Laborers are the mass moral compass that keeps Educators honest. These are not just concepts but observations of the Natural Law constantly at work as much in the inner environment of our bodies as in the outer environments of our communities—extending even to the far reaches of the cosmos. We saw them in action in the brain as the prefrontal cortex (Warrior) inhibiting the deep limbic system (Merchant) in its daily duty to produce thoughtful, appropriate behavior. We shall see them again in matters as disparate as relationships, myths, and the cycles of time.

Like good carpenters Vedic seers used many tools to fashion their vision of the cosmos. There are many ways to approach the same issue, and Vedic texts offer yet another method of looking at the natural roles afforded to each type in society. A case in point is government. Each of the four Vedas has an *upaveda,* or second science associated with it that directly correlates to government administration. For example ayurveda, the science of life, relates to the *Rig-Veda* and the Educator type, whose aim is to teach people how to live with Nature, including the daily health routines and moral values that are foundations of a healthy society. The *Yajur Veda* has as its upaveda the science of warfare and martial arts. These are Warrior virtues designed to protect society from foreign and domestic usurpers. Table 9.1 shows the four Vedas and their upavedas in relation to the dharma types.

TABLE 9.1. DHARMA TYPES AND THEIR VEDAS

VEDA	UPAVEDA	DHARMA TYPE AND MODERN CONNOTATIONS
Rig-Veda	Ayurveda (healing)	Educator. Wellness and lifestyle. The founding principles of healthy living and society.
Yajur Veda	Dhanurveda (warfare)	Warrior. Protecting people from threats to life and livelihood.
Sama Veda	Gandharva veda (music and arts)	Merchant. Inspiring, entertaining, and distracting people. Enhancing the pleasure of living through the sixty-four art forms known as *kalas,* including music, trades, arts, and crafts.
Atharva Veda	Artha shastra (economics) and sthapatya veda (architecture)	Laborer. Securing people's movable and immovable assets. Building structures and growing the wealth of society.

Government in the Iron Age

Warriors are best fit for leadership and rule because like athletics politics is largely a Warrior game—although with the corruption of rulers into warlords in the current Iron Age the divine right of kings has been rejected for more humanistic systems such as democratic and socialist states. In the best of times Warriors are supposed to lead society as philosopher kings—divinely appointed incarnations of law and justice. But in the absence of such righteous lords, and in the wake of the destructive history of petty Warrior tyrants, stewardships of government have been erected, the most current and successful of which is democracy. However, rule by the masses has never been an optimal model of leadership, as few people have the requisite knowledge and experience to make educated decisions about their government. Most citizens are too busy taking care of themselves to worry about the details of running a country, especially in a Merchant society.

> **"The opinion of 10,000 men is of no value if none of them know anything about the subject."**
>
> **MARCUS AURELIUS**

Consider that in the United States alone *fifty million* adults are functionally illiterate—unable to read past a fourth-grade level.* What kind of voting decisions can one expect from such a population? Perhaps this is why it has been so easy for the savvy and the media conscious to manipulate public opinion with sensationalism and sentimentality—emotion rather than reason—for as long as democracy has been around. Politicians readily tie ideas of patriotism and moral superiority to further their political agenda and thus sway public opinion in their favor.

The principle of a ruler genuinely guided by Natural Law and the will of God also runs through the ancient world, from Israel to the Egyptian pharaohs and from Plato to the emperors of China. Though the days of such highly evolved leaders are gone, there are still presidents and prime ministers who pretend to have God on their side, an idea that resonates in the collective unconscious of people.

---

*Forty-two million American adults cannot read at all; fifty million cannot read past the fourth-grade level. In addition 20 percent of graduating high school seniors are functionally illiterate at the time they graduate, and 70 percent of prisoners in state and federal systems can be classified as illiterate. Source: National Right to Read Foundation.

In the Iron Age divinely appointed rulers are hard to find, and it is even more difficult to find a populace intelligent enough to elect qualified leaders. Instead people are fooled into believing that wealth and charisma are adequate substitutes for honor and virtue, electing the leaders with the widest grins or the deepest pockets, ignorant of the fact that they are ill qualified to protect society and dharma. As a result countries and governments are more prone to war, pestilence, and other incursions.

Even when first instituted democracy was a problematic solution, but the best that Educator minds could come up with in an age that lacked virtuous Warrior kings. In modern times the architects of America's constitution attempted to avoid these problems by creating a republic, a system that allowed educated representatives to make their own decisions regardless of the prevailing will of their constituents. This in theory averted the sand trap of public opinion, though in practice modern politics tend to run along party lines and are more representative of capitalist forces, interest groups, and lobbies than the free will of the people or their elected representatives. It seems to follow that even in a democratic government a few people tend to seize and control power while giving the masses a semblance of autonomy and freedom. The question is, are they qualified to create policy and rule, or are they better suited to stay out of government altogether?

> Running a business is not the same as running a country because corporations have profit as their raison d'être, while countries have the protection, safety, and welfare of their citizens as their primary motive.

Electing Merchants to leadership posts, for example, promotes a Merchant system of government that does not suit the best expression of a society's dharma. Running a business is not the same as running a country because corporations have profit as their raison d'être, while countries have the protection, safety, and welfare of their citizens as their primary motive. These two are incompatible and often mutually exclusive goals. What promotes profit does not promote human rights. From ancient

Athens to colonial America—the cornerstones of ancient and modern democracies—we have only to consider the practice of slavery to deduce that Merchant values do not necessarily correspond with human values.

As we can see from the factory farms that perpetrate inhumane practices on the animals we eat, and the factories that devastate the environment, profitability is often at odds with humanity. Yet Merchant society is not all to blame. It is, in effect, trying to do its dharma by providing for the masses, though on a perverted scale. Because there are so many people to feed and shelter it becomes impossible to nurture our lifestyles without raping our resources. Few of us want to give up our lifestyle in order to allow others to live. We would rather grow sick and die than turn vegetarian. We would rather conquer more territory than live in a smaller house. But lifestyle modification is at the heart of any substantive change. This is what the greatest spiritual gurus through time, including our own modern-day teachers, insist when asked how to bring peace to the world.

Real or vertical change must be contrasted with horizontal change. Horizontal change is trading one bad habit for another; vertical change is giving up the habit altogether. Driving a more economical car is a type of horizontal change, like giving up hard liquor for beer. Vertical change is quitting drinking, period, without replacing it with other vices. By trading one vice for another, perhaps a lesser one, we are making only horizontal changes, which does not equate to any real transformation in the final analysis. While driving an economical car is a better alternative, walking, bicycling, or, more radically, turning vegetarian* is a vertical leap in personal and social evolution.

> **"As long as there are slaughterhouses, there will be battlefields."**
> LEO TOLSTOY

---

*This is because meat production not only makes a moral footprint, it creates an even greater carbon footprint, causing more global warming than all the cars, trucks, ships, and airplanes in the world combined, as shown by statistics from PETA (www.peta.org). Visit their site for more information on animal cruelty, sustainability, and the effects of factory farming on the environment.

Merchant values are not compatible with the humanistic tenets of an enlightened society. That is not to say that Merchants are by nature greedy or malevolent; quite the opposite. Merchants are responsible for sheltering and providing for the masses. However, they must be governed by a Warrior-class code of ethics that ensures proper opportunities for them to do so. Merchants cannot police themselves—when left alone they will revert to what seems best, which is to make society profitable. In doing this they may ignore other equally important variables such as the environment, equal rights, and effective, affordable health care, which are neither their duty to address nor their area of expertise. It is asking too much of Merchants to do the jobs naturally allotted for other types.

Matters of humanity and social equality are the concern of Educators and Warriors—it is incumbent on them to fulfill the role of counselors, educators, and governors in society, which is why many turn to political activism and public service. Outsiders also play a powerful role in shaping government policy by showing the world what doesn't work. They are the conscientious objectors and rebels who work from *outside* of government to *change* government. Ultimately it goes against dharma to take away others' right to live out their destiny—by usurping the jobs of Educators, Warriors, and Outsiders, Merchants not only lose out in the long run but deprive others of following their natural destinies.

> **"Economic success needs to be redefined: instead of increasing wealth it should be increasing well-being."**
> NIC MARKS, NEW ECONOMICS FOUNDATION

It is better to live your own dream than to fulfill the expectations and dreams of others. Merchants and Laborers enjoy greater fulfillment doing their own dharma than doing the work of types that either they devolve into (Merchant-Warrior, Laborer-Educator) or who are at best neutral to them (Merchant-Educator, Laborer-Warrior). When they follow their path, Merchants are free to contribute to society by organizing, mobilizing, and optimizing the prosperity of their fellow dharma types. The same is true for Laborers, who are more effective at building community and succoring and feeding others than in running a nation. Such are the redeeming qualities of Merchants and Laborers, and they come out best when there are no complications to get in the way of their expression.

For Laborers and Merchants accustomed to working for material benefits (money and goods), running a country can be a perplexing enterprise. Warriors and Educators, however, whose lives are dedicated to ideas (justice and truth, respectively), are naturally more comfortable devoting themselves to public service in the name of secular and spiritual ideals.

Not surprisingly, Warriors and Educators make more qualified government leaders and are better able to represent the founding principles of their countries without getting bogged down in the day-to-day rat race that can exhaust and blind politicians to their ultimate purpose—public service, not personal gain. The Silver Age idea of selfless public service is so forgotten today as to seem almost naive and impractical, the object of scorn behind the country-club doors of Washington bureaucrats. Such ideas are indeed impractical to Merchant and Laborer politicians, who may possess the requisite education and influence to fill leadership positions but are not qualified to fulfill and improve on a person's ability to exercise political, human, and spiritual rights.

Even well-intentioned Merchant and Laborer leaders encounter obstacles that are ultimately too big for them to handle—arguably the best that Bill Clinton could do as president was to balance the budget, a great achievement suited to his Merchant talents, but he became ensnared in scandals that prevented further progress. Laborer type Richard Nixon reached out to create a global community (a noble goal for a Laborer) with Laborer country China, but his jealousy and pettiness led to his demise—he was too small for the post of world leader.

The Dharma Types in Government

The summary below, by no means exhaustive, is meant to give an idea of the spheres in which each type operates best. You will notice that some areas overlap, as they require the talents of more than one dharma type. Refer also to chapter 14, "Money and Profession," for more detailed information.

Warrior: king (highest executive), military, law and order (police, justice administration), health care, transportation

Educator: diplomat, counselor, advisor, justice, senator/legislator, department of education, health care, scientific research (NASA)

Merchant: Food and Drug Administration, housing and urban development, entertainment, lending/credit, investment, federal funding programs, grants and charities, transportation, trade and commerce

Laborer: postal service, civil engineering (all levels), accounting, banking, treasury, economy, unions, agriculture, construction and works, health care

Outsider: import/export, foreign relations, diplomacy, research, espionage

---

The spheres in the list above can be broken down even further. There are segments in the military, for instance, that appeal more to one type than another. Laborers are attracted to engineering, infantry, and heavy artillery, whereas Educators may prefer communications or officer training. Merchants in the military don't do well in the long run, but Outsiders may be snipers, translators, or other special units, while Warriors make good soldiers and leaders in any capacity. With a little imagination we can see that the U.S. armed forces also correlate neatly into four branches—Army, Navy, Air Force, and Marines—corresponding to the Laborer, Merchant, Educator, and Warrior dharma types respectively. The Coast Guard, CIA, and FBI make up the fifth faction of the armed forces, corresponding with the Outsider. Recall the figure of elements from chapter 1 in figure 9.2 (page 204). To this we can insert the military branches appropriate to each as in figure 9.3 (page 204). With a little imagination we can discover the dharma types everywhere—if we only have eyes to see!

Political Myths and Models

Western political models ignore the dharma type, and therefore the basic nature of human beings. But governments based on an understanding of the four aims of life, as well as the basic drives of the dharma types, can help their citizens prosper by allowing them to express their destinies in full. Even the founding of political systems must involve the talents of the five types.

Like making a movie, forming a government begins with a good script. Without good writing as set down by the Educator, the greatest actors and all the money in the world are wasted—as anyone knows who has seen a bad film with good actors. That is why the Constitution is revered in the halls of American government, and why good movie scripts sell for millions of dollars. Next, it takes an executive type to give life and direction to a project. This is the Warrior's leadership role as president or director. Funds must then be secured to produce it, which is where the Merchant's skill of organizing and moving people, ideas, and currency comes into play. The actual work of building the sets or cities, overseeing the infrastructure and crunching the daily numbers, is done by the Laborer type. Outsiders are the final touch, as actors and audience—after all, the first and last consideration of any project is the citizens. Outsiders represent the proletariat, the masses. They cannot become insiders until they have a role to play. People without a government are Outsiders. Actors without a project are Outsiders. When they step into their role— whether as citizens of a country or actors on a stage—Outsiders begin to embody the character of their script.

Whatever the metaphor, every type contributes to the final result,

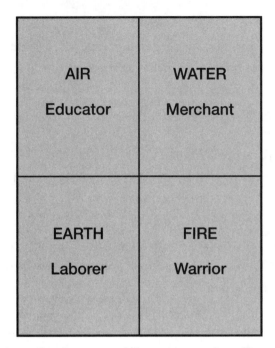

Figure 9.2. The elements and their corresponding dharma types.

AIR Educator (Air Force)	**WATER** Merchant (Navy)
EARTH Laborer (Army)	**FIRE** Warrior (Marines)

Figure 9.3. The elements/dharma types with corresponding
military branches added.

and every type benefits from the completed whole. But not all government models are built to accommodate the dharma of every citizen. Some emphasize one, while marginalizing the roles of others. Let's take a look at some of these below.

Laborer: Communism

Communism is an example of Laborer-type government. While the Marxist ideal of producers sharing in the bounty they produce seems noble in theory, the inherent flaws in the system become quickly apparent in practice. The ideals of camaraderie, solidarity, and working out of love and devotion for humanity are typical Laborer sentiments. However, the real world bears out a few unscrupulous and ambitious types taking over and perverting this ideal into tyranny. Without a system of checks and balances in place to qualify its leaders and balance their power, communism succumbs to the rule of petty dictators. Because it is set up as a Laborer government, Laborer (and also Outsider) types have easy access to leadership, which is evident in the profile of Communist leaders from the past century. Outsider Bolsheviks overthrew the Warrior czarist governments to ostensibly institute a rule of the people (Laborers). But leadership is not the ideal dharma for these types, and such systems fail in practice, or degenerate into a form of slavery, for the inebriation of power is too heady a force for the unenlightened to handle. Educators and the intelligentsia are particularly disadvantaged in Laborer-Communist regimes because the Laborer represents an Educator's devolution point. We have witnessed this in the last century in Mao's China and in the former Soviet regime, which filled Siberia with the bodies and minds of its best Educators and dissenters.

Merchant: Capitalism

Capitalism, though not a form of government, is nonetheless the dictating force behind government in a Merchant society. Much of public policy is dictated to conform to, or at least not interfere with, capitalist markets and the rule of free trade. This is the undercurrent of today's global economy. The pitfall of capitalism is that it creates a government run not by the *people*, but by the *people with money*—a narrow group of political donors for whom those in Congress write policy. As long as the people charged with making laws are owned by the few who stand to benefit from these laws, an unjust system is perpetuated whereby some get ahead while most others remain stuck in a middle and lower class that requires them to work harder and longer hours to survive. At its worst, this system promotes the corruption of society from the inside by deadening the impulses of creativity and growth that are encouraged by leisure and introspection.

The traditions that gave us these dharmic archetypes specified work only as part of an individual's total dharma, putting its upper limit at about six hours per day, while the rest of the time was to be devoted to spiritual, social, and individual pursuits. As an upper limit these hours are laughable by Merchant-class standards, one reason aboriginal peoples who typically require only a few hours a day to meet their material needs have had a difficult time integrating into modern societies.

Natives of the Americas and Australia—and other aboriginal cultures who have relatively closer connections to ancient, sacred societies—have particularly suffered under the global Merchant society.

Outsider: Nomad and Hunter-Gatherer Societies

Nomad and hunter-gatherer societies are structured around free-flowing Outsider principles. A reciprocal altruism exists in these egalitarian societies in which no citizen is above another. All members have the freedom to self-cultivate and go about as they please while remaining part of the community. Freedom, movement, and responsibility are essential aspects of this lifestyle. Members are allowed to judge what is appropriate for themselves and their tribe according to their wisdom, while keeping in mind and abiding by the above three principles. Such societies tend to remain small.

Warrior: Monarchy

Monarchy is leadership by the Warrior class. At its worst, it can take the form of oppressive dictatorships or military tyranny. At its best it is the most natural government according to sacred society and the dharma types. It evokes the myth of a righteous ruler, guided by wise ministers, governing almost unwillingly at the behest of the people. King Arthur's legend in the West and the story of Rama in India exemplify this type of governance, where the precedent for a just monarch shows that he does not seek the crown for himself; it is brought to him, or bestowed from above.

The tale of Arthur relates that kingship is offered to anyone who can perform a specific rite of passage, in this case wresting Excalibur from its stone. Who has set the sword thus remains a mystery, but it is certain that this is no ordinary test. Indeed it takes more than strength or skill to pull it out, for this is a trial of character and virtue—not mere power and force. And, foreseeably, the mightiest warriors fail in their effort to budge the sword. That is, until an unlikely hero gives it a try: Arthur.

The kingship is available to anyone. In previous ages bloodlines were vital, as they carried a physical component of that divine favor bestowed on certain lineages. However, in the modern age, they have become mixed to such a degree that they are no longer reliable for judging suitability and virtue on their own. This is why the dharma types are not hereditary or hierarchical. This is also why monarchy is no longer tenable in our age, for we lack the tests and traditions to elect eligible kings and queens.

As the legend further suggests, authority is not based on brute strength, power, or worldly influence. Instead, everything is decided by divine favor—evidenced by Arthur's ability, against all odds, to pull the sword from its place. While everyone has a shot and fails to even budge the sword, the young Arthur lifts it out effortlessly. We find the same metaphor in Valmiki's Ramayana, the great Silver Age epic of India. Therein Rama, the perfect king, strings and even shatters a bow that a crowd of would-be heroes fails to even lift, thereby earning his maiden Sita's hand. Thousands of years later in the Bronze Age Arjuna follows suit, as related in that massive compendium of Indian history, the Mahabharata. These powerful mythologies demonstrate the divine right of kings by demonstrating that, although perverted by generations hungry for wealth and power, the right to rule is really dependent on divine grace and a supernal rather than earthly legacy.

> "The brahmana (Educator) legitimizes the kshatriya's (Warrior) authority while the kshatriya provides patronage and protection for the brahmana. Secular power, the commodity of the kshatriya, is concentrated in the king, while spiritual power, the commodity of the brahmana, is concentrated in the ascetic."
>
> RAJ BALKARAN, FROM THE ESSAY "LEGITIMIZING RAMA"

It has as its stewards the priestly types who uphold the tests and traditions of that title and its rights of passage. Enter Merlin, Arthur's "guru," or Vasishta, the guru of Rama, both of whom know their pupils' real identities and destinies, both of whom work to guide them on the royal path of responsible kingship.

In modern times we are faced with more concrete, if less romantic, examples of just heroes who become "kings," usually at the behest of their people rather than through personal ambition. Cincinnatus and George Washington come up as salient examples of generals who proved their mettle not just with their skill on the battlefield, but through their character and values in daily life. They stood as embodiments of Warrior virtue and were beloved of their people. In turn they were called again to duty, this time as leaders of nations rather than armies, because of their record for putting God and country before themselves. Here are some qualities that make a Warrior fit to rule.

1. **Adherence to one's word**

   Evolved Warriors hold their word as their bond and would lay down their life rather than betray a promise. As a result they are careful and deliberate in their speech, avoiding boasting, lies, and frivolous talk. This may not seem like a huge challenge for some, but imagine the superstar athletes of today, whose prowess exceeds their prudence, trying to live by this code. It is extremely difficult when you know you can do a thing to not parade it in front of others. It is too often the case that the stronger the person, the looser his tongue, especially among Warriors who degenerate into Merchant-style boasting.

2. **Self-control through devotion to one life partner**

   It is said in ayurveda that the penis is the lower tongue that we use to taste life's pleasures. Devolved Warriors with loose tongues also tend to lead loose lives. Though with power comes privilege, and though one can hold a harem of thousands, the evolved king or queen keeps one spouse for life. Squandering his energy on a harem takes away the shakti (energy) that a king could devote to his people. Shakti is cooked and refined in the secure vessel of a loving, monogamous relationship. This shakti in turn promotes the just Warrior's longevity, reputation, and skill. On the other hand we need only turn to tabloids and TV to see licentiousness and lack of self-control evinced by the motley rabble of wannabe modern Warriors, who seek to squander their honor and energy at every opportunity.

3. **A friend to all—the great benefactor to the world and the people**

   Naturally willing to give their lives in battle for others, Warriors demonstrate this off the battlefield by sacrificing their own happiness for that of their subjects. These sacrifices confirm in them the right to rule; only such a one as this passes the tests of the sword and the bow. The just queen is a friend to all; she does not discriminate based on race, sex, age, or social status, but judges subjects according to their hearts and deeds. Bigotry of any kind is thoroughly inimical to such a person's being, and not tolerated.

Note that power and strength are not mentioned here as prerequisites for the ideal ruler. That is because these qualities flow naturally as side effects of honesty, self-control, and benevolence. In effect they generate power and strength by virtue of their existence and, when cultivated, make their owner indefatigable and undefeatable. That is why these principles apply to Warriors of both genders. Here is another poetic account of King Dasharatha, Rama's father, which enumerates more virtues of the just ruler:

> *Dasharatha crossed a sea of mendicants by giving what was sought. He crossed a sea of knowledge by delving deep into countless books; he crossed the sea of pleasures by heartily enjoying them. He crossed a sea of enemies by destroying them with his sword.*

This snippet from the *Kamba Ramayana* succinctly describes the Warrior's path of excellence: He "crossed" means that he succeeded, passed the test, completed the task he set out to do. It is a defined, finished action that leaves no doubt about the king's ability. Warriors called to action must complete their missions in order to be respected.

A "sea" is an endless, measureless challenge. Warriors' tasks are never easy and their duty never ends. Just as the vast sea cannot be crossed in one day, so the king's responsibility to his people is perpetual. This is why tests of virtue and resilience are necessary to select a proper king. Strength alone fades; power and ambition are fickle. If a Warrior lacks the necessary virtues, he will fall as king and fail his purpose.

What was "sought" is delivered to his people. Not as he wanted, but as they needed. A just king works according to the needs and desires of the people, rather than his own. A wicked king has only his own lust and greed as guides to his rule. One is lasting and sanctioned by Natural Law; the other is fleeting and scars the world by its existence.

"Delving deep" means not skimming the surface. The sea of knowledge is crossed by diving to the depths in order to snatch the pearls of wisdom that lie on the sea floor below. It takes a heroic effort of skill and self-control to find those pearls and retrieve them for future generations. In this example discipline is inherent to the task of learning to hold and control the breath, and regular practice gradually makes one a stronger swimmer. These two qualities of practice and discipline are the foundation of yoga and the Warrior's creed, without which the whole structure of his life becomes unstable and eventually topples down. The just king must have these in abundance if he is to maintain steady integrity in the face of his rule.

"Heartily," not selfishly or with attachments, is the moment enjoyed. The just king takes pleasures where they come, and they are many, enjoying and then leaving them when it is time to move on. There is no harboring or lamenting loss. The wise person knows that when she lives her best life whatever comes to her, pain or pleasure alike, is given full attention and released when its time is over. This does not mean that Warriors are users of things and people, but that they are "experiencers" of the same. They do not hold on to anything against its will, or against the will of their own dharma, but flow along the river of their destiny with effortless skill, navigating the waters of life to reach their final destination.

"Destroyed" implies finality of action (like "crossed" above). The king did not just defeat his enemies but completely finished them, pulling the weeds from their roots so they could never sprout again. These enemies may be anything from social injustices (like slavery) and environmental evils (like greenhouse gases) to personal opponents (like foreign terrorists). Whatever the challenge, the just king walks through it knowing he has justice and divine favor on his side. Accordingly, he does not hesitate to act when action is necessary.

His "sword" is the sharp, decisive weapon that connotes finality of action. It is not words but actions that mark the Warrior. When diplomacy has failed, actions speak louder than words and make the Warrior an effective instrument of the people's will. A sword is sharp and cutting, getting quickly to the point. It does not cause collateral damage but penetrates to the heart of a problem, eliminating it. The sword is also viveka (discernment) personified. A wise king is able to cut through delusion and lies to see people's true intentions. His trenchant faculties of discrimination serve to separate what is eternal from what is temporary, to discern between the false and true, and to deal with each.

Connection to these noble and divine virtues earns Warriors respect in the world and a lasting legacy. In modern times they were well illustrated by another Warrior, General Douglas MacArthur in his famous speech on sacrifice . . .

> *The soldier, above all other men, is required to practice the greatest act of religious training—sacrifice.*

divine justice . . .

> *No physical courage and no brute instinct can take the place of the Divine help which alone can sustain him.*

and self-knowledge . . .

> *Master yourself before you seek to master others.*

CONCLUSIONS FOR EVERY TYPE

Every dharma type has personal myths emblazoned within the character of its destiny; some of these are developed later in this book. The essence of the King Arthur tale is that only by divine grace can one fulfill the highest destiny of dharma type, whether a Warrior, Merchant, Educator, Laborer, or Outsider. What it comes down to is a kind of dispensation, a blessing for the worthy and virtuous that allows them to be the best they can be—and to have respectively justice, prosperity, truth, security, and freedom according to their dharma type. Living myths that illustrate these principles tell us the same thing: live your dharma, and dharma will live in you!

 HOMEWORK

As your homework, take some time to look at governments around the world, as well as your own society, to decide which dharma type fits them best. It doesn't matter if you've been born and raised in one place all your life, for even in America different states and regions have individual personalities. Though the United States is collectively a Merchant nation, there is wide variation between the West and East coasts, between the north and the south, between Hawai'i and the Pacific Northwest. Take a look at your genetic and national heritage to see if you can find which dharma type pertains to your culture, family, or state.

Be creative! Use whatever sources of information you can find. For example, you can deduce a lot from the styles of entertainment found in different countries. England and Germany, both Warrior nations, run more austere, professional television programs than Italian TV—which is more Merchant-like and lively. American TV often portrays devolved Merchant images of violence and terror, while Mexican entertainment runs to more evolved Laborer programs that include dancing, singing, soap operas, and family-based specials. Think about how a country's type affects its image across the globe as well as with its neighbors. Canada, for example, as an Educator nation, has a reputation for politeness, diplomacy, and wide cultural views—though its citizens are also sometimes portrayed as effete, wishy-washy, and indecisive. Think of everything you've learned so far to determine how your culture can benefit from knowledge of its dharma type. If you're more ambitious, you may even wish to ponder how to improve your government using the dharma type tools provided in this chapter.

10
Element, Season, and Taste

ELEMENT

Chapter 1 introduced the five elements and their corresponding dharma types. Now we shall discuss them in more detail. Element theory is the foundation of Vedic cosmology, *samkhya,* and permeates practically every facet of the Vedic sciences. The five elements can even be used as stand-alone personality type pro formas, but they work best when understood side by side with their dharma type. Here is a summary of how the elements and dharma types work together.

Earth: Laborer
Summary
First chakra, instincts of survival and self-preservation. Fixed, durable, and reliable, but also slow, heavy, and materialistic—the most dense of the elements, and the most visible manifestation of reality.

Subtle Meaning
Dense objects create the most gravity. Spiritually, gravity correlates to love, the all-attractive force. When its growth is unchecked gravity turns into a black hole, a force beyond time and space, seeding galaxies

that in turn bring forth new life. Black holes are the organizing principles around which other stars revolve—in the same way that Laborers are the core of their community. And just as black holes are conduits to realms beyond time and space, spiritually speaking love and loyalty (bhakti yoga) are the Laborer's portal out of the temporal world of suffering. There is nothing that a Laborer type cannot absorb and transmute through the power of love and devotion. A black hole is termed such because it is difficult to perceive and its immense gravity allows no light to escape. Similarly, Laborers may appear unremarkable on the surface while being resplendent with gravity and light within. Such persons may only show their light by serving others, without need for gratitude or recognition. The densest element has the potential to become the most potent force in the universe, and it is up to Laborer types to transmute the "stuff" of their petty natures into the power of Nature. In Vedic philosophy Ganesha represents this force of the Earth Element and the root chakra.

> **We are all nomads without the Laborer type's skill and ingenuity to harness the earth's resources and settle us down.**

Usefulness Here and Now

Evolved Laborers have high emotional IQs (explored in the next chapter), for they are patient and strong and learn from experience. Grounded in the depths of their being, they can take everything the world throws at them and still open their arms in devotion. Indefatigable, undefeatable, the Earth Element is the ground of our being, the dust of our bodies, without which nothing can establish a firm foundation. Society is based on the Laborer type, without whom there would be nothing to hold people together—without the Laborer's skill in engineering the material world there would be no cities, machines, or tools to nourish our communities. In brief, we are all nomads without the Laborer type's ingenuity to harness the earth's resources and settle us down. Civilization is impossible without Laborers' homemaking and communal instinct.

They feed us, weave the cloth that warms us, and build the homes that shelter us. They are the very fabric of our material existence.

Precautions

Because Earth is fixed and solid Laborer types can get too set in their ways, becoming rough and immovable, or coarse, gruff, and difficult. They need Water (Merchant) to soften and mold them into a pliable clay adaptable to many uses. Water and Earth mix easily, and their combination brings forth new life when properly harnessed. Agriculture, the foundation of settled society, is a good example, for it represents the cooperation of the Laborer and Merchant types. In fact, it is easy to illustrate evolution and devolution points using the elements. As we shall see below Air (Educator) also shapes and molds Earth, but in a harsh and erosive way. A stone blasted by wind over time becomes rough, porous, and brittle. Thus while culture and philosophy can also hone Laborers, they are happier learning from Merchants, whose approach is better suited to their style of learning.

The Earth Element also relates to smell. Laborers have a good sense of smell and can pick up chemistry, which is why they sometimes like or dislike others for no obvious reason. It is this sense that allows them to love a less than perfect partner. Laborers do not value looks as highly as utility and chemical attraction in a mate. They prefer a partner who feels and smells good to one who only looks or sounds good. Because of the preponderance of the Earth Element, tangible experiences like food and physical affection are more immediate and real to Laborers. Their communication style is also different. They do not communicate in linguistic concepts so much as in the subtle language of the body. It is well known that a majority of interpersonal communication is non-verbal, especially between the sexes. Laborer types understand this well and have a good sense about people, even without knowing anything about them. Of course when devolved this natural gift can turn into prejudice and bias, and Laborers need to take the time to get to know someone before making final judgments. They must back up their first impressions with firsthand experience and give people the benefit of the doubt, something they are more likely to do when evolved.

Water: Merchant

Summary

Second chakra, desire, creation and creativity, wealth, pleasure, possessions, enjoyment. Water is the most sensual of the elements. Without water we cannot taste the food we eat or enjoy life. "Joie de vivre" is based on the French verb *jouir*, which means "to enjoy" but also "to spring forth" (as of water) and "to sexually climax" (ejaculate). The French intuitively knew that without juice there is no joy in life. In Sanskrit the word is *rasa*, the juice and joy that lubricates existence and makes life palatable to the embodied soul—a word particularly delectable to Merchant types.

Subtle Meaning

The Water Element provides for the fluidity and continuity of life. It is the seat of sensual enjoyment and the primordial soup of all creation. Where Earth is rigid, Water moves sinuously and seamlessly to join and harmonize disparate entities with each other, just as the Merchant harmonizes and brings people together. Water is the glue of life that makes humans stick around and desire to experience material existence— it does this by creating relationships and attachments, most notably through sexual union. While Laborers are more concerned with the function of sex (procreation), Merchants are interested in its enjoyment.

Like the depths of the ocean, Water rules forces that are both unfathomable and irresistible—and correlates to all forms of desire and attachment. Water is also sacred in any ritual, spiritual or secular, especially those seeking to evoke the qualities of sacred union, of shakti and shiva, the indelible mystery of the feminine and masculine divine. As an example, wine can be the blood of Christ connecting us to the supernal divine, or it can be the drug of Dionysus for a carnal good time.

By itself Water has no fixed structure; it needs a vessel to hold it and give it shape. Laborers and the Earth Element provide this vessel and give the Merchant meaning and value. Water roams aimlessly without two banks carved in the earth to guide its course. Also, flowing water is free, but water that has been bottled and contained has a price. This mutual evolution between Merchant and Laborer types provides the link between production and commerce and runs the economic machine of human society.

Like Water, Merchants can be a little too slippery in their moral or fiduciary duty to others. Therefore it is incumbent on Educators to provide laws, and on Warriors to enforce them, if the Merchant type is to be made accountable. Water also mirrors the Merchant's general lack of shape and rigidity—physically, emotionally, and spiritually.

1. **Physically:** Merchants may be challenged with weight accumulation, water retention, and an overall lack of physical fitness. It may be difficult for them to stay in good physical condition due to their strong taste for indulgence. Merchants love to taste life, and anything that interferes with this (like diets) gets second billing.

2. **Emotionally:** Merchants can be all over the place. Just as ocean water swells and recedes, so the tides of Merchant emotions, while they run deep, can wreak havoc when not controlled. Devolved Merchants are passionate, impulsive, and prone to bouts of depression and elation, with little real provocation.

3. **Spiritually:** Merchants are the least secure, which is ironic since their path is the clearest and easiest to follow. It suffices for Merchants to let their abundant Water flow in order to walk the path of spiritual fulfillment. Merchants may take a lifetime to learn how to fill their inner void, but it is no more difficult than this: share your abundance with and shelter others, and the universe will share its own and shelter you!

Recalling the circle of life, we see that Merchants' duty is primarily to the Laborer class, as the Laborer's gratitude provides Merchants with blessings twofold—first by nourishing them spiritually, and next by creating return customers for future business. The Laborer type's Earth Element is best at providing healthy structure for the Merchant's Water. Just as earth mixed with water turns into clay that can be molded into infinite shapes, when the Merchant is stabilized by the Laborer type there is infinite potential for utility, creativity, and prosperity.

> **Merchants are the least secure [spiritually], which is ironic since their path is the clearest and easiest to follow.**

Usefulness Here and Now

If Laborers provide the means, Merchants give us the reason to live. Where the Laborer makes a cloth, the Merchant makes it soft, comfortable, and flattering; where the Laborer makes a shelter, the Merchant makes it airy, hospitable, and decorated. That is why Merchants rule wealth and commerce and feel at home in the marketplaces of the world: because humans are willing to pay a premium to obtain the good things in life—and where there is movement of people, there is circulation of prosperity. The Merchant's role is to grease the gears of society and make them work to the benefit of its members. Without Merchants, predominating in the Water Element, we are unable to taste life's goodness or know refinement and grace. Embodied life carries little appetite without Water, which is the primary conveyance of Maya's (Nature's) grasp on the world, holding us as she does 'twixt the dual talons of aversion and desire.

Precautions

Just as water spreads and is absorbed into every space and cranny, Merchant types can become spread out—both physically and emotionally. In the physical matrix too much of the Water Element can lead to indulgence in luxury, gadgets, even drugs. Merchants are into too much stuff. Emotionally, it makes them greedy, pompous, and enslaved to the desire for more experience, pleasure, and stimulation. Merchants need Laborers to ground them in reality. Earth's astringency absorbs excess Water, and contact with Laborer types can help control a Merchant's weight problems and emotional excesses. In Nature the earth guides the direction and flow of water through the channels of its rivers and streams—this is good for Merchants to remember, as they must stay ever vigilant and guided by the boundaries provided by their fellow types. Management must listen to labor in order to be effective. When it doesn't, strikes and revolutions result. In addition, by associating with Laborer types and doing Laborer activities, Merchants are reminded of the simple pleasures of community, food, and shelter.

The most extravagant meal is lonely without company, and Merchants feel hollow when they cannot share their good fortune. Water by itself has no taste or color; only when it is mixed with substance does it take on the color and quality of that substance. In return it gives a medium for any material it contacts to fully express itself. That is how Merchants grease the gears of civilization: they allow people to contribute their gifts by providing the matrix for them to do so. They build stadiums for athletes to showcase their skills; they open restaurants for chefs to wow the world; they build museums, libraries, and universities to allow scholars access to the wisdom of the ages; and they build financial institutions that promote the continued development of Merchant society.

Fire: Warrior

Summary

Third chakra, power, transformation, expansion, penetration, protection. The Fire Element represents change. It is raw, unfocused power that can harm or heal according to its use. The Warrior type has the greatest potential to transform self and others—most drastically through death. Warriors hold the power to kill and to heal, forces represented in their most typical professions: military and medicine. Like fire, Warriors have potential that must be harnessed if it is to be useful.

This takes wisdom and learning, which is why Educators are required to shape a Warrior's evolution.

Subtle Meaning

Agni is the first word of the first Veda, the *Rk Samhita,* the most ancient compendium of continuously practiced spiritual precepts in the world. Recall from the introduction that the first word of any Vedic text is meaningful, giving an account of what is to follow. As the Vedas are divine insights into the spirituality and practicality of human life, agni (fire) represents the medium between our two worlds—the worlds of spirit and matter. Agni also indicates that at our core we are all made of light. Beyond the illusion of solid matter, on the smallest scale imaginable, lie the basic building blocks of our existence, which are nothing but energy. And on the cosmic scale the entire universe came to being through explosion and fire—a fire that disseminated the elements of life. In our solar system we are the products of hydrogen's fusion in the sun; more locally our planet, with its fiery core, is the source, sustenance, and protector of humankind. Dead planets have exhausted their fire and exist in a state of inertia that cannot support life, while our planet is still evolving, growing, and very much alive.

Even at the level of our cells the chemical processes of life are ruled by the Fire Element. Chemistry and electricity galvanize the flesh, transforming food into intelligent tissue, experience into memory, and toxins into waste. Indeed such was its importance to the ancients that fire was worshipped as the link between spirit and matter—the bridge across forever that has been used from the mists of antiquity to modern day to interface with the divine. In the candles of the church or the yogi's *havan* (fire pot), fire makes sacred our most sacred places.

Just as Warriors sanction the Merchant's actions in the circle of duty, so fire sanctions ritual, a Merchant activity. In the spiritual practices particular to each type, penance is the Warrior's domain, while ritual observance belongs to the Merchant. *Tapas,* a word that can mean "penance" as well as "heat," inaugurates the great Vedic epic the Ramayana, the story of Rama, which details the sacrifices Rama endured as part of his Warrior dharma. The Fire Element exemplifies both the physiological processes of transformation (of food, thought, and experience) as well as spiritual penance and the soul's process of en-*light*-enment. Fire also relates to protection. In hunter-gatherer societies fire protects people from the dangers of the wild, while in agrarian societies it serves a more domesticated purpose, protecting the health of its members through cooking our food, heating our homes, and powering our machinery.

Usefulness Here and Now

Fire is at the same time the most useful and destructive tool. Its ability to heal and kill, harm and protect, illustrates the Warrior's double-edged gift. When used indiscriminately fire burns and wreaks devastation; when channeled conscientiously it can bring humankind to the ultra-modern edge of civilization. Warriors are the most skilled type because the Fire Element represents technology. All machines and computers run on Fire—electricity, combustion, and chemistry—which drives the sciences of the twenty-first century. In an internal combustion engine heat is both the propelling as well as the deceleration and degeneration force generated by friction. A nuclear reaction can create energy to heat our homes or burn our bodies, illustrating how Fire represents both progress and destruction.

For Warriors to get the most out of their element they need to channel their energies intelligently, to think like a laser beam, not a forest fire. To do so they must pick their battles, focus their energy, and when their task is met move on to the next goal. When Warriors disperse their energies or have no useful goal, their life force becomes scattered and ineffectual.

Precautions

Just as the Warrior devolves into the Merchant type, so Water puts out Fire and dampens the Warrior's spirit. The goal is not to put out Fire but to channel it constructively. That is why Educators, whose

Air Element gently stokes and feeds Fire, are most useful to the Warrior. Although the Warrior has duties to the Merchant, these at best maintain the status quo. The most optimistic use for a combination of Water and Fire may be cooking and feeding people. This is a noble cause, but it belongs to other types: Warriors can grow irritable if they are forced to cook and clean all day. They need the high and mighty cause to fight for, obstacles to struggle against, and a goal to win. Fire and Earth paired together fare no better, though not as poorly as Fire and Water.

Air: Educator

Summary

Fourth chakra, subtlety, movement, and travel; dryness and intellectuality; liberality, transparency, and high-mindedness; but also fragility, fickleness, and indecision. Any material that becomes infused with air becomes more brittle, and Educator bodies are less resilient than those of other types. Because the Air Element relates to ideas, communication, and the transmission of knowledge, these are essential Educator qualities.

Subtle Meaning

Air travels over the surface of other elements, though unlike space it does not perfuse them. Similarly, Educators may travel to many places and skim the surface of many cultures, but essentially they remain themselves. Just as air may become colored by earth in a dust storm or obscured by water in a downpour, it eventually returns to its original state after the dust settles and the clouds disappear. Like the Air Element, Educators can take on qualities of other types and sympathize with them, learning and growing thereby, but they stay themselves. Outsiders, on the other hand, like space, become infused with other elements to such a point that it is impossible to separate them. We know from physics that matter is mostly empty space, and this is how the Outsider pervades the other types: every element contains and is contained by space, and the Outsider is in everyone, and everyone in the Outsider.

Educators are the Renaissance men and women for the very same reason that air travels around to interface with the other elements. Educators may travel in their minds by reading books and newspapers or by actually exploring other countries and continents, driven as they are by intellectual curiosity. However, though they may be touched by their experiences, Educators are rarely changed the way Outsiders are transformed by their explorations. One is a tourist on safari; the other has settled down in the bush to become one with its people and customs. This does not mean that Educators cannot immerse themselves, but that such immersion is only likely to happen during Outsider life cycles, which many Educators indeed see during the course of their lives.*

Precautions

What does the mountain appreciate of the sky? Not its storms or furies but its high nature, its ability to move above the lowly common world and inspire it—and the same is true of the other types in relation to Educators. What can harm the air? Nothing. Air forgives all, even creatures who devour it, for it cannot be destroyed—Educators established in wisdom know that they cannot be harmed unless it is the will of Spirit. They are protected by truth and dharma, just as they help to protect truth and dharma in turn. Their compassion and forbearance make Educators laudable and set an example for other types. It is not their great gusts or erosive chafing that endear Educators to the world but their ability to be above it all, to soar nobly above the petty cares of everyday entanglements. Educators must take care to rein in their tempestuous tempers and learn to understand why they are valued by others. They must control their passions so they become not a source of harm to the world but a source of inspiration—a wind in the sails of every dharma type.

---

*Refer to chapter 15 for more on life cycles and their effects on the dharma types.

Usefulness Here and Now

Without Earth's atmosphere to protect us we would be subject to the whims and blasts of cosmic radiation, meteors, and random space junk. Though the atmosphere is nothing but air, it prevents destructive foreign bodies from annihilating life on the planet. Likewise, Educators help to secure us by teaching us to understand and live in harmony with our world, from deciphering the will of God to understanding plate tectonics. Though they are less useful in everyday matters—air cannot shield you from a hammer—Educators help us understand why things happen and ensure our safety by creating the invisible blanket of laws and values that protect us. Most people take these for granted, but just as the loss of our atmosphere would spell annihilation for life on the planet, so the loss of these laws and values would devastate society.

In today's world business and entertainment have greater value than education and spirituality, just as gold (Earth) and oil (Water) are more prized than knowledge and wisdom (Air). Is it a wonder that in the modern age our atmosphere has eroded due to a Merchant society's values that put material gain over personal fulfillment? Physical reality reflects the evolution of humanity—during the Golden Age material advancement was simple enough to promote a clean and harmonious life with the elements. In modern times the heavy emphasis on material production (oil, plastics, metals, and even food overabundance) destroys our relationship with the elements and disturbs the balance between Nature and humankind.

The Iron Age bias is toward Iron Age technology. We assume that advanced civilization is built around machines, metal, and electricity. Not finding these in our excavations of ancient cultures, we assume that they were primitive, less advanced than ours. This may be true for societies in the Iron Age of the past 4,000 years, but when we go further back we run into astounding contradictions to this view. We find ancients possessing knowledge of precession, a complex astronomical reality that takes 26,000 years to detail. We find them capable of moving massive monoliths that only our heaviest cranes can wield, and placing them with computer precision relative to geological and heavenly coordinates. We find them capable of astounding feats of memory and mathematics, all without recourse to books or calculators.

According to sacred history, metal and machines actually represent crude tools of a *devolved* culture. According to *shastra,* spiritual literature, in previous Silver and Golden ages manipulation of the mind superseded mastery over metal—rather than writing software ancients wrote mantras to access the technology of the soul. If sacred rituals could produce food and rain, of what use is a tractor? If mental communication connected people, of what use is the cell phone and that bane of Merchant society, the phone bill? We assume that we represent the most advanced version of our species, when in fact we are shorter-lived, smaller, duller, and less technologically advanced than our predecessors in the Bronze, Silver, and Golden ages, according to shastra that has survived these periods.

It is not to lament our fate but to help us become aware of it that this is highlighted. These are the times we live in. It is not to overvalue Educators or Outsiders, but to give every dharma type equal rank. Vedic tradition states that spiritual advancement is actually easier in the material modern age. Because the world is starving for it, our slightest effort to know the Self yields fruit; our every desire to find purpose is supported. Any alignment with or knowledge of Natural Law immediately puts us ahead in the race, for the converse of Kali Yuga's detriments is that God is more likely to take our call because the line is rarely busy. People are more concerned with the temporary constructs of material identity than their eternal selves. Concordantly those who do strive to realize their undying nature have less traffic to contend with, and their "highway to heaven" is clear and uncluttered. Self-cultivation in the Kali Yuga is like driving on Sunday—because fewer people are doing it, there's no traffic, the ride is fast, and we get to our destinations without accident or mishap!

Space: Outsider

Summary

Fifth chakra, empty spaces, speech, and hearing. Spreading, invisible, black as well as transparent, empathic, and universal. The darkness of space makes its natives unable to see their own failings, which is why they need guides, teachers, and counselors to lean on. The transparency of space makes its natives uncertain about who they are and how to find themselves. Their empathy allows them to blend with others; their universality can make them see social customs, laws, and morals as limiting structures and lead them to create their own.

Subtle Meaning

The subtlest of all elements, Space is everywhere and nowhere. Each of the other four are discernible to the senses: we can see fire, smell earth, taste water, and feel the movement of air on our skin—but space is invisible, just as the Outsider can be invisible to society. The other types have preset paths to follow in fulfilling their dharmas—even air currents travel in discernible patterns—but there are no paths in space. The Outsider's path is everywhere and nowhere. This makes the Outsider at once the most populous type and the most overlooked.

Precautions and Usefulness Here and Now

The fifth chakra covers speech, and although the Space Element is associated with the organs of hearing and sound, Outsiders do have a special relationship to speech and words. Words express truth, but truth and language are relative, and Outsiders are most familiar with this paradox of symbol and reality. As a result they have the loosest conceptions of literal truth and can become great liars, or great actors. They can reinvent language or simply spoil it. Outsiders plunge into the unknown to find truth beyond the artifice of speech, and fulfillment in life comes when they bring that truth back and tie it to speech. Their challenge is to be relevant—when they tie their self-expression to the language of society, they become understandable to others. When Outsiders find a way to express their complex destinies, they become rewarded according to the quality of that expression. We said before that the goal for Outsiders is to find their purpose, but that's only half the battle. The other half lies in expressing that purpose intelligibly to others. When Outsiders coherently integrate purpose and expression, great forces reward them in turn.

Outsiders emerge from the shadows to pronounce the plight of humanity and offer it solutions. The outcasts from society come back to save it. This is the real meaning of *avatar*,* which comes from the Sanskrit prefix *ava* and root *tri*, literally meaning "to cross (down) over." Avatars are the ultimate embodiment of the Outsider virtue of returning back to society in order to save it—crossing over into the world to offer the gifts of their transcendence is Outsiders' ultimate journey.

But we don't have to rise to the exalted level of avatars or saints to be effective Outsiders. Since Outsiders are the most populous type, and true exceptional beings come along only once in a generation or millennium, what are the rest of us supposed to do? The fact is that every Outsider has a unique gift. There is something *you* do better than anyone else—find it, and express it to the world! How refined this expression becomes depends on your personal evolution, but every Outsider is a revolutionary in his or her own way—just as the feral tiger roars even in the hearts of the tamest kitten.

In the final analysis Outsiders are not builders but destroyers—it takes other types to implement their suggestions into effective solutions. This is why Outsiders should work with Educators to record these ideas and make them socially tenable. Then Warriors can execute, while Merchants may put them to use in growing society. Finally, Laborers can build the housing and infrastructure to make them last. This model is apparent in everything from the establishment of a religion to building and running a business.

---

*Avatars in Vedic cosmology are holy incarnations of the divine who take birth on Earth in order to restore dharma. Among the orthodox avatars are Rama and Krishna; most also consider the Buddha and Jesus as incarnations of the divine, or at least avatar-like.

FOUR SEASONS

One of the oldest concepts of Vedic society is the institution of *ashrama,* or stages of life. In the West these four life stages correspond to childhood, adulthood, retirement, and old age. Childhood ends at about the time kids graduate from college and move out into the world. Adulthood ends at about the time male/female menopause signals a change in the priorities of men and women. The so-called midlife crisis is Nature's way of redirecting people into new territory in which they release the obsession with achievement and security and begin to share their wisdom with the world. The retirement stage is completed at about the time most Americans finish sharing their lessons and retire from the world, usually by age sixty-five. The stage of old age is completed by death.

In Sanskrit the four stages of life are called *brahmacharya, grihastha, vanaprastha,* and *sannyasa,* represented here by nature's four seasons. Like the four great ages of the world and nature's seasons, time is cyclical in the ancient worldview. In chapter 1 we saw that over thousands of years the world ages come and go as civilizations die and are reborn, and that great world changes occur at the junctures between one age and the next. Likewise the human soul evolves with the seasons of the body, changing direction at each stage until it drops the body and takes birth again, beginning the cycle anew. This view of time singles out life's crucial transitions and teaches us to gracefully flow with them. Not knowing what we're supposed to do during each stage of our lives leads to identity crises, stress, and other psycho-social problems. Our ancestors advised us to follow the cycle of life seasons in order to ensure the proper discharge of our dharma and karma.

The four life stages or seasons each cover about a fourth of our lives. Depending on our definition of an optimal life span, this could mean twenty to twenty-five years each, for an eighty- or hundred-year duration of life. Like the Bible, Vedic texts allot people about 108 to 120 years' life span, in accordance with natural and cosmic rhythms. By modern standards these may seem ambitious figures, but if we average an eighty-eight-year life span, the stages break down into segments of twenty-two years each, marking the ages where most people experience transitions in Western society—completion of education, completion of family and security, retirement, and death. Nature of course reflects these stages by the four seasons, and each season has a special affinity with a dharma type. Let's take a look at them in table 10.1.

TABLE 10.1. FOUR SEASONS OF THE DHARMA TYPES

DHARMA TYPE	SEASON	AGE SEASON ENDS
Laborer	Spring	22–25
Warrior/Merchant	Summer	44–50
Educator	Autumn	66–75
Outsider	Winter	Death

Spring: Laborer

Spring is the season for birth, growth, and optimism. It is when we discover the earth and begin to enjoy the fullness of its bounty. The springtime of our lives is our youth, in which our duties are simple: to grow and to learn. This is the time when we attend school, develop our bodies, and obey our parents. It is not yet the season to enjoy the world in its fullest sense because we are still dependent on others. It is the time for simple pleasures and tastes, before the mind and senses have developed enough sophistication to fully discriminate good from bad, desirable from undesirable.

It is a plentiful season that shares its foremost quality with the Laborer type. Although education is an aspect of youth, growth is Nature's primary concern during the first season, and a hale and vital physical body is a core attribute of the Laborer type. Physical development is more important to Mother Nature than how many facts can be stored in your head because physical vitality allows you to procreate and continue the species. Early education is more about discipline and social training than real learning; it is the time during which we discipline our brains with rote memorization and rudimentary knowledge that in later years, if we're lucky, turn to wisdom. In the Vedic view we are not truly capable of attaining higher knowledge until our minds have a) fully matured and b) become tempered by experience. The first step happens by the end of Spring, the second by the end of Summer. Thus wisdom usually dawns during the Autumn season of our lives.

Western medicine seems to agree, affirming that our brains do not complete their wiring until our early to mid-twenties. Our anatomy mirrors the sacred cycles of the four seasons just as our social customs do: in the West the formal end of education (four years of college) at about age twenty-two coincides with the end of Spring and the beginning of Summer, during which basic training is left behind for real-world applications. Summer is the time when we put all the education and social skills we learned in Spring to use.

Like children, during the Spring season Laborer types enjoy being trained. They respond to firm, loving authority and right influence. And whether shaping a spousal relationship or molding an employee, the same strategies that give kids boundaries also work to keep Laborers evolving—repetitive tasks, constructive distraction, and a healthy respect for authority keep Laborers on the right path. From singing a song to poring over spreadsheets, keeping busy keeps Laborers' minds from obsessing on negative thoughts and moving toward constructive uses. Going to a movie or even taking a coffee break can distract Laborers and put them in a positive state, reminding them of just how enjoyable simple pleasures can be—reminding them of the Spring season when time has no meaning. That is why smart employers allow breaks for their workers, especially Laborer types.

People live according to the laws of Nature whether they are aware of them or not, and savvy observers can advantage themselves and others by understanding this.

But distraction can also be dangerous and is one way that Laborers pick up addictions to cigarettes, coffee, and alcohol. What begins as an innocuous habit can become an addiction. It is well known that habits we pick up in the Spring season tend to stay with us for the rest of our lives, and this is one reason tobacco advertising actively targets kids and adolescents. Whether we know it or not the savvy world of Madison Avenue is well aware of Spring's sticky quality and is quick to take advantage of the impressionable nature of those in it, whether it is directly cognizant of the four seasons and the brain's wiring or not. People naturally live according to the laws of Nature whether they are aware of them or not, and savvy observers can advantage themselves and others by understanding this.

Summer: Warrior/Merchant

Summer is the season of the Merchant and Warrior. It is the time to earn a living and make a mark on the world. It is the season to be outside and active. Those who live in colder climates can appreciate the gift of summer for the paucity of its days and the blessing of its warmth. The summer heat compels us to Warrior activities like competition, physical exertion, and work. Why waste a perfect day by staying inside? This is the time to go out and experience the natural world for all its challenges, surprises, and rewards. School ends for the summer for just this reason. The Warrior, though benefited by knowledge, is usually not hell-bent on acquiring it, especially when there are other more immediate tasks to be done. Thus during the second portion of our lives we are concerned not with education, but in putting that education to use. This is the time for cultivating family and social dharmas and building the pillars of society. Between the ages of twenty-two and forty-four the body is mature and hale, able to perform the tasks we require of it. We are all Warriors at these times, carving out a niche for ourselves, dealing with the competition, and building a reserve for those who will follow.

> **If children in the Summer of life do not reproduce, they bear the burden of attachment to their parents and must replace the role that grandchildren play.**

This is also a Merchant period during which men and women work to secure a future for their families. Prosperity, progeny, and profession are the focus, and Summer is not the time to withdraw from the world, unless becoming a monk is one's chosen path. But even then, monasticism becomes the profession, fellow monks the family, and students the progeny, so even for spiritual aspirants the Summer years are the time to interface most with the world and fight for realization of one's aspirations.

Autumn: *Educator*

Autumn teaches non-attachment. Just as leaves begin to detach from trees, between the ages of forty-four and sixty-six our own grownup children now in the Summer of their lives begin to leave home and start their careers and families. Men and women in the Summer season do not have time to spend with their parents, as Nature pulls them to fulfill their own dharmas, and people in the Autumn season of life are left alone. This is their first test in detachment. They may also lose their jobs, their hair, their memory, and in the case of women their ability to reproduce. The loss of these and other nonvital functions begins to teach them the difference between what is permanent and what is fleeting, and to value the essential in life. This quality of viveka, discernment, and the transition to full detachment becomes complete when they enter into the final stage of life, where, tired of the entanglements and attachments of family, society, and even their spouses, the elderly take off into the wilds of Winter to hibernate until the coming of the next thaw. This hibernation takes the form of meditation and making peace with their spiritual selves, until sleep comes in the form of death to take them to a new body and a new Spring. To make the transition easier for people in the Autumn season, Nature provides them grandchildren to look after—in this way, though grandparents do not see their own kids much anymore, they still have someone to care for and teach.

It is the role of men and women in the Summer of life to produce children and to enlist their parents' help in raising them. Procreation is part of the dharma of an adult human body, and an important duty to one's family, because it replaces the attachment that an aging parent has for a child with another, more needy being in the Springtime of its life. This releases people in their Summer periods to fully actuate their dharmas and gives the grandparent a new perspective and appreciation for the innocence of Spring. If children in the Summer of life do not reproduce, they bear the burden of attachment to their parents and must replace the role that grandchildren play. This can be difficult, for adults in the Summer season are more interested in diving into the world than being doted on. Nonetheless, it is a child's duty to look after his or her parents, especially if there are no grandkids to fill this role.

Autumn brings an end to the fiery race for self-actualization, as the competitive juices of the Warrior subside and the Merchant's desire for wealth and experience is gratified. We begin to slow down and appreciate our exploits, relishing more the passing of days and caring less about their outcome. This is a time to observe the change in the cycles of Nature. Leaves begin to turn red, even as our hair turns white. The weather is cooler and our bodies stiffer, and we are no longer able to dive into the waters of the wild. Our ability to interface with the physical world becomes more and more restricted. This is the time to take stock of our accomplishments and everything we have done in Summer and Spring. This third season is characterized by wisdom. It is incumbent on those in their Autumn periods to consolidate their experiences and share what they have learned with the world. Whether or not it is our intention, we all become Educators in the Autumn as the younger generation looks to us for guidance.

Educators by their nature are not as hardy and hale as the other types, but they command respect by their self-control and the example they set. No matter what our dharma type, we all have something to teach during this time. Grandparents now, we can lend our wisdom to the rearing of our grandchildren and allow our grown children to experience their Summertime unimpaired. Grandkids and others in their Laborer (Spring) season are the worthiest recipients of our knowledge, and we must associate with them as much as possible, as it feeds our souls while nourishing their minds.

Traditionally it "took a village" to raise a child, especially the elders in a community, because they were at an optimal time to share their gifts. Grown in patience and diminished in ambition, they have the best interests of their pupils and progeny in mind.

Winter: Outsider

In America retirement officially starts at about age sixty-five, which coincides with the beginning of Winter season, though for some Winter may start sooner or later. Some people may work well beyond their retirement years, effectively extending their Autumn period, while others may retire early, ready to settle into the warm shelter of solitude and self-reflection. Whatever the variance, there is a natural transition around this age that affects people in specific ways.

> "This kind of retirement plan requires no social security, only the maturity to walk out as a renunciate. Since the Indian society respects the Sannyasa [Winter] stage of life and the Veda enjoins it, naturally the basic needs of a sannyasi are taken care of by the society. Although some people postpone this stage of life, every one is expected to become a sannyasi in the end."
> SWAMI DAYANANDA, FROM HIS COMMENTARY ON THE BHAGAVAD GITA

This period is characterized by isolation and change, qualities that befit the Outsider type. In Western societies the elderly are sent off to nursing homes or hospitals, sequestered away from the mainstream world. For the average Westerner the thought of death is oppressive, and we do all we can to sanitize ourselves from it. Despite the fact that it is the only certainty in life, we vainly screen ourselves from its reality, hoping it will go away. The elderly or sick who have death upon them are a reminder of that ultimate change, when the physical body gives way to the spirit self. Thus people in the Winter of life become Outsiders, shunned by others not because of any lack of virtue but for the same reason we shun other Outsiders—we do not understand them or what they represent; they threaten the status quo of our daily existence.

Old people are less concerned with propriety—they have earned the right to speak their mind, to burp and do as they will, to hell with the consequences! They are Outsiders because they care little for the ordinary decrees of social decorum, aware that they can be snatched from the game of life without warning.

But Winter doesn't have to be laden with the hoary frost of bitterness. Nor, in the words of a famous dub poet:

> *How, passions spent, we droop like sapless vines / in the winter of our minds.*[1]

It is the happy redemption of our immortal soul, for the pledge of our mortality. It is a time of bitterness indeed, but such bitterness that makes the sweet taste sweeter. It is here that we understand what the Vedic saint Shankaracharya meant by "throwing off the world with disgust." Men have lost their *shukra* (brightness), their juice, their seed, and women their shakti, the feminine power. All that's left is a dry shell that once harbored the flames of passion but is now home to the light of the spirit. The fire of youth that burned so strong must now be transmuted into the steady light of wisdom, wisdom gone beyond the mundane world of time and space into the far realm of the spirit. Whose mortal eyes fail now has the faraway look of one who beholds a distant shore and looks upon the inner spaces of the mind. Nature, in her ever present goodness, trades one gift for another. If we have the wisdom to exchange our expired tools for the new set that she gives us, we can continue to enjoy the protection of Natural Law, the dharma of life's final stage.

People in the Winter of their lives, like any Outsider, must be honest with themselves and face the truth of their immanent reality. They must own the present and prepare for what Nature has in store for them. This whole book is about following the Natural Law of the universe, the dharmas of body, mind, and soul. Having reached Winter, we can't stop now. In fact, this is the most important time to heed the call of Natural Law, for here it promises to take us to its highest fulfillment, the realization of our true Self. Whereas the dharmas of the lower world offer temporal returns—health, wealth, name, and fame—the dharma of the spirit holds eternal rewards for us such as cannot be fully redeemed in the body.

We should remember that the four seasons not only are religious or philosophical designations but have real and practical correlations. Research shows that between the ages of fifty and seventy-five our health declines relatively slowly. But after age seventy-five physical ability drops off more drastically, reflecting the transition between the Autumn and Winter seasons. During Autumn we can still make use of our body to share wisdom and experience with younger generations. But with the onset of the final season our duties to others come to an end, and our bodies begin to withdraw from the world in preparation for their final transition. This does not mean that we have to go meekly into the night. In fact, people in the Winter season are encouraged to exercise and remain active both mentally and physically. However, the emphasis here is not on creating more attachments to the world, such as having a beautiful body or a glowing reputation, but on relinquishing them. We can remain hale until our dying days so long as we are also aware that the body and all of its connections are impermanent expressions of a permanent Self. During the Winter phase Nature encourages us to get to know that Self by shaking, and even breaking, our attachments to anything that stands in the way of that knowledge.

Applying the Seasons to Your Life

The four seasons of life are well known to most Indians. However, most people do not make the connection between the seasons and dharma types. Understanding the permutations of these connections can open up our world in new ways. For example, Laborers love to reminisce and wax eloquent about their "good old days" when they were young and strong and the world seemed to shine with the brightness of Spring. Older Laborer types may disparage the present, and things associated with it, and drone on about how things were better in the past. Since Spring is the Laborer's season, the time between birth and age twenty-two, can you see why Laborers would have a fondness for their youthful years? It is not about a particular time in history, but about when they were young. And because Autumn represents the time of the Educator, a Laborer's devolution point, is it a wonder that Laborers get cranky between the ages of forty-four and sixty-six, when their bodies no longer move the way they should and their ability to be good nurturers and providers begins to wane?

On the other hand, Educators do not mature until their forties, fifties, and sixties. Since wisdom does not fully ripen until Autumn, Educators may spend their early years in painful but gradual learning. Spring is hard for them because they devolve into the Laborer type, and Educators are often teased or pushed around, or feel clumsy and awkward during this time. They begin to hit their stride and shine in the Summer season, an evolutionary time for them, though they do not really come into their own until their later years. Summer is both a Merchant and a Warrior period, during which Educators look to get ahead (Warrior) and profit from their knowledge (Merchant). From software engineers to astronomers, teachers, and professors, they make their mark in the world and profit from it best in the Summer season. But since Educators' priority in life is not profit, they do not find full satisfaction until Autumn.

For their part, Warriors shine during Summer. Since they have to use their bodies and life energy (prana) in order to be successful, they are at their peak between the ages of twenty-two and forty-four. For athletes this is generally the season of greatest accomplishment, when most world records are broken and money is made. Since Summer is also a Merchant period it can be a time of stress and overwork, which is why Warrior types can die from heart attacks and strokes in their Summer years. Warriors devolve into the Merchant and should watch out for pushing too hard during this time. In their zeal to achieve and be somebody, they must be guided by wisdom to know how much is too much and what boundaries must be respected.

We can also use the four seasons to look at how people relate with each other. Educators, for example, are sometimes awkward with children, since kids represent the Spring season, their devolution point. Much better are Laborers, who enjoy being parents, caretakers, and nurses, because the freshness of Spring that is still on children rubs off on them, reminding them of their youth. Or like Bruce Springsteen or Kid Rock (an Outsider playing a Laborer), they may use memories of their "glory days" to inspire them in their careers.

A quality of the naturally devotional Laborer type is to sit and learn at the feet of parents and mentors. Be it life skills and morals or athletics and arithmetic, the devotional spirit of children is cultivated in the first stage of life as they are taught to obey and serve their elders and follow social standards. We do not judge our children as being inferior or lesser citizens. In fact, this is when we love them most, when they are brimming with innocence and the freshness of life. The same is true of the Laborer type, who is also beloved of the dharma types when evolved. Laborers in line with their dharma have the innocence and freshness of Spring ever about them, even into their Winter season. For the same reason Educators tend to look or feel older than they are because they represent Autumn, while Warriors seem to always have an air of energy and danger, be they eight or eighty!

The seasons of life, along with the five elements (and the six tastes, which follow), are tools to help guide our life transitions, understand our psychologies, and pattern our behaviors. We can use them in new and innovative ways to shed light on our professions, relationships, as well as our spiritual lives. The remainder of this book covers these topics in depth, but the only real limit to how we use the dharma types is our own imagination—the permutations are endless.

TASTE

In ayurveda, the Vedic science of life, six tastes are classed according to their effects on the body and mind. Each taste represents a discrete part of our existence, and taken together they mirror the totality of the human experience. They are sweet, sour, salty, pungent, bitter, and astringent. Their effects are indicated in table 10.2.

TABLE 10.2. TASTES OF THE DHARMA TYPES

TASTE	DHARMA TYPE	SEASON
Sweet is a taste of Heaven. It is anabolic, relating to growth, optimism, and everything that is good in life. It is the reward for good deeds or a job well done. Yet too much sweet promotes fantasy and immaturity. It represents the baby stage of life, and of all stages this is when we need the most sweetness from our environment, food, and relationships. This is when we need to be nurtured and cared for by the world.	Laborer	Spring
Sour whets our appetites for other tastes. It represents the school age, when kids are forced to learn, which though sometimes deemed unpleasant opens their minds to other possibilities and makes them hungry for life experience. An excess of sour turns to "sour grapes"—when we want things so much for ourselves that we cannot enjoy sharing them with others.	Laborer	Spring
Salty taste makes us thirsty and kindles our appetites in a different way than the sour taste. Sour is slow to work, but salty makes us want food immediately, which is why we can't get enough of salty snacks or treats. It represents the middle of life in which we desire to improve ourselves. Too much salty taste leads to water retention and represents greed and accumulation.	Merchant	Summer

TASTE	DHARMA TYPE	SEASON
Pungent is the spicy hot taste that drives us to compete and gives us energy, passion, and desire. It clears our head and makes us push to achieve. It also represents adult life, when we are at the height of our power and most able to affect the world. The pungent taste is the most dangerous in that a little bit goes a long way, and too much can be painful!	Warrior	Summer
Bitter taste makes us appreciate the sweet. It shrinks our tissues and repulses us from food. Like the Autumn stage of life, the bitter taste sets limits on how much we can ingest and makes us turn our minds to other things. It sometimes makes us long for sweetness. Bitter is catabolic, beginning the breakdown process that encourages us to fast from the everyday menu of worldly life and look to other forms of sustenance.	Educator	Autumn
Astringent taste is like an unripe banana: it dries up the tongue and sucks out the juice from the tissues. Astringent, like Winter, is catabolic, breaking down and purifying the body further until little excess remains.	Outsider	Winter

Too much or too little of any taste can spell too much or too little of its qualities in our lives. For example, let's say Joseph eats too much sweet taste—he is compelled to reach for a candy bar or soda at the slightest sense of uneasiness or hunger. This demonstrates an immature mentality that lacks impulse control and cannot grow up. Joe needs some bitter taste to balance out the sweetness because bitter relates to maturity and realism, whereas sweet represents idealism, fantasy, and puerile behavior. People who overeat sweets are hooked on the fantasy of the short-term high but ignore the reality of the long-term deleterious effects of sugar.

Another example is Jane, who can't get enough salty snacks—potato chips, French fries, you name it, she can't stop eating it. The more she eats, the more she buys. Salty taste relates to greed and our desire for more things in life. It is appropriate at a certain age and in judicious quantities, but our culture is inundated with sweet and salty tastes, thereby addicting people to fantasy and greed—we spend more and more on goodies and objects, thinking that everything will pay for itself as we get deeper and deeper into debt. This mix of naiveté and desire spells disaster for our bodies and pocketbooks alike, and eventually for the economy itself.

What is needed is a healthy helping of bitter and astringent tastes to balance sweet and salty. Dark, leafy greens are great sources of bitter, and in the words of Dr. Vasant Lad, "Bitter is better for the liver." The liver, our primary detoxifier, benefits from generous servings of salads and leafy vegetables.

The fiscal equivalent of leafy greens is self-restraint. Restraint and contentment are especially healthy for Merchant types, and Merchant society itself, though they may be an acquired taste like dandelion and sprout salad. Contentment is also one of the observances of the yogic path that is particularly useful to the Merchant, as illustrated in table 10.3.

TABLE 10.3. SELF-REGULATIONS FOR THE DHARMA TYPES

DHARMA TYPE	MORAL RESTRAINTS (YAMA)	OBSERVANCES (NIYAMA)
Educator	Nonviolence (ahimsa)	Self-study (svadhyaya)
Warrior	Truthfulness (satya)	Austerity (tapas)
Merchant	Non-stealing (asteya)	Contentment (santosha)
Laborer	Continence (brahmacharya)	Cleanliness (shaucha)
Outsider	Non-grasping (aparigraha)	Surrender to God (ishvara pranidhana)

Though the Yoga Sutras tell us that all of these codes of self-regulation or restraint "become a great vow when they become universal and are not restricted by any consideration of the nature of the kind of living being to whom one is related, nor in any place, time, or situation,"* in practice it is useful to focus on one or two of these, especially as they pertain to our dharma type.

For example, Warriors sometimes have dilemmas about nonviolence because this may appear to interfere with their dharma of protecting others or clash with other lifestyle choices, such as eating meat, that otherwise promote their well-being. But for Warriors truthfulness, or doing what they say and saying what they do, is the first and foremost vow they must master. In fact, this alone can take them to enlightenment, because going deep enough into any one discipline can lead a type to the other side.

Likewise, continence is the vow particularly useful to Laborers. For householders continence means not abstaining from sex, but using sex for procreation in the crucible of their marriage. Laborers thrive on their communities, and building a big family goes along with their dharma. Saving their sexual ardor for their loved one and sharing it in this context, rather than wasting it frivolously, bears great fruit for a Laborer type.

For Outsiders, who have a harder time finding their dharmas, it is tempting to grasp and try to be somebody else. Though this is useful for a while, ultimately all Outsiders must come up with their own unique expression and share it with the world, and thus nongrasping becomes the vow best suited to their highest purpose. In the same way special attention to cleanliness for Laborers, contentment for Merchants, self-study for Educators, austerity for Warriors, and surrender to God (acceptance of their life circumstances, which leads to responsibility, ruth, and respect) for Outsiders lead to an optimal life experience.

---

*Translation of verse 2.31 of the *Yoga Sutras of Patanjali* by Swami Jnaneshwara Bharati, available at www.swamiji.com.

A Memorable Fancy

In speaking with teachers from different traditions I have had conversations on a variety of topics, from pets in America to war and warriors. Here is one I had on vegetarianism with a mentor from India, an expert on ayurveda and classical Vedic subjects. My questions are in bold.

What do you think about the rise of veganism and vegetarianism in the West?

"It is funny, you know, that we Indians are preaching vegetarianism for the last 3,000 years, but who is listening? Perhaps yoga and meditation have come to the West to solve these problems. People like yoga, so they are also considering other Vedic solutions like ahimsaa, nonviolence toward creatures, and dharma, how to live with the Natural Laws of your body and the universe."

Maybe one reason some Americans don't think they like vegetarianism is they really don't know how to do it because they haven't yet learned how to cook vegetables and what to eat.

"You are right! [laughing] I would not eat this food either. If I grew up here I would probably be a meat eater too! You know, this tofu, it is not real food. I know the Japanese eat it, but it is never a main dish. But you Americans are crazy when you grab something. We need to teach you how to cook so you can digest your vegetables and your tofu and not become sick from malabsorption and bad food combining. That is why you must teach ayurveda here."

It seems that the Vedas have a lot more to teach us than spiritual values.

"Why not? It is about the total experience of living. From how to caress your wife, you know, in the Kama Sutra, to how to build your house with [the principles of] vastu shastra, there is more practical knowledge coming out of the Vedic tradition than just chanting 'Hare Krishna' and twisting your body into a pretzel!

"Being vegetarian is not for everybody. Some Warriors need meat to keep their bodies strong and healthy, and milk is such a wonderful food—that is why we drink it when we are young. But what we do to get these resources is the terrible thing. How we treat our animals is the terrible thing. If eating organic and humanely treated animals and dairy means we have to spend a little more, then what is the cost? We save our souls by spending a few dollars? I say it is worth it! [laughing]

"Vegetarians do not understand that the land that gave birth to the practice of nonviolence and not eating meat has the most know-how about the topic. They don't understand that it is okay to drink milk if it is from your own cow that you raised and loved, or from the neighbor that you trust. But these hormones and chemicals, and the violence we use on animals today just to get them onto the trucks and into the slaughterhouse—it is killing us, and them. It is killing our souls by killing their bodies. That's why you must teach people ayurveda!"

Using Taste in Your Life

As we grow older we appreciate bitter tastes more—adults learn to enjoy drinking beer or eating salads as a natural mark of an evolving maturity—but too much bitter or astringent curtails our enjoyment of life. These tastes relate to people who willingly or unwillingly throw off the world, like ascetics and mendicants. Too much of anything is unhealthful, and balance is necessary to obtain satisfaction in life. Vedic wisdom encourages the skillful use of all six tastes to promote a unique rasa, or sense of enjoyment, in our degustation. Likewise Vedic philosophy encourages knowledge and skillful use of its many disciplines,* and the yoga principles previewed above, to create a superb rasa in the totality of our life experience.

As we saw with the four seasons, the six tastes lend themselves to

---

*Ayurveda (self-care); jyotisha (astrology); vastu (home arrangement); samkhya (cosmology).

different applications and are used in ayurveda to treat disease and restore balance to the body. But leaving aside their health implications, we can see again why Educators are more serious than other types due to their affinity to the bitter taste and the Autumn season. We can find a physical correlation to the Laborer's jealousy in the sour taste. Laborers are the most jealous type, one of their few shortcomings, and the sour taste predominating in them can describe character traits like jealousy and sour grapes as much as actual taste preferences.

Warriors can be harsh and unyielding, and of all the tastes, pungent is the most potentially harmful. While other tastes can kill you slowly, the effects of pungent are immediate and acute. Pepper spray is concentrated pungent taste, and whether defending against charging bears or attacking criminals it has direct uses for self-defense and law enforcement. Not surprisingly, pungent taste in the form of cayenne pepper improves blood flow in the body and is good for the heart. Recall from chapter 8 that the heart and blood are Warrior organs, circulating energy and courage to every system in the body. The links between the types and the various categories enumerated in these chapters go on forever, and ultimately we cannot describe every nuance of embodied life as it relates to the dharma types. It is up to you, as a reader, to form ever new correlations that benefit you and others!

✦ HOMEWORK

Your homework in this chapter is to start making connections between the dharma types and your world, using the categories we have learned so far. These categories are interface mechanisms for applying the dharma type technology to our lives. You may ask yourself, "If I'm an Outsider and linked to the astringent taste, what does that say about my food preferences?" Since the astringent taste is rare and unusual, you may like interesting foods or have diet and lifestyle preferences that are different from your society's. You may be vegan, while living in a small town in Texas. You may love Indian curry, though hailing from Minnesota. Combining this with the connotations of death in Winter season, we may find that Outsiders eat canned or leftover food. Canned food is considered "dead" in that many of its nutrients are robbed from it. Furthermore, astringent taste breaks down tissue, which is again why Outsiders make good troubleshooters but not necessarily builders—they can break down and critique what's wrong, but not necessarily know how to build it up. Try using the elements, tastes, seasons, circle of duty, five bodies, brain systems, anatomy, and other categories to interface with your life. Even table 8.2 (on page 176), describing long-term versus short-term effects can be profoundly useful once you know your type. Are you generally ruled by emotion or intellect? By objects or ideas? How does this affect your relationships or work performance? Consider these categories, as well as the ones to follow (intelligence, speech, and secret fear), on a regular basis, and your world will open up to you in new and fresh perspectives.

11

Intelligence, Secret Fear, and Speech

INTELLIGENCE

The word *intelligence* comes from the Latin *inter-legere*, to "read between the lines," to understand the underlying dynamics of a given situation. Each of the five yoga bodies discussed in previous sections has a specific intelligence. Let us take a look at these here, with some of their keywords in table 11.1.

TABLE 11.1. YOGA BODIES AND THE DHARMA TYPES

	LABORER	OUTSIDER	WARRIOR	MERCHANT	EDUCATOR
Yoga Body	Food/Flesh	Bliss	Vital/ Breath/ Energy	Sensate	Wisdom
Intelligence	Emotional	Mystic	Energetic	Aesthetic	Intellectual
Attributes	Capable, practical, intuitive	Iconoclastic, experimental, empathic	Ambitious, skillful, coordina-ted	Convivial, clever, sensitive	Sophisticated, ideological, wise

Intelligence denotes sophistication of an emotional, energetic, sensate, intellectual, or mystic nature, according to the five yoga bodies. Thus, while some people may have intellectual sophistication, they may possess a paucity of emotional or energetic intelligence. Likewise, some people who are physically skilled may possess little openness to the mystery of life.

Laborers, for example, have the highest emotional IQ, as they are better able to grasp and deal with the emotional currents in the human body. We should not wonder why emotional intelligence is associated with the Food/Flesh Body, since science tells us that emotions are carried and catalyzed by our neurochemistry and hormones. Long before modern medicine the ancients knew that emotions were physical things, which is why they can be manipulated with drugs, food, exercise, and touch.

> **You can't solve an illogical problem by thinking about it logically. Outsiders offer new solutions to old problems using their radical intelligence.**

Laborers make the best caregivers. They are grounded, down to earth, and not easily shaken. Their deep reserves allow them to cope with a crying child, a complaining mother, or a dying patient with dignity and compassion. No other type has the potential for emotional maturity that Laborers are capable of, which is why they are perceived as practical, stoic, and nurturing. Though Merchants rule the Sensate Body, they can be emotionally immature because they are not grounded in the Food/Flesh Body like Laborers.

In the same way Educators have intellectual or philosophical intelligence, the kind most commonly measured with intelligence quotients, but IQ tests ignore the other four human intelligences. Only in the Educator type is this rational, linguistic intellect emphasized; other intelligences are nonverbal. When a baseball player sights a ball rapidly traveling toward his body, for example, his Energy Body allows him to correctly adjust the vector and timing of his bat to produce the intended outcome—hitting the ball out of the park. This is a nonlinguistic intelligence particularly useful for survival in which the brain and nervous system fire electrical and neurochemical impulses to coordinate movement for a specific purpose. Warriors possess this type of energetic intelligence.

For their part, Merchants have a high sensual, or aesthetic, IQ. They know how to value things such as art and manufactured goods, which is why they are the primary producers and consumers of luxury. From Godiva chocolates to Aston Martin sports cars Merchants, tend to enjoy things more for their glamour and style than for their usefulness, as discussed in chapter 4. Their affinity with the Sensate Body can also refine their senses and make them sensitive to emotional slights, which may lead Merchants to create great music and art—or to simply act out.

Finally, Outsiders are the mystery seekers and explorers of the dharma type family. They possess a mystic or radical intelligence that allows them to probe the hidden aspects of life. Another word for hidden is *occult*, and from UFOlogists and conspiracy theorists to theoretical physicists, Outsiders' abilities to sense and experiment with the extrasensory is unmatched. You can't solve an illogical problem by thinking about it logically. Outsiders offer new solutions to old problems using their radical intelligence.

It is not the quantity but the quality of intelligence that separates one archetype from another. It is not how much intelligence we have, but what type predominates in us. Martial artists possess intelligence, though not the type we think of when we consider someone smart. Finely tuned athletes are in fact supremely intelligent at the energetic level, where they can make their bodies move with a degree of sophistication unavailable to those who do not possess such intelligence. The Warrior's Energy Body is tied to the breath* and the movement

---

*Prana (life energy) is termed *vital breath, chi,* or *ki* in different disciplines.

of electrical and neurochemical impulses that coordinate mind and body functions for a specific outcome, such as scoring a goal or killing an enemy. Contrast this with the Laborer's Food/Flesh Body—more typical of muscle, sinew, and flesh—which is less concerned with the goals and achievements of the Warrior type and more with what can be touched, felt, and manipulated with the hands.

These distinctions have practical applications in daily life. Being tied to the thinking power of the body, Laborers have stronger gut feelings and hunches and learn kinesthetically through touch and movement. Laborers must feel people before they can like them, which is one reason Educator politicians like Barack Obama have difficulties connecting with their Laborer type constituents—they fundamentally speak different languages and think with different intelligences.

A genius who probes the unfathomable mysteries of space but cannot balance a checkbook may possess the mystic intelligence of the Bliss Body but little savvy or street intelligence, which is the domain of the Sensate Body and the Merchant type. In fact, few are gifted with intelligence in all five areas. Most people operate on one or two levels of competence, with less development in the other three. Knowing your intelligence can help you obtain success in life by singling out your strengths, so that, for example, you can get a job that best suits your high points while de-emphasizing your dummy areas. Of course it is important to develop a well-rounded personality, and this map also helps us distinguish which areas we need to shore up. Learning the intelligence of our evolution point, as we shall see below, is vital to making us well-rounded human beings. Mastering at least two intelligences gives us two legs to stand on and the ability to actualize our talents while hedging against our vulnerabilities.

Language of the Dharma Types

To read between the lines implies the ability to discern implied, hidden meaning not overtly expressed. It is truly the ability to speak a language. In turn, each of the five bodies speaks a different language that only those versed in it can fully appreciate. When Warriors learns a tennis stroke they learn it faster and master it more quickly than the other types because they speak the language of coordination and skill. Their bodies and minds are wired to naturally figure out the nuances of energy and control. On the other hand, when Merchants learn a card game or a sales pitch they are better at it than their fellow dharma types because of the inner intelligence that steers them to the most powerful way to affect people, and the most profitable strategy to make money. In addition, those who speak the same language are more at home with each other than those who don't, which has repercussions on compatibility between the types.

> The more intelligences we understand, the more we are able to relate with others clearly, rather than through the stained glass of our own perceptions.

It is in the evolution point of the types that we find the most useful second languages to learn. The Educator, for example, must learn the Warrior's ability to express prana, while Warriors must learn the Educator's linguistic skill. For Merchants and Laborers it is again reciprocal. Each type should learn the language of its evolution point to improve its own capacity to communicate. Just as a child born to Mexican and American parents learns to speak both Spanish and English, we must ideally learn two languages and master two intelligences if we wish to fully express our talents—those of our original dharma type and those of our evolution point.

Ultimately it is also useful to learn a third language, that of the life cycle we are in when this is different from our dharma type. Like it or not, we have to speak the language of our life cycle, just as the English- and Spanish-speaking child must learn German if the family moves to Germany. Life cycles can last years, even whole lifetimes, and the more languages we speak, the better our ability to navigate through them with ease. The more intelligences we understand, the more we are able to relate with others clearly, rather than through the stained glass of our own perceptions.

In chapter 8, we saw what every type has to do in order to obtain fitness, allowing for optimal vitality to experience life, health, and longevity based on the affinity between the dharma types and their yoga bodies. Recall that Warriors have to master the first two bodies to have health, while Merchants have to master three, Educators four, and Outsiders all five bodies. Like Russian nesting dolls, each body fits within and is encapsulated by another. In the same way, Outsiders must learn to speak and understand all five of the body's languages and intelligences, a skill they are particularly good at.

The Five Bodies

The Food/Flesh Body	Laborer
The Vital/Breath/Energy Body	Warrior
The Sensate Body	Merchant
The Wisdom Body	Educator
The Bliss Body	Outsider

To translate this into real-world applications, Outsiders are best at learning second, third, and fourth foreign tongues* like Spanish or Italian because they are able to blend and assimilate better than any other type. This explains their affinity for strange customs, foreign relations, and the other Outsider categories covered throughout this book. On the other hand, Laborers are usually not required to learn many of the body's other intelligences, except perhaps that of their evolution point, because their Food/Flesh Body does not require them to. Their dharma is such that they are quite happy speaking one or two of the body's languages, obtaining fulfillment therefrom. As a result they do not learn and assimilate foreign tongues well—whereas Outsiders

---

*The word *tongue* in this section is used to refer to foreign languages, like Italian or Spanish; the word *language* refers to the intelligence and skill of a specific yoga body.

may roll their *r*'s with a perfect Spanish or Italian accent, Laborers will struggle to grok proper pronunciation, bedeviled by the limitations of their type.

That does not mean that Laborers should not study foreign tongues—though they may not come easily, learning new tongues and skills like jyotisha, Sanskrit, or vastu shastra* can do wonders for the health, wealth, and personal development of a hardworking Laborer type. Laborers appreciate these skills more than anyone else, because they've had to work harder than anyone else to acquire them. Outsiders may take their talents for granted, but Laborers cherish everything they've learned by the sweat of their brow. Learning a foreign tongue can change a Laborer's life forever, while for the Outsider such a skill may be less earth shattering. Even Educators, when they acquire foreign tongues, are less moved than Laborers. These Educators will also retain more of an accent and sound scholarly when speaking, for as subtle as Air is it cannot blend as perfectly as the Outsider's Space Element—unless, of course, those Educators are living in Outsider life cycles.

The potential to speak many of the body's languages is why Educators can make good teachers and why Outsiders may have good perspective and problem-solving acumen. When evolved they are able to see the world through different lenses and relate to people on many levels. They are able to make laws that are inclusive or abolish practices that are restrictive because they understand the plight of other types—but when devolved they may never realize this potential and may be as narrow-minded as any other devolved type. The key is that they have the gift, and it is up to them to use it.

When types devolve they become oblivious to other intelligences and unable to speak languages other than their own. This is tragic on interpersonal as well as global levels, in relations between people as well

---

*Jyotisha and vastu shastra, like many classical subjects, use language that allows us to interface with the world in specific ways and employ similar learning pathways in the brain.

as countries, which also have dharma types and are ruled by the Natural Laws that govern individuals. Throughout history some of the unfortunate venues for misunderstood intelligence have been religion and male-female relations. We will now look at how intelligence relates to, and can improve, gender dynamics.

Dharma Intelligence in Men and Women

Archetypally women have a greater affinity to their Food/Flesh and Sensate bodies and men with the Vital/Energy and Wisdom bodies. The Food/Flesh and Sensate bodies are closely tied to the Earth and Water elements and physical chemistry, which is why women are attributed with higher emotional intelligence than men. Men for their part relate better to the Vital/Energy and Wisdom bodies and their corresponding Fire and Air elements. Fire relates to sight, goal setting, and the transformation of other elements, which is why men tend to have a stronger need to manipulate their environment, make and use tools, and set goals. This is reflected in our anatomies, where men possess greater physical strength while women have superior emotional integration via more sophisticated anatomical structures, such as the corpus callosum

TABLE 11.2. DHARMA TYPES ASSOCIATED WITH MEN AND WOMEN

	MEN	WOMEN
Yoga Bodies	Vital/Breath/Energy and Wisdom	Food/Flesh and Sensate
Elements	Fire/Air	Earth/Water
Brain Hemisphere	Left	Right
Dharma Types	Warrior (primarily) and Educator	Laborer (primarily) and Merchant
Intelligences	Energetic and linguistic	Kinesthetic and sensate-emotional

and their complex hormonal systems. Thus one is able to *do*, the other to *feel* and *express*, more adeptly. This also relates to a goal-oriented, left-brain, rational, problem-solving mentality attributed to men and a holistic, right-brain, visceral, emotionally integrated intelligence attributed to women.*

The Food/Flesh and Sensate bodies relate to the Laborer and Merchant types, who are characterized by the Earth and Water elements. These elements are usually, though not always, represented as feminine traits in mythology, like Mother Earth and Mother Nature. Nature's life-giving qualities are most conspicuous in the water we drink and the food (Earth) we eat. On the other hand, Fire and Air tend to be represented as masculine traits and are associated with the Warrior and Educator types. The Sun (Fire) is male and paternal, as is Father Sky. In this way our ancestors related the macrocosm of the universe to the microcosm of our bodies. Without a key we lose the relevance between the eternal nature of these myths and our momentary existence. Understanding the intelligence of the five bodies, elements, and dharma types allows us to link ourselves to our environment in the fluid, intuitive, and holistic manner of our ancestors.

Practically this means that it is useful for men to learn the Laborer and Merchant languages if they are to have success communicating with women. Men who are already Laborer or Merchant types have

---

*While the Food/Flesh Body represents muscle and flesh, it is the energetic impulses from the brain that actually generate strength. Thus men are generally physically stronger than women, even though women are more closely allied with the Food/Flesh Body. On the other hand, women generally have greater pain tolerance, a greater affinity to touch, and better "gut instincts" than men, all qualities of the Food/Flesh Body and the Laborer type. The corpus callosum mediates between the left and right hemispheres of the brain, allowing them to communicate. The corpus callosum is shown to be more integrated in women and homosexual men, allowing them to *express* (left brain) what they *feel* (right brain) more effectively than straight men. (For more on this see the studies found at http://news.nationalgeographic.com//news//2008//06//080616-gay-brain.html and http://news.softpedia.com/news/Scientists-Have-Found-a-Difference-Beetween-the -Brains-of-Straight-and-Gay-Men-70527.shtml.) In the end, it is not that men do not feel but that for many their intellectual, rational brain is not *in touch* with these feelings.

an advantage, whereas Educator and Warrior men are not as handily equipped to interact with the opposite sex. Take a look at the list of Laborer and Merchant type men from part 1 and you will find that many have reputations for being attractive to women: Warren Beatty, Bill Clinton, Muhammad Ali, Elvis Presley, Frank Sinatra, and Sean Connery among the Merchants, and Harrison Ford, Kevin Costner, Dean Martin, and Marlon Brando among the Laborers.

Now take a sample from the Educator side: Woody Allen, Billy Graham, Bob Dylan, and George Lucas don't exactly invoke the same kind of sex appeal. Though there are some Educators, like Barack Obama, who have charisma and charm, Educators are usually beloved for other qualities. Warriors, on the other hand, though they do not naturally speak the Merchant or Laborer tongues, tend to embody a sense of masculinity, making them appealing despite this failing. Thus, though they may not communicate perfectly with women, Warriors usually do not have a problem attracting them. The almost universal popularity of Paul Newman and Robert Redford with women is a good example of this.

It is useful for women to learn to speak the language of the Warrior and Educator to better communicate with their male counterparts. Unfortunately, however, Warrior and Educator women, though better equipped to communicate with and understand men, are not necessarily the most desirable *to* men. Just as Warriors embody masculinity, Merchants and Laborers embody femininity. Thus, many men prefer a Merchant type woman regardless of whether she can communicate because men are often more fixated on physical appearance, whereas women may prefer other intangible qualities like charisma, self-control, power, leadership ability, and success. Take a look at Marilyn Monroe, Paris Hilton, and Michelle Pfeiffer, Merchant types who are some of the most desired women on the planet. Men, like Warrior types, are ruled predominantly by the Fire Element, which relates to sight, so men tend to respond better to visual stimulation, explaining why they might crane their necks and use their eyes to identify a potential mate.

Current studies indicate that hip-to-waist ratio, breast size, and other biological, visually discernible factors often dictate female attractiveness for a man.*

Women, like Laborer types, tend to use other senses to feel out a man. Women often factor in a good scent, good chemistry, and the ability to move them emotionally when determining the attractiveness of a man.

SECRET FEAR

The Educator type's secret fear is for survival. Because Educators lack physical skills to fully care for themselves, they are often the most physically vulnerable. Their antidote is to surrender to the forces of Nature, allowing Nature to take care of them. This is difficult, but an Educator surrendered to the greater will becomes invincible. Gandhi is an example of an Educator who harnessed the forces of surrender to achieve superhuman results.

The Laborer's secret fear is of being ridiculed—perceived as stupid or not knowing enough. The antidote is love and devotion. Linguistic behavior, facts, and information do not stand up to pure, unalloyed love. Oprah Winfrey and Mother Teresa are example of Laborers whose ability to love transcended their secret fears of ridicule.

The Merchant's secret fear is of being worthless. There is an emptiness inside Merchants that is filled only by giving. This is the spiritual paradox of the hungry ghost: no matter how much they eat, they cannot be filled. External things cannot rid them of this feeling. The antidote is to give the very thing they crave, and in doing so to be released from the desire for it, which is the cause of their suffering.

The Warrior secretly fears God. Warriors are masters of the

---

*For more on physical traits and attractiveness see studies found at http://www
.ncbi.nlm.nih.gov/pmc/articles/PMC1634963/, http://www.dailymail.co.uk/femail/
article-1306012/Beauty-summed-To-tell-womans-really-attractive-figures.html,
and http://divyapahwa.com/2013/05/24/on-the-myth-of-the-0-7-waist-to-hip-ratio/.

material plane, where they can control themselves and their environment. They fear that which they cannot control, which is the spiritual. Right knowledge protects Warriors and assures them of their just place in the world. It also sanctions their actions when they are performed with the proper intent. This type of right understanding is the central theme of Krishna's teaching in the Bhagavad Gita.

Ironically, though they are the most willing to give their lives for another, Warriors also secretly fear death, or what lies beyond death, because it is an enemy they do not know how to conquer. Death and God are things they do not easily understand, and they may devote their entire life to doing so. Those people who understand death, and what lies beyond, are revered by Warriors—which is another reason why Educators and Warriors share a bond of need. The first has the theory, the second the power and patience to make it work. The Buddha was a Warrior who transcended death by his intense practices, many of which he learned from his Educator comrades in the forest.

Outsiders fears being caught and restrained. As a result they tend to hide themselves or conceal their intentions. The answer is to be plain and honest with people. Freedom comes not from skulking in the dark, but in turning the light onto your self. Outsiders can only be restrained when they deceive themselves and society—therefore for Outsiders "the truth will set you free" is not a cliché but a mantra for personal emancipation.

SPEECH

Speech is life energy organized and expressed with the intent to communicate. Communication can be achieved through bodily movement (dance), symbol (writing and art), sound (music and speech), and more, but in this section we will focus particularly on the language of the spoken word. In bygone days adherence to one's word was vital, as speech was perceived as an extension of one's self. When people spoke they exhaled not only prana (life energy) but their soul—life energy combined with intention and intelligence. Though modern attitudes regarding speech are less rigorous, what we say and how we say it is important, and every type has special injunctions that govern how it should speak.

For example, words can be weapons for Warriors. They can be tools to protect people or cut them down. As it is up to Warriors to protect dharma, they must craft words to suit their purpose. A knife in the hands of a surgeon can be used to cut out disease, in the hands of a butcher to separate meat from entrails and bone, and in the hands of a soldier to destroy an enemy. But whether coming from a lawyer or a soldier, words on the Warrior's lips should reflect the Warrior ideal: incisive insight, accurate judgment, and uncompromised truth. Warriors can be brutally honest, though experience usually teaches them that tact can be just as useful as force.

Warriors are by no means always outspoken, however. "The Warrior's speech is soft, but his heart is sharp" is a Vedic adage that attests to the Warrior's ability to speak softly and carry a big stick. Heroes speak kindly from a place of strength, though they may not always have the well-wishing nature of the Educator type. Warriors are wary and on the lookout for a fight, so they keep their senses about them; they know all too well the craftiness and exploitive nature of the human beast and are quick to pounce and punish others when they step out of line. The politeness and civility of Warriors are not to be mistaken for weakness, as their tongue can turn razor sharp as the need arises.

When they lash out Warriors can be severe, especially those hardened by the crush of humanity, using words that penetrate to the quick. Such an approach becomes useful for law enforcement officers and people who need to cut through lies and deceit to get at the truth. But whatever their profession, Warriors can be recognized by their ability to communicate a strong presence, even without saying a word. When they evolve into the Educator they become soft-spoken, humble, and forthright, the ideal of the perfect leader who commands others not with bluster but with quiet respect earned by actions instead of words.

For Educators' part, "the Educator's tongue is sharp, but his heart is soft." This second part of the Vedic adage applies to many Educators whose crusty, gruff exterior belies their inner tenderness. The priestly class ultimately wants the best for all beings and endeavor to bring it to them, however well or ill conceived their methods.

In the action-movie extremes of hero and villain we sometimes find devolved Educator masterminds explaining to no end the devious machinations of their plots, leading of course to their ultimate demise. Such comical scenarios illustrate Educators' motivations: masterminds who must inform everyone of their brilliance and daring, out of conceit, but also from a sincere desire to educate and enlighten those who have not been blessed with their vision! They have conceived that by their twisted intrigues they can create a new utopia, and that no matter how destructive, the results of their actions must ultimately benefit the world.

Mythic caricatures on TV and in comic books sketch out strengths and flaws in the basic archetypes and can be ingenious at showing the circle of duty in operation if we have eyes to see and decode these dynamics. For example, it takes a hero following priority to foil the plot by striking at the heart of the Educator's well-conceived but impractical plans. Recall from the circle of duty that in times of extreme stress one type can rise up to thwart its particular priority, as in Laborers striking against unfair Merchants or Educators outwitting Outsider terrorists. This way the Warrior hero thwarts an Educator villain's plans while teaching the Educator a lesson in the process—that is how the types help each other, especially those that evolve into each other. In this case the Educator learns from the Warrior that this bullshit cannot fly, and that it is best to return to the surrender and benevolence that are the Educator's basic traits rather than trying to become a master of the universe. Then the Educator can learn that despite his wild dreams and passions, in practice he must be true to his essence, which is wise and compassionate, not dark and scheming. Reprimands from the Warrior work wonders to keep the Educator honest.

An Educator's words must serve to enlighten and brighten, to encourage and counsel, to fill others with hope and goodness—that joy born not of objects but of good deeds. Like the feeling you get when helping a friend in need, or someone stuck on the side of the road. Educators can have a calming effect upon others with their speech. Barack Obama was noted by supporters and critics alike for having a reassuring, soothing influence on his staff as well as his opponents. His speech as an Educator was one reason he was elected; it embodied the composure, learning, and nonjudgment that are hallmarks of evolved Educators. The ability Educators have to give hope is not based on encouragement (Warrior), hype (Merchant), devotion and zeal (Laborer), or profound inspiration (Outsider)—it comes out of their ability to see all sides of a story and offer solutions that are both morally and intellectually satisfying.

> **The ability Educators have to give hope is not based on encouragement (Warrior), hype (Merchant), devotion and zeal (Laborer), or profound inspiration (Outsider)—it comes out of their ability to see all sides of a story and offer solutions that are both morally and intellectually satisfying.**

Yet while some Educators are eloquent, others can be stiff and pedantic, especially when devolved. Others still are mild and withdrawn, reticent even to speak, as if the effort were draining to their energy. Though they have much to say, some Educators cannot find the best ways to say it, or their words fall on deaf ears so they prefer to say nothing at all. In such cases art, music, or their professions become outlets for these Educators, who express themselves through their work rather than small talk or social graces. These Educators must find their passion and speak it—then they can be heard, as much for their enthusiasm of expression as for what they have to say.

As for enthusiasm, none can match the zest of the Merchant, whose speech is the sweetest of all. The most voluble, clever, and glib of the dharma types, Merchants are never at a loss for words and know how to use them to affect others. Even if they are not educated Merchants know how to paint pictures in the minds of an audience and have the best appreciation for shakti. They are able to link words and speech with intention in such a way as to persuade people to align their life energy with theirs. Because they can easily make friends and convert people to their cause they are the best salespeople, for people prefer to give their money to a friend, not an enemy. The Merchant's speech greases the grooves of everyday conversation, and at its best can soar to become the highest music and art.

Whereas Laborers underpromise and overdeliver, Merchants talk a good game but rarely deliver in full on their promises. The mantra when dealing with Merchants is "don't hold your breath"—learn to expect less to avoid disappointment. This is not because Merchants are intentionally deceptive, but because their exuberance is difficult to rein in. Recall from chapter 8 how Merchants are ruled by short-term, acute passions that can make it challenging for them to follow through on their ambitions. Unlike Laborers, who are more long-term oriented, Merchants are quick to shine and quick to burn out.

Sometimes Merchants have a hard time containing their enthusiasm, and whether telling a story or selling cars they may exaggerate in order to make vivid pictures in the listener's mind. Other types should not hold them to the fire for this tendency, unless it is specifically intended to deceive or swindle. Then Merchants must be made accountable so they do not repeat their mistakes—this constitutes the Warrior's duty and the Laborer's social priority to Merchants. When Warriors fail to keep Merchants in line in their daily duty, Laborers must rise up in priority to censure the Merchant class, as we saw with the Warrior's priority to the Educator in the comic book example. In recent times, the world witnessed just such an outcry during the global economic crisis of this decade. Where Warriors failed to uphold the laws that prevented plundering by Merchant institutions, an uproar from the general populace demanded that lawmakers do something about Wall Street. A complete overhaul of the commerce system was then proposed, with purported greater transparency and accountability.

The Educator-Laborer Speech Dynamic

The Laborer's words can be square and heavy, economical and earnest. The Laborer's language is kinesthetic, with the power to move people and make them feel. The Laborer's speech is direct and true, even laconic. It is plain, practical, and delivered in a "take it or leave it" manner that can make a Laborer type appear gruff or insensitive. But Laborer types are quite the contrary. They feel deeply, but they may not necessarily possess the words to convey their emotions. And they don't need to, because their actions communicate better than words. Consider Laborer-style music. You don't listen to the blues for its lyrics—it is the emotional power of the blues that affects its listeners. It is sufficient just to be around Laborer types to understand who they are and what they're about—there is little need for words or explanations.

Laborers prefer plainness in their speech and in that of others. That is why Educators have difficulties relating to the Laborer type, for they tend to be spacy and elliptical, whereas Laborers are direct. Each party can feel misunderstood and misrepresented. On the one hand, Educators feel invalidated because despite their efforts they cannot make themselves understood by Laborers. This feels like a major failing, as Educators are supposed to be the teachers of the dharma types! On the other hand, the Laborer type may fall into the trap of "I'm stupid; I don't understand enough; I have no value." Both of these attitudes are illusions created by each type's inability to understand the relating process of the other. It is important for Educators to know that Laborers understand actions better than words, and it is through their behavior that they can reach the Laborer type, not through their sermons. On the other hand, Laborers should appreciate the complexity of Educators' task, which is to learn, absorb, and transmit knowledge, and to cut them a break when they slip up and fall on their faces.

This is in line with the Laborer's basic instinct, which is to nurture and feed others. A handshake and a smile, a shared meal and a drink—these can promote better understanding between Laborers and Educators than debate and argument. In fact, this method of sharing love is efficient in communicating with every type. Though they may not word it that way, it is essentially love that Laborers share with the world when they devote their time, energy, and emotion to others. And love is a language without nations, without borders. It is understood by black and white, young and old, Muslim and Jew, and for this reason makes Laborers the best communicators of all!

Laborers and Preachiness

Laborers, however, love to preach—even when they are not qualified to do so. Preaching is for Educators, and as we know Laborers devolve into Educators. The problem is that when types devolve they begin to look and act like each other, so that it may be tough to tell them apart. When you see a Laborer look and act like an Educator, watch out, because something is wrong! The same holds true for Educators who behave like Laborers—they are not in line with their dharma and will not have satisfaction. They need to look to their point of evolution to actualize themselves. Of course when types evolve they also begin to look like their evolution points—Merchants resemble Laborers, and Educators look Warrior-like when in the flow of their dharma. (Refer to part 1 for more on the evolution and devolution of the types.)

With Laborers' narrow and parochial attitudes toward knowledge, preaching can be a dangerous road. On the one hand, their focus on personal experience and "walking the walk" makes Laborers passionate and convincing on topics they believe in—they experience a truth and believe that everyone should have the same experience. Insofar as this comes from a genuine desire to benefit others, it can be nurturing and satisfying to those who partake in the Laborer type's causes. Here we have the impassioned pastor, sweating it out on the stage in an ecstatic swoon, singing praises to the Almighty.

On the other hand, when Laborers' narrow focus prevents them from acknowledging other ways of doing things, an ugly type of bigotry and pettiness can rear its head. Racism, fanaticism, jingoism, and other forms of intolerance spoil Laborers' genuine zeal. Far beyond religion and politics, this form of small-mindedness can insinuate itself into their lifestyle and become a hallmark of their personality.

Few can stir up tears or pluck the heartstrings of emotion like impassioned Laborers. In this kind of pathos lies their nobility, and in their earnest devotion Laborers stand above all others in inviting the heart to feel. But in their pettiness and smallness none are more reviled and despised. When they speak with their heart intent on teaching there is no force more passionate and moving than the Laborer type. Be it in daily life or on the stage—in work or politics, music, or religion—Laborers can reach and grab our hearts and send us into ecstatic union. Bruce Springsteen is an example of an entertainer whose Laborer roots run deep through his music.

On the other hand, corrupted Laborer types have used this ability to connect deeply to take advantage of people on massive scales. Communism (a Laborer type system) had the appeal of uniting the underprivileged classes into solidarity, but in practice it was perverted by Stalin and other communist leaders who used their Laborer appeal to preach peace to the masses while stabbing them in the back. From the corner Bible thumper to the next-door politician, the road is narrow and fraught with peril when Laborers impose their views onto others.

Here are some rules to follow in order to get the most out of the Laborer type's advice, and some pointers if you are a Laborer intent on sharing your wisdom:

1. Laborer types are qualified to give advice mainly to other Laborers, Merchants, and Outsiders. When they dispense wisdom to Warriors and Educators it is not as effective, for these types think with different intelligences and have methods of obtaining knowledge unavailable to the Laborer.

2. Laborers understand the power of their emotion and assume that it carries with it truth. "If I feel it then it must be right!" is the mantra in this type of thinking. A little education and experience, however, can contextualize Laborers' emotions and help them temper their passion with knowledge. This is what Martin Luther King Jr. endeavored to bring to the black church, which he felt disempowered its members by stressing *emotionalism* over *education*. Instead he sought to feed people's minds—as well as their souls—and give them power through knowledge. In this way Laborers must be open to being wrong, and to constant reeducation.

> *I wondered whether religion, with its emotionalism in Negro churches, could be intellectually respectable as well as emotionally satisfying.*
>
> MARTIN LUTHER KING JR., REFLECTING
> ON HIS EARLY LIFE IN THE MINISTRY

Refer back to table 8.2 (page 176) to remind yourself about the two basic camps among the dharma type family—Laborers and Merchants, who are ruled by feeling, and Warriors and Educators, who are ruled by thinking. Outsiders are excluded because they take on qualities of the type they are emulating. Thus, Outsiders playing Warriors move to the thinking duo, while those playing Laborers will be in the feeling group.

Warriors and Harshness

We may think of Warriors as harsh and unyielding, but they can be remarkably polished and polite. Observe how professional adversaries like politicians, athletes, and businesspeople communicate. They can be complimentary and courteous on camera but ready to pounce on their enemies when need be. This is because Warriors respect the rules of a game and are ready to play it. Publically they may observe social etiquette, but when it is time to play, they play to win. When not constrained by the conventions of proper conduct the Warrior's speech is often direct, to the point, and rarely superfluous.

Take Warrior doctors, who may look cold and professional to the point of seeming hard-hearted. They treat people as cases, and their bedside manner may appear uncaring, even cruel. This type of doctor gets into medicine to battle disease, not interact with patients; the goal is to affect a cure and prevent suffering. Educator types, on the other hand, may be more sympathetic to the personal issues of the patient, depending on their theoretical outlook—if there is something to learn from, or to teach them, Educators will interact with patients readily, just as Laborers may commiserate with the suffering by virtue of their human touch and sensitivity.

Yet it is not because they are hard-hearted but because they are conscientious that Warriors assume a role of professionalism and wear it like armor. It is to keep their hearts from being broken by every terminal case that Warrior surgeons gird themselves with protection. The challenge for Warriors is to protect themselves without shutting others out. When they become blinded and desensitized to suffering they begin to lose their life purpose, which is to ease that suffering. Therefore they must strike a balance between too much and too little. For the intense and excess-prone personality of the Warrior, however, this remains a lifelong challenge.

This is where some find help in Eastern traditions, like Buddhism, Taoism, Hinduism, and other philosophies that stress a type of ease and harmony with Nature. The Buddha did not hesitate to push the envelope on human endurance and potential but ultimately found value in a middle ground of effort combined with surrender. Wind too tight, and you break the string; too lax, and it will never sing. From Shaolin monks to samurai swordsmen, Eastern spiritual traditions are famous for producing warriors of legendary mien. Such Warriors achieved their mythic status not by the number of armies they conquered, as do Warriors in the West, but by the quality of their interactions and the degree of skill they exhibited in the dispensation of their duties.

Supernormal powers and hairsplitting skill are attributed to such masters, but these feats do not come out of an excessive physicality or bloodthirsty rage. Instead they arise from an even-tempered zone of stillness in action—like the eye of a hurricane. Warriors attain this by integrating qualities of the Educator into their nature. Here are some of the Educator's traits Warriors can absorb, and how they are benefited thereby.

1. **Knowledge** grows their strength and influence, is power for Warriors, and can be used as leverage to help them intelligently navigate through their duties.
2. **Diplomacy** helps them win battles they need to win and avoid battles they don't need to fight.
3. **Compassion** drives them to justice and fans the desire to fulfill their destiny.
4. **Surrender** is what balances the Warrior flame. When in balance Warriors become conscientious and skillful, and skillfulness in action is one of the definitions of yoga.

When yoga is achieved Warriors' speeches become gentle yet firm, direct but all embracing. They say little but intend a lot. Their tone conveys compassion tempered with accountability, and like fire their speech is used to heal as well as to kill, enabling their words to become instruments of progress and evolution.

Outsiders

Speech is a marker of identity; it tells people who you are. You cannot understand someone unless you speak his or her language. Outsiders are adept at learning new accents, tongues, and identities. However, this ability can also keep them from finding themselves, and they must eventually learn the language of their own souls to discover who they are as individuals. Outsiders must discover their unique expression and share it with the world if they are to find a place and feel understood by others. They cannot expect to be heard by society unless they teach the world to sing their song, thereby refreshing the social harmony in revolutionary new refrains.

Outsiders have the loosest concept of self-expression. Nothing is off limits, and they express themselves in unique ways, from the most vulgar to the most profound. In Latin *vulgar* means "of the people" and referred to the proletariat, the working class, the largest section of society. While in other ages the proletariat idea was associated with Laborer types, in the Iron Age the Outsider's numbers outstrip other classes. The Roman Empire effectively created whole nations of Outsiders by conquering tribes and assimilating their cultures under the aegis of Roman rule. Their speech and customs, being different from those of their conquerors, relegated them to lower ranks in society as slaves or workers because it is impossible to access the higher echelons of a culture without being fluent in its language and traditions. The same is true of our global economy today, where industrialized societies assimilate migrations of Outsiders on massive scales, making it easier to be an Outsider but harder to find yourself in the fray.

> **Jewish Educators need to learn Hebrew to understand the roots of their culture; Educators who meditate, do yoga, or otherwise study the Vedic traditions this book is based on should study Sanskrit.**

One result of the Roman Empire's conquests was that as a group Outsiders contributed their unique expression by creating the Romance languages—French, Italian, Spanish, Romanian, and others that emerged from the vulgar vernacular of a society in which Latin was spoken by the elite. English is another such mélange, a product of the linguistic melding of conquering influences in the British Isles. Today English is the language of worldwide currency and diplomacy, which underscores the influence Outsiders have had on the Iron Age. Outsiders as a group literally found their unique expression in the many languages they left behind.

Just as Outsiders do this collectively on a global scale, Outsider individuals must find and add their voices to the chorus of society. By adapting to society Outsiders change it, so much so that it begins to sing their song. After all, the Romance languages today resonate all over the world, while Latin, their progenitor, is relegated to the stained-glass halls of academia and ecclesia.

Language and the Educator

This Outsider influence over the fourth age of man has also had negative effects. As mentioned, there are very few pure languages left in the world, and where these exist they are mostly used for sacred purposes, such as maintaining the myths and lore of a tradition. Examples of such languages include Hebrew and Sanskrit, or Greek and Latin for Westerners. Other less well-known linguistic traditions, like Gaelic and Finnish dialects, are also notable keepers of lore. Because linguistic intelligence is specific to Educators, learning the sacred language of a tradition is particularly important for them. Jewish Educators need to learn Hebrew to understand the roots of their culture; Educators who meditate, do yoga, or otherwise study the Vedic culture this book is based on should study Sanskrit. This is because reading secondhand interpretations is not sufficient for Educator types—they must access lore *directly* if they are to teach it to others.

Even on a practical level, going to the source is always useful for Educators. Politically minded Educator types do better to source their news from C-Span rather than the plumy late-night "politicasters" on the local news or CNN. Science-minded Educators get more out of reputable scientific journals than glossy magazines because to get to the truth they must go to the root. A mathematician's language may be calculus; for computer programmers it may be HTML or Java. For students of the sacred sciences getting to the core of their field requires plunging into the lake of sacred dialects that remain in this age.

Language changes the structure of thought and how we see the world. In the words of Outsider-playing-Educator Gabriel Byrne, "To be robbed of your language is to be robbed of the way you think."[1] The language we speak affects our reality, and every type should endeavor to learn its own tongue, as discussed previously. And while Laborers learn through touch and Warriors through movement, Educators learn through reading, discussing, and listening to words.

One drawback of English as the world vernacular is that English as we know it has no sacred history or literature. China has the Tao Te Ching; Hebrew the Torah; Greek the New Testament and Plato; Sanskrit the Vedas and Upanishads; Latin Virgil and Augustine—but what does English have? The greatest English writers, like Shakespeare and Milton, drew wisdom from Greek and Latin. They sourced what they could from the wellspring that was ancient even in their time. The spiritual traditions of the English language pale next to those of the more ancient languages of the world. Therefore, to truly understand ancient thought, we must learn the language in which it was transmitted. Reading in translation is seeing the world through a muslin screen. We must have firsthand experience of a thing for it to be real to us. We must speak the language of a place to interface with its customs, for in the words of Nobel laureate Czeslaw Milosz, "Language is the only homeland."

12

Music, Myth, and Poodles

MUSIC

All musicians play or sing according to the characteristic of their dharma type. Warriors sing of struggle, Laborers of drama and suffering. Outsiders rebel, Merchants revel, and Educators contemplate the nature of their world. When Outsider-playing-Educator Alanis Morissette sings, "Thank you frailty, thank you consequence, thank you, thank you silence,"[1] she expresses the Educator's vulnerability (*frailty;* see the "Body Type" section in chapter 8, pages 158–65), propensity to instant karma (*consequence;* see chapter 2), and love of quiet self-reflection (*silence*).

The same is true of Pavarotti when he sings from Tosca:

> *O! Dolci baci! O! Languido carezze . . .*
> *O! Sweet kisses! O! Languid caresses . . .*

Awaiting execution, reliving the taste and feel of his passionate lover, this Laborer's heart pours out the drama of the moment. Laborer music is gutsy and devotional. It relies on instinct and emotion to hook its listeners, not on the refinement of its content. Being also workingman's music, it can be sung in the neighborhood tavern or in the army foxhole to boost morale and build camaraderie. Because its roots run deep, it is passed down from generation to generation. Patriotic, traditional, blues, gospel, religious, and other styles that share the above qualities exemplify Laborer music.

Like the Merchant's easygoing nature, Merchant music makes you feel good. It is foot-tapping, hand-clapping, lighthearted entertainment. And like their music, Merchants have a knack for raising spirits. That is why they are successful at making money, and the reason pop music sells millions of records. People pay to be reminded of their precious joy as human beings, and Merchants are the beneficiaries of that need. Because they have a gift for ornamentation and embellishment, Merchants' music is also flashy and trendsetting, inspiring fashion movements, hairstyles, and the like. Though it may lack substance it is catchy, hummable, and easy to digest. It is easy to market as it is quickly appreciated—and usually quickly forgotten.

Where Merchant music is designed to make you feel good, Warrior music often does the reverse: its intense, driving melodies come from the Warrior's need to fight. Where this fighting spirit is directed determines how the music comes across. From provocative, in-your-face attitudes to fighting for justice and the rights of the underprivileged, Warrior music carries a message that highlights injustice. Here, Warriors walk hand in hand with Outsiders, who have similar agendas. Because it evokes the ugliness in society, the hard times of personal relationships, or individual struggles and addictions, Warrior music does not carry the sing-songy, feel-good message that Merchant music does. Consequently, it is usually not as popular, though that is hardly a concern for Warriors. Like the Outsider who brings them up for society to look at, the Warrior's job is to redress social evils. This can take place on the personal (a battered wife), social (police brutality), and even global (war) levels, and it serves the Warrior's deeply driven need to correct and control, as noted in chapter 3.

Warrior music is hard driving, intense, and powerful. Like Laborer type music it is also repetitive. Its hooks, rhythms, and melodies pound into us over and over until they conquer the senses and overwhelm the palate to bring the listener to an altered state of awareness. Hard rock and gangsta rap are good examples, though it can span any style that has force as its hallmark. The Warrior's mind is constantly racing after a challenge and a goal, and Warrior music provides a track for that mind to follow. When the mind has been properly harnessed or overthrown a sort of trance, peace, or equanimity emerges wherein the Warrior earns a moment of respite.

When Warriors evolve they seek to teach and show the world its shortcomings, using knowledge and wisdom. Educators also do this, but their music comes across with less force and more subtlety than Warriors'. Educator music is softer, has a lighter touch, and when understood can be profound. Though it may not be as melodic (Merchant), inspiring (Laborer), or powerful (Warrior), it is seeded with the purity born of the Educator's heart and can be a medium to our highest selves. However, poorly made Educator music may just seem wishy-washy, spineless, and boring—it depends upon the skill and personal evolution of the composer. Educators pursue their craft to express a higher truth through music, often with little recompense. They may not be recognized for their gifts, or at best they may be appreciated by a select few (other Educators mostly). Nonetheless when done right Educator music can touch the hearts of the masses, stirring up echoes of the numinous self, and reminding us of who we are as spiritual beings. Educator music is the most cerebral and socially conscious—think Bob Dylan and Joni Mitchell. Not necessarily the easiest to understand or appreciate, it relies on its content to appeal to the public. Folk and classical are primary examples of this type of music. Not surprisingly, in a highly publicized study students scored higher on IQ tests after listening to ten minutes of Mozart, and babies responded positively when it was played during pregnancy. It is not a stretch to believe that Educator music, like Educators themselves, can make you smarter!

Finally, Outsider music is always fresh, always different, and sometimes shocking, offering new paradigms to its listeners. Also, one country's pop music can be another culture's Outsider fare. In Jamaica reggae is the norm, whereas in the United States it is Outsider music. In the same way, world and other musical imports are considered exotic. Outsider music is often an amalgamation of different styles meshed together in the musician's soul and emerging as a totally different genre. From punk rock to jazz and world fusion it is an eclectic, heterogeneous mix of kooky and cool, odd and audacious. It can come from left field to knock your socks off, redefining music standards—like rock 'n' roll in the fifties—or it can simply degenerate into vulgarity and cacophony, becoming untenable as music.

MYTH

Myths are archetypal images and stories that we use to generate, maintain, and transmit *lore*, which is knowledge with a living spiritual essence. Such knowledge has lasting, universal value and appeals to different civilizations over the expanse of time. When its spiritual center is lost or forgotten lore degenerates into fantasy or superstition. This deterioration is sometimes inevitable, especially as we move from age to age. It is almost impossible for people in the Iron Age to understand the myths of the Bronze or Silver ages, no less the Golden Age. As a result modern storytellers must make do, and sometimes turn what was once living lore into a spectacle for the sake of money, or to satisfy their misguided desires. It is difficult for one age to understand the myths of another, particularly because the spiritual reality behind them is no longer apparent. Living lore is passed down from person to person and cannot survive on paper as written word—like a living soul it needs a body to give it proper shelter and expression, to translate its reality for a new generation.

> Living lore is passed down from person to person and cannot survive on paper as written word—like a living soul it needs a body to give it proper shelter and expression, to translate its reality for a new generation.

The written word is so often misinterpreted that it engenders more entropy than enlightenment, but living breath gives direction and meaning to the dry and lifeless page. That is why ancient societies cherished oral tradition over its written counterpart, sacred wisdom (shruti) over secular knowledge (smriti). But in movies and TV, in our books and media, and in the way we live our lives the current Merchant culture places a high value not on hidden spiritual realities but on their manifest, gross appearance. An example is the way we value gold for its surface quality rather than its intrinsic meaning.

> **The king's crown is the earthly counterpart of the saint's halo.**

Before gold became sacred to Merchants as a mark of wealth it was sacred to Warriors as a sign of higher authority. Ancient kings wore gold crowns as symbols of their divine right to rule. Gold was considered solidified light representing *sattva*, the anointed halo of purity, truth, and divine radiance. The king's crown is the earthly counterpart of the saint's halo. Just as the poet's laurel wreath marks the poet's favor with the lesser gods of poetry and art, the king's crown designates him as favored of the One, the central Sun around whom all great bodies are but planets, revolving according to His will.

From Egypt to the Americas, from Vedic to Nordic lands, this link to our divine origins was vital to our ancestors. The king's right to rule was given and taken away by God. Its symbol in heaven was the sun; on earth it was gold. Yet everything degenerates over time. Yesterday's spiritual truth becomes today's cult and superstition. The lore and learning of previous ages become the lies and legends of our age. From astrology to religion the insights of previous epochs have dimmed into dark superstitions. The same is true of gold in the Iron Age, which is precious less for its intrinsic value than for the remnant cachet of its supposed allure.

Merchant society has appropriated gold as a marker of value, not understanding or caring about its original significance to the kings of previous ages. As a result world leaders grab at gold and other so-called precious metals as sources of wealth and power rather than symbols of divine mandate. But a king must be as equal in valor as in wisdom, in justice as in judgment. Leaders who take power only to feed their coffers, who fail to recognize the connection of their exalted position to the exalted source of their authority, also fail to bring positive change to their kingdoms and ultimately suffer a karmic hell for doing so. That is why Warriors make the best rulers. Even if it is subconscious and forgotten, inherent in Warriors is an abiding respect for the divine source of their power, represented and interpreted as that is by the Educator type.

Outsider Heroes

From James Bond to Beowulf the most common heroes are Warriors, populating myth and legend from the beginning of time to our modern era. Whether folk legends or superspies, Warriors are famed for rising up to save the day from the endless evils that beset the world. They are also today's sports superstars, conferring honor to their teams and nations through their exploits. In times of peace sports rivalries substitute for real conflicts, and Warrior champions shine on the playing field rather than the battlefield.

But as this is no longer a Warrior age (as mentioned in chapter 1), Warrior myths have been given a spin and Outsiders *playing* Warriors have become archetypes of the modern protagonist. From Spider-Man to the X-Men, today's Outsider heroes are freaks of nature who are as valuable to society as they are different from it. The Iron Age reflects the lower instincts of every dharma type, and Outsiders are the heroes who emerge to redress evil in the Kali Yuga. The stagnation of the Iron Age is impossible to overcome unless one adopts radical measures. The world's avatars and holy incarnations, sources of great myth and lore, are all Outsiders. Ironically, Outsiders are also the age's worst criminals. These two extremes, hero and villain, represent juxtaposed Outsider types each trying to escape the clutches of their age—one by wisdom, the other by selfish means. One by *releasing* ego, the other by *embracing* it.

Ultimately it takes the ingenuity of both types to redress the calamities of the world. It takes one Outsider to destroy the status quo while another offers solutions to rebuild it. Destruction precedes renovation, and for Outsiders the lines between right and wrong, good and evil, are rarely clean and clear. The sacred and profane have little meaning for a person who is an amalgamation of both. In fact, the only way for superheroes to defeat their villain foes is to really understand them, by being part of them. Spider-Man knows how to defeat his nemesis because he understands his strengths and weaknesses. He understands them because he has them himself. It is only a matter of choice that separates one from the other. It is only a matter of spiritual evolution that marks the hero from the villain.

In ages past that line was clearer. In the Silver Age when the Vedic avatar Rama walked the earth the guise of evil was embodied in his counterpart Ravana. As an incarnation of the divine Rama stood for all that was good and just, while Ravana was his opposite. Today it is harder to tell good from bad, partly because the standards have loosened. *Tapas,* the first word of Rama's epic the Ramayana, recounts the austerity, discipline, and self-sacrifice he endured to save his people, with little thought for himself. These words, which summarize tapas, also embody the ethic of the Silver Age. While these ideals remain with us, modern mores are more flexible and less demanding. It is impossible to be that good and virtuous in the modern era. Modern myths emphasize this struggle to become the best we can be regardless of our social standing, gender, race, or economic status. This makes the dharma types all the more important for this age, where people have lost sight of their inner archetypes and have no personal myths to guide them to fulfillment.

Every age has its heroes. In a Golden Age, Educators are revered as exemplars of evolved humanity. Seers and sages are the champions who remind us of our spiritual essence. In the next age, Warriors become emblems of truth and justice alongside Educators. Then, in a corruption of the Silver Age ideal, Warriors take over as sole heroes of the Bronze Age, only not for truth and justice but for power and dominion. Finally, in the Dark Age, Merchants and Outsiders become the heroes of our time. Merchants are the real-life idols, while Outsiders become the larger-than-life, mythic icons of the world.

Entrepreneurs and entertainers are today's royalty, the dream of teenage boys and girls and the envy of the working classes. They epitomize the glories of wealth and fame and are hailed by the Merchant media. On the other hand our sports heroes (the long-haired soccer geniuses and tattooed basketball mavens who travel around the world wowing audiences) tend to be Outsiders. There is something about Outsiders that makes them appeal to a wide audience on the one hand, and to seem untouchable on the other. It is no wonder they are called "Untouchables" in Indian society—they are a source of awe and inspiration as well as fear and disgust.

Modern Myths

Mythology is the language of the dharma types. Myths and archetypes live deep inside our collective consciousness, transcending surface values of mode and fashion. In modern times movies and comic books have replaced ancient epics as conveyors of archetypal images, and when well conceived they are as powerful as any of the myths born of ancient Greece, India, Scandinavia, or Rome. If anything, they are more pertinent than their antiquated counterparts, for the gods of Greece and Rome are dead, or lie embalmed in heavy tomes on dusty shelves, nevermore to feel the cleric's ardent breath. But our TVs crackle every day with electric life to feed us the fast-food imagery of modern mythology.

> **"A coward is a hero with a wife, kids, and a mortgage."**
> **MARVIN KITMAN**

Today, myths exist under our noses—the original pinup girl, Venus, was replaced by Marilyn Monroe and Angelina Jolie in modern culture's equivalent of the femme goddess. Sylvester Stallone and Arnold Schwarzenegger have exhumed Hercules, while Johnny Depp dubs as Apollo. But the best myths are the dharma types, and we can see them hard at work in pop culture, from the silver screen to our favorite sitcoms.

Laborers

In chapter 5 we saw that Laborers make the best sleuths and detectives. Because of their dogged determination they can persevere to get to the bottom of practically any case. Laborers are also thick-skinned and naturally ingenuous types, so they don't mind asking questions that other types might cringe at for fear of looking stupid. The detective Columbo in the eponymous 1970s television program embodied this archetype. Patient, rough around the edges, and seemingly facile, he was also a master sleuth capable of following his instincts and sniffing out malfeasance. Laborers think with their bodily intelligence, using their gut feelings and nose to lead them, and these rarely fail to steer them in the right direction.

> The gods of Greece and Rome are dead, or lie embalmed in heavy tomes on dusty shelves, nevermore to feel the cleric's ardent breath.

It is difficult to lie to Laborers. Unless they choose to ignore their instincts, they, like Warriors, have a nose for deception. The only time their senses become scrambled is when they have strong feelings for someone. Laborers will allow love to override their basic instincts because their communal and family spirit is stronger even than their own sense of self-preservation! They would rather believe the lie their lover tells than trust in what they know is true, just to keep a relationship going. This is why Laborers are unreliable lie detectors when they have a personal stake in the matter, and why Warriors are ultimately better at ferreting out the truth. Warriors can separate emotion and logic, ultimately proceeding based on rationality rather than romanticism.

This spells the difference between police and private detectives—the former being Warriors, the latter Laborers. The first need a structure and rules to work within; the latter prefer to work for themselves, use their own tools, set their own hours, and turn down cases they don't like. These qualities come out in the professions preferred by each type, as discussed later.

Rocky Balboa is another tough-as-grit Laborer character. He is all heart, and despite what people think about him he is not dumb but carries an inner intelligence that is usually foolproof. He is beloved for his plainspokenness and has simple tastes and needs, and unscrupulous people try to profit from his sincerity and popularity. He knows everybody on the block, is great with kids, and supports his neighbors. He has to work tooth and nail for everything he gets and earns his bread by the sweat of his brow. Typical of Laborers, he is self-deprecating but inwardly confident—a confidence born not of egotism, but of intimate self-awareness: he knows his limits and what he is capable of. Laborers know their inner strengths, which makes them able to withstand the blows the world throws at them. They do not try to go where it's not their business to go but stick to what they know—though that never keeps them from dreaming big!

There are real Laborer types who have little in common with the trappings of Rocky's life, but all Laborers share certain inner qualities. Real-world Laborers like Harrison Ford, Bruce Springsteen, and Oprah Winfrey are living embodiments of the Laborer myth. What they have in common is the practical, loyal, rough-necked and raw-wristed spirit that lives in every Laborer type.

Another iconic Laborer personality is Clint Eastwood, who embodies this spirit in his movies as he does in real life. From the early days of Dirty Harry and spaghetti westerns to the last decade in his attempt to preserve the memory of war veterans in movies such as *Flags of Our Fathers,* Eastwood stuck to his guns in detailing the outwardly tough, inwardly sensitive Laborer persona. This is especially evident in the patriotic and emotional reminisces of his World War II biopics. Clint's journey from Dirty Harry to Walt Kowalski (in the movie *Gran Torino*) hallmarks the evolution of this Laborer hero on the silver screen.

Merchants

Oskar Schindler's story, as popularized in the 1982 book *Schindler's Ark* by Thomas Keneally and the 1993 motion picture *Schindler's List* by Steven Spielberg, shows the extraordinary things Merchants can accomplish with their wit and panache on one hand, and their compassion on the other. It exemplifies the Merchant myth of caring for others.

> Itzhak Stern: "Let me understand. They put up all the money. I do all the work. What, if you don't mind my asking, would you do?"
>
> Oskar Schindler: "I'd make sure it's known the company's in business. I'd see that it had a certain panache. That's what I'm good at. Not the work, not the work—the presentation!"
>
> DIALOGUE ENCAPSULATING THE MERCHANT-LABORER DYNAMIC
> FROM STEVEN SPIELBERG'S *SCHINDLER'S LIST*

A Christmas Carol is another Merchant myth that teaches an unrepentant hero, Ebenezer Scrooge, the true value of wealth late in his life. More lighthearted popular myths that typify the Merchant's social ease and gift for gab are the *Ocean's Eleven* series, as well as their real-life counterparts of the original Rat Pack that featured Frank Sinatra, Dean Martin, Peter Lawford, Sammy Davis Jr., and Joey Bishop. Marilyn Monroe, Angie Dickinson, and Shirley MacLaine were the female members of this group. Though not all of them were Merchant types, together they embodied the Merchant ethic of high-spirited hedonism.

Outsiders and Warriors

The Outsider hero is the most prevalent in today's myths. One has to effectively buck the system to express one's true nature, as Merchant society is not built to support heroic self-fulfillment. Therefore, Outsiders assume roles and personas to hide their true selves from the world. Clark Kent is the Educator mask of an Outsider Superman. He can never fit into society because he is physically and intellectually different. Stories like those of Batman, Spider-Man, and even Indiana Jones, in which our hero has a public persona radically different from his private face, illustrate the Outsider archetype. And from burly, tattooed basketball millionaires to extreme and exotic illusionists, real-life Outsider heroes have captured the attention of society while keeping their private faces hidden.

Like superhero costumes the dharma types embody five distinct myths that teach us to harness our special powers. People do this every day when they go to war in the name of God and country, as the martyr or patriot archetype allows them, for good or ill, to put aside their normal lives and do extraordinary things in the name of their ideals. Imagine what you can do when you don the costume of your dharma type and custom-tailor it to a perfect fit using the four seasons, the circle of duty, your language and intelligence, and (discussed later) your particular life cycle. Imagine becoming larger than life when you tap into the ready source of strength and inspiration that is your dharma type!

Hollywood regularly employs archetypes to create successful blockbusters and memorable characters on the big screen. The Disney formula works over and over again because its characters are archetypes that audiences intuitively connect to, often without knowing why. Talented artists attain success when they link their subject matter to such characters. Archetypes exist within us, with or without our conscious knowledge. When we link ourselves to their subtle power we as people become successful and memorable, just like the movies and stories that use them for the same reason.

Now let us take a look at the Educator. Since Outsider and hero myths prevail in popular culture's movie, book, and TV landscape, let us move on to an archetype that does not get as much press but is just as important.

Educators

Educators are unlikely heroes. Harry Potter from the popular children's book series and Gandalf of Lord of the Rings fame typify the Educator in popular myth. In fact the Lord of the Rings trilogy, though an Educator tale, portrays all of the dharma types with an equal mastery of execution. There we find the circle of duty demonstrated over and again: Laborer to Educator (in Sam's loving service to Frodo), Educator to Warrior (in Gandalf's dutiful service to Aragorn and other worthy heroes), Merchant to Laborer and Outsider (in Pippin and Merry's service to Sam and all of the Outsiders they encounter, from Ents to Elves), and Warrior to Merchant (in the lords of Gondor and Rohan's protection of Pippin and Merry). Devolution is shown in Boromir's fall to greed (Warrior to Merchant), just as evolution is demonstrated by the king to be in Aragorn's service to Gandalf and his embrace of wisdom and lore (Warrior to Educator). These and other relationship dynamics consistently permeate the trilogy, as well as *The Silmarillion*, its prequel. It is testament to the author's deep understanding of myth and archetype, and one reason his work has endeared itself to readers through the years.

Practically every myth demonstrates archetypal dynamics between the classes, from the simplest fairy tales to our most complex and modern legends like those of Middle Earth. Tolkien understood the value of sacred lore and worked to bring it into popular culture through the vehicle of fantasy fiction. As a creation myth his *Ainulindalë* is as beautiful and stirring as anything extant among the world's spiritual epics. Though Christian, he populated his works with divine and semi-divine beings coexistent with humans in a world similar yet categorically different from our own, a world that moved in cyclical time through four great ages rather than in linear history.

Unfortunately, the movies that brought his works to wide acclaim could not convey this lore, the real-life essence of Tolkien's world. This is a trenchant example of a Merchant ethic unable to understand Educator values. Not surprisingly, the movies were still wildly acclaimed by the

Merchant culture, too distracted as it was by the gross spectacle to miss the subtle force Tolkien worked painstakingly to create.

The purpose of myth is to teach. Every tale has at its core the lore that enlivens and gives it its essence. At its worst consumerism turns lore into a whore, prostituting it for profit. Just as love is lost in the mechanical act of sex for hire, so the essence of myth is lost in its mechanical replication through the Merchant media machine. We have seen tales imbued with lore become mere "action flicks," built to satisfy a temporary desire for distraction and be forgotten, until the next myth is chopped up and served to us again, a fast-food rehashing of the same unsubstantial and unfulfilling fare.

> **Just as love is lost in the mechanical act of sex for hire, so the essence of myth is lost in its mechanical replication through the Merchant media machine.**

Real myths fill us, live in us, and inform our souls for life. They teach us by inspiring, frightening, and stirring us to action. Some movie critics give five stars only to those movies that readily pass the "re-watch test"—films they would gladly watch a second and third time. Really great movies, like great myths, reveal more and more layers upon every viewing, becoming part of our lives by changing the way we speak, act, and see the world. Outsider-cum-Educator George Lucas accomplished this with his first Star Wars trilogy, just as Tolkien did with his books, plumbing the riches of ancient lore to bring out myths for their generation. Both of these Educators' epics depict journeys into darkness to confront the depths of fear and pain, only to fail and be saved by grace. This is the essence of good myth: that *alone* we are doomed to fail, but for the supernal favor of grace; that in the world evil always appears stronger than good; that the path is perilous and fraught with obstacles—and that all these are as nothing to the hand of divine grace.

Grace saves people living the essence of their archetype. In the Lord of the Rings trilogy it is Educator compassion that ultimately is redemptive. When Educator types Frodo and Gandalf spare the wretched Gollum, their redemption comes from Gollum in the end. It is Warriors' self-sacrifices that save them—not for their own glory but for the highest cause do they fight and stake their lives. For Merchants grace comes from feeding, supporting, and cheering others, even when they have no food, nor strength, nor cheer for themselves. Grace follows the unquestioned faith and devotion of Laborers, the unheralded backbone of any story, who accrue the rich spoils of their duty in the end.

> **Grace saves people living the essence of their archetype.**

The popular Harry Potter books show us another Educator hero. Unlike the august Middle Earth epics, the Harry Potter series is more plainly an adolescent Educator story. Wizards are, after all, pagan priests, ministering to the world and communing with Nature's hidden powers. The Educator's dilemmas and sticking points are illustrated here, from Dumbledore's lust for power to Harry's anger and longing for something he cannot have. Dumbledore sums up the Educator's need to control his senses and resist temptation when he says, "Power was my weakness and my temptation. It is a curious thing, Harry, but perhaps those who are best suited to power are those who have never sought it."[2] How appropriate a lesson this, for Educators who grasp at power when they should be reaching for providence. We have seen this throughout history, as when the pope's reach exceeded that of the state and he imposed the terror of excommunication, as well as execution, upon the bewildered masses. Harry Potter is a cautionary tale against such perversions of power directly aimed at young Educators.

But the series also shows the flip side—Harry's deep surrender to his destiny, his sincerity and solicitousness for his comrades, and his acceptance of his fate, demonstrating the Educator's indomitability of spirit once his destiny is embraced. When Harry, the Educator/wizard, surrenders to his fortune and accepts what *is* as Nature's reality, he becomes part of and supported by Nature, a force so powerful that it cannot be defeated, only surrendered to in turn. That is also what separates a wizard from a sorcerer—one is bent on protecting Natural Law, the other on bending and breaking it.

Dharma Types on TV

These examples from movies and books illustrate how powerful modern mythic images can be. From *Scrubs* and *Seinfeld* to reality programs, archetypes exist in the ensembles of the most popular TV shows. A mix of every type makes for great drama, and viewers who understand the dharma type model are treated to extra insights. Let us take the cast of characters from *Friends* as a case study, including their fictional professions (see table 12.1).

TABLE 12.1. DHARMA TYPES OF THE *FRIENDS* CAST

CHARACTER	TYPE	PROFESSION
Joey	Warrior	Actor, playing a doctor
Rachel	Merchant	Mass media
Ross	Educator	Teacher
Chandler	Merchant	Business
Monica	Laborer	Catering (feeding others, hospitality)
Phoebe	Outsider	Music/other

Perhaps one reason for *Friends'* popularity was the accuracy with which characters represented their dharma types, right down to their professions, a credit to writers who were able to tap into the strengths and weaknesses, the dark and light spots, of each dharma type and bring them to the screen. As viewers we pick up on these archetypal images and resonate with them on a primal level. Any writer or producer who can do this is ahead of the game when it comes to ensuring a successful program. On the other hand, programs with an incomplete ensemble of dharma types find themselves weighted toward the types they use, and against the missing types.

For example the show *Lie to Me* incorporated a cast of characters that included Educators, a Laborer, an Outsider, and a late-addition Warrior. With prominent Educator personalities, the show appealed to Educators but had some or little allure for Merchants, who were not represented in the cast. This is a dangerous strategy, for Merchants are synonymous with entertainment, and successful, entertaining shows need to have them represented. *Friends* attracted America's Merchant culture with massive appeal because it had two Merchant main characters, Chandler and Rachel.

The Public Broadcasting Service is less known for its entertainment value than for its educational programs, such as *Sesame Street*, which is appropriate since it is patently an Educator station. For the same reason, however, it relies on pledge drives rather than Nielsen ratings and commercials to stay on the air.

 ## TV HOMEWORK

As your homework assignment take some time to discover who is who on your favorite TV shows. Ensemble casts make for great television and allow us to view the evolution of the dharma types in real time. Some shows with five main characters, like *Entourage,* are easy to decipher; others may take a little more time. List the characters by dharma type and include reasons why you think they embody that archetype. What mannerisms, quirks, and other telling qualities give them away? What type was Carrie from *Sex and the City,* or Cliff from *Cheers*? Good luck!

> **Without lore there is only action without accountability, hijinks without heart, metal without meaning.**

The Value of Myth

It was reported recently that a piece of Star Trek memorabilia sold for half a million dollars at auction—a trivial item with no real, intrinsic value, it was nonetheless instilled with the aura of myth. Like gold, whose mythic value was discussed at the beginning of this section, we cherish things that represent the sacred, things imbued with lore. We are so moved by the meaning that heroes and myths bring to our lives that we pay anything to keep them around, as if losing them could mean our deaths. And perhaps it could. Perhaps a life lived without meaning is empty, and tantamount to death itself.

Inventive, resourceful idea-agogues have profited by providing people a semblance of meaning and associating their products with myth and lore. George Lucas recast the hero myth into a likeness comely to the modern eye in the guise of Luke Skywalker and Han Solo, creating a billion-dollar empire based on the dreams and ideals of viewers. He transposed mythic messages to give meaning to a new generation. Ironically, when he abandoned mythic images, as in the later Star Wars trilogy, he also failed miserably. Without the masculinity and magnetism of the Warrior there is no real hero. Without the idealism and wisdom of the Educator there is no lore. And without lore there is only action without accountability, hijinks without heart, metal without meaning.

It is the role of Educators to provide that meaning, Warriors to live it out, Merchants to glorify it, Laborers to preserve and enjoy it, and Outsiders to inspire and redefine it. Every class has its role, every class has its place—it is no more the part of Educators to profit from memorabilia than for Warriors to rest on their laurels. Warriors fight and do not have time to sit back and enjoy their work. Like a doctor who has cured a patient, or a lawyer who has won a case, these types cannot rest on yesterday's triumphs—they must seek them out ever anew. Laborers for their part are the spectators, the audience that recounts and records the hero myths of their generation. They are the great storytellers, helping to preserve the essence of a culture's myths, while the Merchants propagate them with fanfare and panache.

> **Only those who court their death become fully engaged in life—those who flirt with disaster marry sweet success, and to the hero go the spoils, while to the layperson go only daily tribulations.**

Ultimately heroes are important because they are precious and few. Today, heroes are people who stand up to the Merchant society assembly line to make their voices heard. They do not have to be Warriors or Outsiders—every type has a heroic gift. The hero is a man or woman who undertakes to fully embody the highest aspects of his or her dharma type, for only those who court death become fully engaged in life—those who flirt with disaster marry sweet success, and to the hero go the spoils, while to the layperson go only daily tribulations.

We cheer those who break from bondage to pull away from the crowd, but we also jeer when they fall under the grind of the Merchant machine. Stories of fallen heroes serve as cautionary tales to keep us in line. As a result most people don't get to live up to the silver screen ideal. Instead of persevering on the quest for self-fulfillment they are left slaving away to stay out of debt and fulfill their financial obligations to the world.

Nonetheless, aware of humankind's need for good and true role models, the Merchant machine still tries to fill that void, even while cashing in on the process. From video games and movies to books and comics, modern myths still make their way to the starving public, though they are often outnumbered by inferior fare. The pop star imbroglios and bubblegum fairy tales fabricated by modern storytellers have monetary gain, not moral instruction, as their incentive, and these pseudo myths and images are not the same as the flesh and blood of real people and living heroes. As a result we are left unsatisfied and must turn to other sources that temporarily fulfill our need for wholeness—like shopping, sex, food, drugs, and even pets.

PETS

Merchant society's fascination with pets comes from the Merchant's natural instinct to shelter and care for others. It also arises from loneliness and a need for company. Merchants use pets as substitutes for partnerships to help fill the void that people often can't. In this respect, pets are a blessing to Merchant cultures like the United States, for they teach responsibility and care for others. But they can also become a negative fixation that leads people away from real human interaction.

It is not surprising that we dote so much on our pets—after all, they are human creations designed to augment our lives and keep us company. The breeding of dogs and cats into customized human companions has taken millennia; we can even trace the history of our relationship with animals to the cycle of the ages. In a Golden Age people coexist with creatures of the wild in a way consistent with Educator values, adopting a "live and let live" attitude with Nature and using their superior spiritual development to communicate with animals on their level. In a Warrior period, tired of being attacked and ravaged by certain beasts of the wild, humans begin to hunt, capture, and domesticate them for the good of society. These animals become valued as hunters and warriors themselves and are rewarded for their service to humankind. In such a Silver Age they are treated with respect and honor, securing a role in the tales and myths of the time.*

In the next age, dominated by lower Warrior instincts and conflicting Merchant values, animals become people's instruments of service and commodities rather than sentient equals. Because it is still a Warrior age, beasts of strength and power continue to be respected

---

*The Ramayana provides a good example of the human relationship to animals in a Silver Age, presenting animals that coexist with people in a time dominated by Warrior virtues. Bears, monkeys and other creatures of the wild fight side by side with humans, winning laurels and infamy according to their deeds. Warriors judge actions, not appearances, and in the Silver Age creatures are judged by their valor and character, not by their outer appearance. Accordingly, many are depicted possessing character flaws and virtues just like humans, and like people they are shown to be capable of both good and evil deeds.

and feared, but they become less our allies and more our tools, bearing the yokes of the farmer and packing our larders with milk, cheese, and their own flesh. As society grows animals become more and more sources of food, not company. Our ability to communicate with them becomes lost by the end of this age, and the gap between man and beast is permanently widened. This is also the time when mythical creatures depopulate Earth. The faery folk and their lore begin to leave us as humans become increasingly deaf and blind to the subtleties of their existence. By the onset of the Iron Age they are almost completely gone, and their legends become nothing more than fairy tales.

In the present age, the Kali Yuga, as societies and populations exponentially increase, animals entirely become a commodity. From the abattoir to the zoo their use becomes restricted mostly to our sustenance and entertainment. This is also where manipulation of their genes becomes an art form, as in the domestication of the dog over the last four thousand years, surpassing every other animal in the shape, size, color, and variety of its breeds. Consider the journey from wolf to Chihuahua to see the progression of people's fascination with pets over the years and through modern day.

It is no wonder that our pets are so dependent on us. They rely on us for food, grooming, exercise, and entertainment. It is up to us not only to walk them but to keep them clean, well nourished, and happy. This is a burden we take on when we manipulate their genetic structure to our ends. It is also a burden that takes significant time and energy. Another downside of having pets is that sometimes we forget they are animals and that their consciousness is different from ours. Excessive emotional investment in them can tie us down and prevent us from living out our own destinies. It is one thing to love a pet, but quite another to smother it with sentimentality to such a degree that it substitutes for our own experience of life.

But the mantra for the Age of Kali is to "use what you've got." We can use the values of the Merchant age to evolve out of ignorance. Our pets can be conduits to a better understanding of ourselves, teaching us to relate with others by generating greater authenticity, warmth, and compassion in our relationships. How much of a leap is it to care for another human being or do something nice for our neighbors when we find that they are also animals requiring the same warmth, food, shelter, and exercise as our pets? How difficult is it to say "Hi!" to someone when you know that they also share your passion for Labradors and take the same time to care for, groom, and love them as you do? The beauty of living in an Iron Age is that by opening our eyes to the tools life gives us we can use anything to rise up from the droning darkness of routine existence to harmonize with the light around us.

A Memorable Fancy

As I walked with an elderly philosophy teacher along the streets of our city it was impossible not to notice people with their animals. The conversation naturally turned in their direction. My questions are in bold.

What do you think about many people's obsession with pets in America?

"People feed their poodles designer baked biscuits but turn their noses at volunteering at a shelter to feed their fellow human beings. Engrossed in vanity, these people congratulate themselves on being a 'good person' though there is nothing in their actions to account for this self-image. Actions must be judged by the objective barometer of shastra [scripture] to correctly calibrate the inner gauges of the subjective account.

"They say the road to hell is paved with good intentions, and most people walk that road every day, unable or unwilling to change their trajectory. But shastra tells us what each type must do to reverse their steps and walk the road of heaven. There is little excuse for ignorance, much less for those who know the right path and fail to walk it still."

But isn't the attention people give to animals a type of blessing?

"It's a fact of life that what you give your attention to rewards you in like kind. Devote your time to insentience and dullness, like sitting on the couch, drinking beer, and watching TV, and sure enough next lifetime you'll make a fine rock that even the animals of the wild will enjoy sitting on! Mind you, it's great for the pets—they're practicing being human, and next lifetime they'll be holding the leash!"

He laughed and continued.

"But the best way to handle pets is to let them be animals: respect them, feed them, take care of their survival—and let them live their lives. One of the problems with owning pets is the responsibility you have to them. They become like children, and in a place like New York City you can't let your dog run loose like he wants to, so you have to walk him, groom him, give him love and attention. It teaches selfless service. If only people could treat each other the same way!

"It's okay, you know. In the midst of selfless service come those mindless moments while walking 'Buster' or grooming 'Fluffy' during which you can turn your mind to spiritual things, while the body and senses are distracted by their habitual duties."

He paused and laughed. "Ha! So you have the Yoga of Cat Grooming and the Tao of Doggie Doo—only in America!"

So, what do you tell students who have pets?

"It is okay to love your animals, you see. We need to learn to love this way, at this level. We need the comfort of a fellow soul. But we need to take it to the next stage too. That is the hard part. We snuggle Fluffy but bite the husband's head off when he comes home. The problem is that Fluffy might become the husband in the next life!"

He turned to me, as if in warning. "Don't forget that!" and we both laughed.

HOMEWORK

Part One

A revealing exercise I used to give fitness seminar attendees was to have them go home and find their totem, or spirit animal. This is the creature in Nature that best resembles you on a material, psychological, and spiritual level. The next day many people who had done their homework would come back with a glint in their eye, ready to share.

"So, what's your spirit animal?" I once asked a lively woman in the back.

"I'm some type of bird, for sure," she replied.

After a brief discussion I asked her, "So, what do you like to eat?"

"Well, I like bread and cereals, and I really like nuts and seeds."

I smiled, paused, and then, "What type of foods do birds like to eat?"

She opened her eyes big and laughed—apparently she hadn't put it together.

Your totem animal can give you new insight into matters as diverse as diet, appearance, physical habits, even psychology. Another man raised his hand and volunteered his results.

"Well, I meditated all night on it, and the only thing that kept showing up was a coyote!"

Of course when it came down to his favorite snack he gave a wily grin and said, "Just give me a good steak and I'm set for the night. You know, I don't like to eat much during the day, but give me a steak dinner and I'm happy!"

Everyone murmured as they began to appreciate the correlations between their spirit animal and eating habits. Those who had flaked out on the exercise swore to do it that night and come up with their totem animal the next day.

Finally, a burly guy from the back volunteered, "I'm a bear. And it's funny, I always thought my diet was all over the place. I mean, I love fish—tuna and salmon, actually—but I also eat a lot of bread, candy and sweets, and I've had a hard time figuring out what to feed myself to be healthy."

Another class member then piped up, adding that bears love to forage, but eating sweets, especially refined sugars and alcohol, was terrible for them and made them fat and listless.

He laughed, "Yeah, I can relate to that!"

Diet is just the beginning of discovering the secrets your spirit animal has for you. Along with types of exercise (fast and explosive for cats, slow and studied for elephants, for example), we can discover social habits, appearance, haunts, and even the dharma type that goes along with your animal. How well an animal matches you depends on your ability to imagine the correlations and make the connections.

Totem animals carry a personal meaning for every individual—my totem bear and yours might mean different things. They may describe features about us that range from the spiritual to the mundane. Take time to research and meditate to find out what animal best fits your personality. Remember that in many traditions the totem animal is not shared with anyone—it is for your personal evolution only. Also it does not have to be your favorite animal; in the beginning you might not even like it! But there is nothing wrong with pigs, rats, and snakes if we understand their motivations and how they resonate with our deeper sensibilities. The rat, for example, is associated with luck, charisma, wealth, and intelligence in China. Representing the first year of the Chinese zodiac, rats hold a place of honor and are said to have first introduced rice to humankind. And though black rats were the harbinger of the flea that caused the plague in Europe, their bigger brown rat cousins are believed to have ended the plague by kicking them out and taking over. Take time to research the deeper meaning of your totem animal and you might discover that even the lowliest creatures have noble virtues worthy of guiding us on our paths!

Having a friend's help in this process is also helpful as friends are more objective about us than we are. Don't be too literal in trying to make everything fit—not everything has to match precisely. It is the essence and spirit of the animal that you are looking for, not every one of its habits, though many habits do reflect that essence. Use your totem animal as a guide to help you tune in to Nature and how it connects to you. After all, the dharma types were designed to work with other systems, not as an exclusive technology.

Part Two

Perhaps the reason we as a culture love pets is that they remind us of the stripped-down essence of our dharma type, teaching us to be good Merchants, Laborers, Educators, and such. Sometimes the qualities of the dharma types are displayed most purely in animals. For example, dogs are archetypal Warriors. They can be trained and disciplined and make good, trustworthy companions. They are thoughtful and goal oriented, learning from past mistakes. Cats on the other hand are Merchant creatures. They become more affectionate when they want something, and though they are concerned primarily with their own survival, they can be irresistible nonetheless, with a grace and charm that make us happy to provide for them. Unlike dogs, which have a significant prefrontal cortex, cats have none at all. They do not reflect on actions or possess self-control. Recall that the prefrontal cortex is the Warrior part of the brain, and it is fitting that dogs have it well developed, while cats are completely lacking in it. Cats are more representative of the limbic system, which governs primal emotions and libido, which is why cats are more leisurely and affection seeking while dogs are more rigid and loyal.*

As a homework exercise try listing animals according to their dharma type. Consider how the world treats them, what they give or take from the environment, and their role with humans. For example, turtles could be Educators because they are generally harmless creatures, benevolent and honored for their wisdom in many cultures. The Laborer-type cow, on the other hand, is the only animal that freely gives of its milk to other species and loves all equally. Sweet and doe-eyed, cows sustain communities with the work and food they provide. It is a shame that we treat the animal responsible for nurturing and sustaining humankind for millennia with

---

*Cat owners, retract your claws, I am the proud and happy owner of two cats myself!

the least care, affection, and courtesy. Could it be that for the last 5,000 years we have also treated Laborers this way, basing our society on their hard work and selfless service while keeping them down as second-class citizens? There are countless implications between an animal, its dharma type, and our relationship with it. Cows will never be as sexy as Chihuahuas or kittens, which is precisely why Laborers must incorporate Merchant qualities if they are to get their due. We have to give Laborer-type animals an image makeover if they are to receive recognition for their contributions, and if we want to align our culture with the tenets of an enlightened, sacred society.

Mistreating the animals that give us the most with torture, punishment, and little more regard than objects is a reflection on our own humanity, the lower values of the human animal. What type of animal are we who do these things? Humans must certainly be Outsiders, as evidenced in the extremes of our behavior—in our ability to do enormous good and terrible evil, as in the mystery of our origins and the complexity of our evolution.

Serpents are also Outsiders, maligned and misunderstood though holding powerful medicine for society. Their sheer mystery inspires terror and panic, earning them a bad reputation. Tigers are often represented as Warriors, but how about canines, whose values are loyalty, hierarchy, leadership, and efficiency? When it locks its eyes on a target, there is no stopping a wolf from attaining its goal. And can we see the Merchant type in parrots, lovable for their loudness, temper, and mimicry? Or how about the ludic dolphins,* for their carefree, charming nature?

Fundamentally, all animals are Outsiders on this planet. Biologists tell us with some certainty that the seeds of our existence, the amino acids and peptides responsible for creating life on this planet, were carried to Earth by meteorites and comets crashing down from outer space. We are stardust, nomads from afar, a fact on which both our spiritual as well as secular texts agree!

---

*Dolphins are said to be the only species other than humans to engage in sex just for pleasure. Closely tied to the Water Element, they seem to share the playful, pleasure-seeking qualities of the Merchant personality.

In these chapters we have classified much of Nature into dharma type categories, as our ancient ancestors did before us. From the elements and seasons to the music and sports we play the dharma types inform our everyday reality. As an extra-credit spin on this exercise, try taking a look at the different breeds of your pets through the lens of the dharma types. Though dogs are Warriors, are some breeds Merchants, and others clearly Laborers? Can you come up with a way to relate with them that befits their dharma type? Does your Warrior shepherd benefit from discipline and exercise? Does your Educator retriever seem almost human at times, considering how smart she is? Or does your Persian cat have different needs from the Russian Blue? Can you use this to figure out your pet's dharma and what behaviors are best suited to its type, just as you would with humans? When you begin to see the world through the lens of dharma, you may come to recognize the supreme order and variety in the universe, while enjoying your own place in it.

Enjoy!

We are stardust, nomads from afar, a fact on which both our spiritual as well as secular texts agree!

13

Sport, War, and Warriors

SPORT

Sport involves the concerted movement of body and mind, force and intention, to obtain a specific goal. It is the creative expression of prana for play and recreation. Recall that prana is the breath of the Vital Body, called ki or chi in some cultures, and the life force that animates our flesh. As the Bible says:

> *And the Lord God formed man of the dust of the ground, and breathed into his nostrils the breath of life; and man became a living being.*
>
> GENESIS 2:7 NKJV

As any athlete knows, it is difficult to express your talents without proper conditioning, for conditioning is up to 90 percent of athletics. In Western sports prana is harnessed for the purpose of obtaining a particular goal; in the East harnessing prana is the goal itself, as in practices like t'ai chi and pranayama. However, one cannot excel at sport unless the Energy Body has been mastered to some degree in conjunction with the muscles, bones, and fascia of the Food Body, and this mastery means that sport has wider applications than putting a ball through a hoop or conquering an opponent.

Sport as Metaphor

Old-time fitness guru Jack LaLanne used to say that training was his penance. Sport and training are ways to get out physical toxins, to express and release pent-up emotions, and to discipline our mind and spirit. In ancient societies sport was a spiritual event, especially for Warrior types. From the ancient Maya to African tribes it was a metaphor for perfecting the self by surpassing the limitations of the human body. Few historians remember that the sports events of the Olympic games were originally an adjunct to a grand religious festival that also included poetry, singing, dancing, and religious worship. The ancient Greeks believed Olympia, a city on the Peloponnesian peninsula, to be the center of the world and Mount Olympus the home of the gods. Olympia was a place of sanctuary and worship, and even warring cities would postpone their conflicts in order to partake in its religious festivals. Consider how far the modern Olympic spectacle has strayed from this ideal and you will notice that while we idolize the Greeks for their gifts of logic and democracy, we have a long way to go to understand their embrace of natural spirituality. Today's sports festivals are more famous for advertising goods than admiring gods, and more closely aligned to Merchant values than to Educator or Warrior virtues.

> While we idolize the Greeks for their gifts of logic and democracy, we have a long way to go to understand their embrace of natural spirituality.

Sport is a natural outflow of spiritual worship, and many athletes have had their religious experiences on the playing field rather than in church. Professor and author Joseph Campbell relates that he felt his first epiphany while running track. When the field becomes your altar and your breath the offering, the heat and sweat of your body can represent your purification, a transformation into something more refined. The mechanics of this become clear when we look more closely at how skill and mastery are acquired.

Sport in Practice

Mastery of sports skill begins with thinking (see figure 13.1). One must first learn the rules of a game and logically analyze its movements. A tennis stroke is broken down intellectually into its component parts. Next, physical training takes center stage. At this middle step, one begins more *doing* than *thinking*. Reflexes become automatic by assiduous repetition and disciplined practice. Doing requires a different intelligence, synchronizing the Food and Breath bodies in movement. Here, intellectual concepts are subordinated to the body's physical intelligence. Thinking is buried at this stage, because it is a hindrance. If you are thinking, "Now I must flex my wrist and jump and push my hand in order to make the ball drop into the hoop," you will probably not only miss the shot but never really master the skill. This second level of learning is kinesthetic and must rely on the pranic intelligence of the body to impose its will on the ball and make it go where it needs. This requires present-moment awareness.

Being in the present is crucial for any sport. An athlete who is in the now, the "zone" of witnessing awareness, is capable of astounding feats. This state allows one's prana to coordinate movement without egoic or intellectual interference. Intention unchecked by thinking is a powerful force. It has the capacity to orchestrate muscle, sinew, and bone into a symphony of movement that achieves its end without effort, without thought, without attachment to an outcome. In the zone, to Michael Jordan the hoop looked enormous, the path through the lane appeared obvious, and missing a shot seemed a ridiculous concept. There was no thinking, only action, for at the second level of learning, intention produces its desired result without interference of rational thought.

Finally, at the third level, subtle thought comes back into the equation to guide our intention, without overburdening or blocking the flow of prana. At this point Roger Federer can guide the ball to the baseline corner with astounding precision; Tiger Woods can align his shot with the hole from twenty feet away and sink an un-makeable putt. This final level of learning is the level of mastery. When skill has become

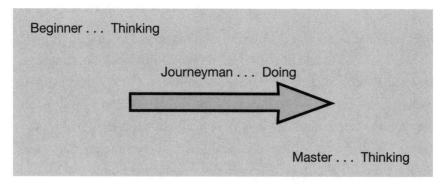

Figure 13.1. Levels of learning.

second nature through learning and then doing, it is refined at the third level by guided intention—thought and action working together.

These three stages of skill acquisition have correlations to other parts of dharma type philosophy. They represent the seasons of life, where we begin by *learning* in Spring, *doing* in Summer, and applying *wisdom* to doing in Autumn. As students, our job is to acquire theory during our formative years. In the next season, as we strike out in the world, we become doers, learning by experience and leaving behind our studious ways. Then, in the Autumn of our lives, we start to learn again and apply our wisdom back into the world, this time tempered by experience. The Winter stage of life represents retirement, giving up all that has been learned for rest and emptiness, freedom from the rules and requirements of the game. This is not the devolved Merchant's emptiness but the Outsider's void of experience, the blissful absence of *vritti* (fluctuation), also known as nirvana, the absence of suffering and agitation.

A lesson for Warriors, for whom sport is a metaphor, is that in order to evolve they must begin by acquiring knowledge. In the middle stage they are responsible for developing skill through the intense application of intention. Then in the final stage they must return to using their mind so that they do not curtail their growth at the second level. Evolution thus begins and ends with coaching, and Educators and their concepts are integral to a Warrior's development.

Play

In the animal world play is a natural component of growing up. It hones and sharpens a young animal's physical repertoire while building valuable social skills in a pressure-free environment. For a cub chasing its mother's tail is fun but it also develops the agility and timing necessary for the hunt, qualities it will need for survival later in life. It is through play that a baby evolves and learns to become an adult. And unlike animals, who stop their evolution when their bodies reach maturity, humans have the potential to continuously evolve even into their waning years. One of the common ways we do this, as with animals, is through play. Sport is the combination of play and exercise, an activity that involves skill, coordination, and discipline along with a feeling of enjoyment. It is through the sports we play that we become stronger, healthier, and wiser individuals.

Sport can be an avenue for our evolution, as the skills we put into hitting a good topspin forehand can serve us equally well in our daily relationships with others. Unfortunately, most of us don't regard athletics this way. We step off the court a more tired but essentially same version of ourselves than we were before we stepped on. But as we have seen from the animal kingdom, there are valuable life lessons to be learned from leisure physical activity. Aside from the physical implications, there is an opportunity for psychological and spiritual self-inquiry when we engage in any rigorous practice and challenge our mind and body to excel. It is through this challenge that we can find aspects of ourselves hitherto untapped, to see who we really are when put under the gun. For its part the military, another side of the Warrior coin, makes it a point to emphasize that its personnel be trained to parlay their skills and discipline into everyday life. When this actually works it makes better people and citizens; when it doesn't it can create monsters instead of men, or traumatic situations like PTSD that can scar a Warrior for life, as we shall see below.

"Playing sports, or even just watching, builds a stronger understanding of language."

University of Chicago press release, "Playing, and Even Watching, Sports Improves Brain function," *Science Daily*, September 3, 2008

Sport and Dharma Type

Educators are benefited by sport because they evolve into Warriors, and sport is a Warrior activity. Not surprisingly, movement and sport are shown to have direct correlations with enhanced cognitive skills. Thus, just as meditation and self-study produce better Warriors, movement and sport enhance Educators' intelligence by moving their life force and inspiring new ideas.

Sports that are more uplifting for the spirit, with less the dominion of the body as their aim, are Educator pursuits; tennis, hiking, and horseback riding are some examples. We do not find Educators to be well suited to brutal sports, such as rugby or wrestling, because Educators are essentially harmless. They may, however, take up martial arts for the philosophy of self-cultivation and self-defense. They participate in sports for the sake of the game, enjoy being challenged to learn the techniques and nuances of a new endeavor, and find the challenge of the game is more fun than beating an opponent at it. Therefore games of skill that require a lifetime to learn, like chess or tennis, are beloved of Educators.

Warriors can excel at any sport. From archery to weightlifting Warriors can be champions at anything, though they prefer activities that stress competition and, to a lesser degree, recognition of achievement. Horseback riding is fine, as long as you are riding against someone. Hiking is great, so long as you reach the summit first. This is the challenge of the Warrior, who prefers the glory of achievement to the quiet exaltation of the spirit that is Educators' reward, even when this achievement is only recognized by themselves.

Merchants, on the other hand, are often interested in sport for tangible rewards such as money, fame, and popularity. Or they may prefer the aesthetics of sport—the subtle pleasures of faking out an opponent, or refining their motor skills to such a degree that they become art in motion. Some of the most memorable athletes of the last century have been Merchants, with their showmanship flair and fun personalities.

Merchants' interests run along lines of profit, and they may also become team owners or agents or otherwise benefit from the business of sport rather than its practice. These Merchants find the same fulfillment, the same tests and challenges, in the economic marketplace that an athlete finds on the playing field or a soldier on the battlefield.

Laborers prefer sports that emphasize teamwork and community. They also make good boxers and weightlifters because of their hardy constitutions, and they can excel at any sport that requires heavy work. In addition they do well at endurance events that challenge physical as well as mental toughness, such as marathons. Outsiders, by contrast, have different reasons for going into sport. Unlike Warriors, who want to challenge themselves and be number one, or Merchants, who crave aesthetic refinement or financial reward, Outsiders go into sport to express something unique or to escape from their status quo.

Snowboarding and mixed martial arts (MMA) fighting are examples of Outsider sports. MMA in particular is an example of a popular Outsider sport because it blends different fighting styles into one amalgam, something Outsiders excel at doing. Outsiders may also be attracted to sports that are not as well known, such as parkour or luge, though that does not mean that every luger is an Outsider. It does mean that Outsiders gravitate to things that are different, edgy, and slightly subversive.

That basketball is the sport perhaps most synonymous with African American inner-city youth culture is no coincidence, since the black experience in America is tantamount to the Outsider's experience of the world. As a form of personal expression, culture, and even community, basketball has done more to bring Outsiders together than perhaps any sport in America. One cannot distinguish a baseball player or a golfer in a crowd—but basketball players cut a swath much different from their surroundings. Because of their height basketball players are Outsiders, and basketball an Outsider sport, one designed for persons otherwise ill suited to other activities.

Because they like to fly and are ruled by the Space Element Outsiders also favor aviation as a hobby or sport. Because of that element's unpredictability, their interests are also impossible to define. From X Games to aerobatics Outsider activities favor the underdog in society—the loner or the individualist who does not otherwise integrate into mainstream culture. Because Outsider sports are a vast genre it is impossible to describe them in one breath. However, it is easy to spot them when they take place, because they are different and, like MMA, often incorporate elements of various other disciplines. Table 13.1 shows some individual sports and the dharma types they relate to most.

TABLE 13.1. SUITABLE SPORTS FOR EACH DHARMA TYPE*

WARRIOR	Archery, auto racing, boxing, dance, diving, equine sports, football, gymnastics, hunting, martial arts† (weapons, grappling, striking, mixed), motorcycle racing, rowing, running (esp. short to medium distance), speed skating, surfing, track and field (esp. running)
LABORER	Animal sports (rodeo, horse racing, angling), auto racing, baseball, bodybuilding, boules, bowling, boxing, fishing, football, hockey, motorboat racing, rowing, rugby, running (esp. long distance), track and field (esp. throwing—shot put), soccer, weightlifting
OUTSIDER	Aerobatics, auto racing, basketball, cycling, dance, diving, gymnastics, motorcycle racing, parachuting, rock climbing/mountaineering, soccer, surfing, track and field (esp. jumping and pole vault)
EDUCATOR	Aikido, archery, chess, dressage, golf, hiking, polo, rowing, running, skiing, t'ai chi, tennis, volleyball, yachting
MERCHANT	Cue sports, figure skating, golf, skiing, soccer, swimming

*Note that some sports fit more than one dharma type.
†All combat sports generally belong to the Warrior type, though specific martial arts that also benefit other types, such as t'ai chi or boxing, are listed accordingly.

Golf doubles as a Merchant-Educator game, and soccer as a Merchant-Laborer sport. It is not surprising that soccer is the world's number one sport since Merchant society recognizes Merchant values and aesthetics above all others. It is, however, strange that soccer is not more popular in the United States, the prototypical Merchant country where we are crazy about Warrior spectacles like American football instead. This speaks perhaps to the disintegration of our society, which favors Warrior instead of Laborer values, which are more representative of its evolution point. In the last century baseball's popularity in America has been eclipsed by that of other sports, perhaps to the detriment of the best values of the country.

> That basketball is the sport perhaps most synonymous with African American inner-city youth culture is no coincidence, since the black experience in America is tantamount to the Outsider's experience of the world.

Baseball is a Laborer game, as it emphasizes many qualities of this type. Baseball players are superstitious and sometimes have elaborate pregame rituals they perform to help them win. Baseball is also a slow game that is family oriented and grounded in down-home, earthy values. There is a relaxed sweetness, a youthful wonder that draws Laborer and Merchant types to play and watch it. That is perhaps why it has lasted so long as "America's game," especially during the Laborer era of the mid-twentieth century. With the coming of the 1960s and '70s America entered an Outsider period during which sports like basketball and others became more prominent.

Laborer sports have one thing in common: they are simple, require little equipment, and serve to gather community together. They can be practiced at any age and are accessible to everyone. Unlike sports that require special terrains and equipment, like polo or tennis—which are aristocratic, Educator pastimes—baseball needs only a stick and a ball, while soccer goes one step simpler and eliminates the stick. Even sports like weightlifting, which do require special equipment, begin as Laborer activities like lifting and carrying large workloads.

Team and Community

It is safe to say that in interpersonal relationships, in love and sex, Merchant society exalts the virtues of variety while sacrificing intimacy. Lasting profundity is traded for temporary excitement, a trend that encourages less satisfaction and increased desire to consume more. It promotes the sense of emptiness that Merchants are prone to, and ironically it reduces their ability to really enjoy themselves. The antidote is the Laborer's loyalty and stick-to-it-ness. As in daily life, in sport we need to marry our athletes to their teams in order to gain the benefits of a lasting union—longer life, better prosperity, and greater professional success, benefits that accrue to married couples and can accrue to loyal athletes as well.

> **Merchant society exalts the virtues of variety while sacrificing intimacy. Lasting profundity is traded for temporary excitement, a trend that encourages less satisfaction and increased desire to consume more.**

Loyalty to team and community is part of a team's success—not just in the stadium, but also in the real world. An athlete's effect on his or her city can be more important than success on the playing field. From modeling good behavior to actively contributing time and money to social causes, players with roots are likely to feel more grounded in their professional and personal lives. This is especially crucial for Outsider sports and their athletes, who are prone to feeling left out, judged, and even discriminated against.

In the 1970s and '80s sport became big business as it teamed up with TV and other media to become "sports entertainment." The unfortunate spawn of this union has been the destabilization of teams and communities by the marketing of players to the highest bidder. Nowadays it is rare for a team to stay the same for more than a year, as players and coaches are traded back and forth to build the best organization. As a result fans are left with little to cheer about as the athletes they just learned to love are scuttled off to another team, and they are left grasping to fill a void. This kind of impersonal business-first atmosphere is good for neither fans nor athletes. Spectators become more critical and demanding of players in order to compensate for the constant manipulation of their emotions, while players withdraw and learn to play for money, rather than love, as their loyalties to place and team are replaced by the bottom line.

In the final picture what does it mean to be a Phoenix Sun, or a New York Yankee, when the players that make up a team are neither raised in Phoenix or New York nor spend enough time there to even learn the street names, no less get to know the local culture? What does it really mean when "your" team wins? Is it really Phoenix or New York triumphing, or an eponymous business that has no devotion to place or player? We must understand how we spend our energy, and where we devote our attention. Do the sports we follow really reward us and uplift our community, or do they suck our resources and attention while leaving us with fluffy hometown souvenirs as keepsakes—souvenirs that have themselves been outsourced to China?

Ultimately, the value of sport comes from the amateur level, where athletes play for love of the game rather than financial remuneration. College teams tend to stick together and play with more heart and passion than their professional counterparts. It also lies in individual participation. We don't have to be Kobe Bryant or Roger Federer to enjoy a game of hoops or tennis. In fact, games are more enjoyable when there is less pressure to succeed. Sport is about cultivating perfection, not profit, as per the Warrior's credo, and the challenge and reward of perfect execution is a lifetime pursuit that has lessons for every type.

A Memorable Fancy

Athletes and soldiers are both Warriors, but the former build their bodies and play for a living, while the others brutalize their bodies and serve for a living. I asked one of my Indian teachers about these differences as we sat watching a game on TV. Here's what he said (my questions are in bold):

■ ■ ■

"Athletes are reincarnated soldiers. When a soldier has given himself for God, honor, and country, shouldn't he get to play? Doesn't he deserve to enjoy the benefits of his good karma? And the more valorous he has been as a soldier, the greater his reward in heaven and the next life."

Muslims believe strongly in heaven as a reward for death in a righteous war.

"Yes, and so did the Scandinavian, Germanic—actually all of the ancient peoples believed it, because it was true. It still is true. But this heaven is not just a place somewhere in the atmosphere; the rewards of good and bad deeds are enjoyed right here on earth!"

So you're saying that Michael Jordan was a war hero in a past life?

"Ha! Who can tell? The ways of karma are mysterious. Nadi readers* and gurus sometimes reveal such things. But for every good deed there is reward; for every misdeed there is penance. The secret is to know the difference. It is all about viveka—discriminating between actions that lead to happiness, and those that drag you down to more experience and suffering. The ultimate end is freedom from bondage. And even though these sports players are enjoying their time, they are still in bondage. Viveka is discernment, and discernment leads to action that is free from any suffering—and then one goes beyond the short-lived heaven of good deed."

What's that like?

"Go see for yourself!"

We laughed together. Later, I asked his definition of yoga.

"Long ago, yoga was designed to dismantle the body, mind, and soul structures that limit the self. To demolish limitations of the body, asanas [postures—disciplined physical activity] are practiced. To destroy negative patterns of the mind and emotions, pranayama,

---

*Nadi readers are a sect of astrologers in India who use proprietary techniques to determine past life karma.

yama, and niyama [disciplined breath control, moral restraints, and observances] are cultivated.

"To develop the spiritual self, starting with the moral restraints and observances, the higher practices of dharana [one-pointed focus], dhyana [meditation], and samadhi [concentration, full absorption] are cultivated. Ultimately, yoga is about freedom from the things that bind you. Freedom is the ability to express yourself limitlessly."

What about Warriors who are not part of the formal school of yoga, not on the spiritual path?

"Every Warrior is doing yoga, even if they are learning a sport or just studying a skill. Warriors know the hard work, self-sacrifice, and one-pointed focus necessary to be successful at anything. This is yoga in action. They understand sacrifice, just as the Brahmin [Educator] understands surrender. Vyasa says, 'Yoga is available in all states of mind.'* The difference is that in our [Vedic] tradition, these skills were codified not for the sake of reaching a worldly goal—like becoming a doctor or an athlete—but for the sake of the skills themselves; greatness is a side effect of yoga, not its aim!

"But practicing yoga helps you in anything you do. Becoming detached from winning a game usually helps you win the game! That's the paradox of life. Being detached means not being afraid to lose. When the fear is gone, you let go. And when you let go, your creativity is channeled so you can do great things. Haven't you noticed that when you really want to impress a girl, she pulls back because she feels your desperation? But when you don't have anxiety about the outcome, you're detached, and she feels your 'coolness' and pulls in toward you? That's the real definition of being 'cool'!"

---

*Vyasa is the foremost commentator on the *Yoga Sutras of Patanjali,* one of the seminal texts on yoga philosophy.

I chuckled to myself, remembering the too many times in life I had pushed girls away because I wasn't "cool" enough. So I asked the smart-ass question: So, yoga can help me pick up chicks?

"Ha ha! Yes, Warriors should practice yoga philosophy to be happy in everyday life. Real wisdom never goes out of style. Let them read Sun Tsu's *Art of War* to be great at battle; let them study the Gita and the Yoga Sutras to be effective on the internal battlefield of the soul!"

WAR AND WARRIORS
Post-Traumatic Stress Disorder

Let us now examine another type of Warrior, the soldier. According to statistics as many Vietnam vets have committed suicide as died in Vietnam itself. In 2007 alone 12,000 American Iraq War soldiers attempted suicide—1,000 attempts per month. This deadly cult of guilt and shame can be stopped if Warriors and those acting as Warriors understand what it means to be a protector of dharma. When Warriors cultivate the skills they need most—not strength and killing techniques, but good judgment and a just cause—they can reintegrate into society without suffering the fallout of post-traumatic stress disorder (PTSD).

> Merchant society is more interested in proliferating automatons than in nurturing informed and thoughtful Warriors who are masters of themselves and their surroundings. This is because automatons are expendable, predictable, and therefore easily controlled.

PTSD and similar afflictions can follow when Warriors doubt their life purpose and the cause they are defending. When Warriors' inner consciences cannot reconcile the actions they have performed, dis-ease is the result. On the one hand Warriors believe in the code and camaraderie of the armed services, which turn them into refined instruments of law enforcement. However, when they are thrown into situations that are ill conceived by their superiors, or when their ethical and moral compass contradicts the actions they are forced to take, a powerful rift develops—like tectonic plates moving in different directions inside them. It may not be apparent on the surface until the stress builds up to a breaking level, and their world shakes with the power of released violence and emotion.

Warriors have no problem with violence or extreme situations. It is when these are undertaken for ignoble purposes such as profit and dominion that Warriors suffer. They are willing to kill and be killed to defend their sons and daughters, their loved ones, their country, and their faith—but when Warriors become instruments of profit for a Merchant society their inherent noble cause is lost, and the inner compass that guides them with such certainty becomes turned around. They begin to wander, half pulled to the thing they love and hate, the armed service, and half repelled by its egregious misapplication in world affairs. In the words of one soldier, "I love being a soldier; the only bad thing about the army is you can't pick your war."[1]

Sometimes Warriors defend the blunders of their leaders, even to the point of violence, because to contradict these would be to implicate themselves in those very blunders. This dissociation is evident when talking to Warriors whose brains have been disciplined to believe in something their hearts cannot conceive. Again, such a powerful juxtaposition of conscious and unconscious attitudes is strongly divisive, both to the Warrior's inner self and to relationships. There is nothing more stress releasing, enjoyable, and healing to Warriors than to personally invest fully, totally, 100 percent into a noble effort. There is nothing as stressful and eviscerating to Warriors as uncertainty and doubt about their cause. Therefore Warriors can empower themselves with knowledge in order to find a just cause, or they can plunge into complete denial so they can never be blamed for actions they undertake.

The first option offers a way out for Warriors who have lost their compass, the magnetic charge that inspires their lives and guides their destinies. The second option creates mercenaries, automatons who march themselves and others to spiritual annihilation. Sadly, Merchant society is more interested in proliferating automatons than in nurturing informed and thoughtful Warriors who are masters of themselves and their surroundings. This is because automatons are expendable, predictable, and therefore easily controlled. The offer of a bit of money and the illusion of security and happiness for family and country is enough to get some Warriors hooked. It is ironic that the leaders who offer these incentives have no real regard for their soldiers, though they are eloquent at paying them lip service when necessary—at enlistments and funerals.

At its worst Merchant society betrays the faith of its fallen by prostituting itself to the highest bidder, creating wars that make murderers of men, and corrupting its children because it does not know how to raise them; this all occurs because education is compromised to favor earning potential rather than general wisdom. For children to become adults they must be inspired and taught by their tribal elders, but when tribe and leaders are only after gold and profit—because they themselves were never properly trained—children become incomplete creations of an imperfect society. It is up to us in the twenty-first century to reintroduce proper values to our children, and even our government, in order to herald a new era. Recall from the four seasons that for the first twenty-two to twenty-five years of age, children are in their Spring season. At this time they are learning, growing, and obeying their elders. Unless we find something integral to teach them, inspired by Educator, Warrior, Outsider, Laborer, *as well as* Merchant values, they will become the next generation of imbalanced citizens and leaders in the Summer of their lives. If it is too late for those of us who did not receive a complete upbringing, it is not too late for those who are still fresh and ready to learn, because the lessons we teach them now shall temper the world for fifty years to come.*

---

*It is little wonder that the most brilliant mathematical minds of this decade went to work on Wall Street rather than Main Street, resulting in the greatest world economic catastrophe since the Great Depression. In a Merchant society the short-term lure of money sometimes overwhelms the long-term rewards of your dharma type.

Teaching boys to become men does not mean purging and brutalizing the female essence within them, though this is exactly what the armed forces do in order to create killers. That essence is inside every male. Jung called it the *anima*, just as the *animus* is the male counterpart inside every female. These must not be eliminated but brought into balance, and the only way to accomplish this is to be taught by someone who has already learned and experienced it, a leader who exemplifies this balance within. In Eastern traditions great Warriors are marked by this dynamic equilibrium of yin and yang. The anima in men gives them compassion and caring. Without it they more easily become mercenary killers and automatons. The attempt by certain sectors of the armed forces to erase compassion and caring is one of the causes of PTSD—they do enough to get boys to kill and even perform atrocities, but after killing these same boys become tortured by their conscience, which has not been wholly destroyed. The only way to prevent this is by educating Warriors about their purpose, and how to protect it.

> "Remember that education gives you not only knowledge, which is power, but wisdom, which is control."
>
> "It is possible to affirm the existence of God with your lips and deny his existence with your life."
>
> MARTIN LUTHER KING JR.

Real Warriors are conscientious—evolved Warriors take qualities of the Educator into their personality, like consideration and tactfulness, and use them to become better Warriors. Recall from the discussion of anatomy (chapter 8) that the prefrontal cortex of the brain is concerned with thoughtfulness, planning, and learning from mistakes. Since Warriors are strongly led by this part of the brain they cannot count on forgetting things they've done; their bodies and minds simply will not allow them to.

PTSD Prevention

Many soldiers have dreams that haunt them after war. The brutal deeds of the battlefield are replayed upon the movie screen of their minds often for years on end. This happens when they are forced to perform or have witnessed acts that are not consistent with their normal reality. That is why it is vital for soldiers to have proper ideals and personal integrity in place before they go to war, so that they can sleep at night after they return from war. When soldiers are made to deviate from their moral purpose they must search their hearts and ask themselves, "Will I be able to sleep at night if I do this?" Usually the answer is instantaneous, as it should be, for excessive thinking can get you killed on the battlefield. Answers come quickly, especially to Warriors who have been trained in proper discrimination, judgment, and personal morality. The decisions they make on the war front can have telling consequences for the rest of their lives.

War is hell. It is brutality and carnage. To survive it, a base instinct is sufficient. However, to survive the consequences that follow takes a moral purpose and understanding that support soldiers in their toughest battles on the field and give them good account off the field. Everyone wants to live, but Warriors can just as easily override this animal instinct in order to save a life. It's a curious trait. They are ready to sacrifice themselves for their fellow soldier or their cause. The decision of when, how, and for whom is up to them—and usually instantaneous—but when Warriors give themselves for another they fulfill an essential part of their dharma: self-sacrifice. Putting another before yourself is the greatest penance a human can perform, and Warriors are ready to do it. Living in this spirit of sacrifice takes an inner compass that is specially tuned by proper physical training, moral education, and spiritual orientation.

Warriors who suffer PTSD have lost their orientation. They either resign themselves to brutality as the reality of life, taking a "if you don't kill them they kill you" attitude, or they suffer from the conflict of values that creates a rift in their being, as described above. The way to deal with these is to understand that we live in an imperfect world, and that few actions will be neat and clear-cut, especially in war. The important thing is that we nonetheless *strive* for perfection. Knowing that we will never achieve it, and yet doing our best, is the hero's journey. The more dire the situation, the more heroic the deed—the more hopeless the battle, the greater shines your struggle for victory. Heroes are not great because they live in a perfect world; it is because they *don't* that their deeds carry weight and meaning!

So what to do? Sometimes the best fight is not to fight. Insubordination, or peaceful refusal to cooperate with a regime of wrongdoing, is sometimes enough. Imagine if enough German soldiers had stood up against the atrocities at Dachau and Auschwitz. They may have been killed for their actions, but dying to defend dharma is better than killing in opposition to it. Sometimes Warriors can embrace a better fight and battle evil in a way that upholds their dharma. Even after battle, they can attempt to redress wrongs perpetrated during the fog of war. These are difficult choices and every soldier must consult his or her inner compass for support. All Warriors must use skillful judgment to obtain a perfect report of themselves from the greatest commander there is, the inner Self. In sports we know that every generation breaks the records of its predecessors. Perfection is constantly redefined. But the Warrior's secret is that perfection is not an external benchmark but an internal event. In Sanskrit, this type of personal perfection is called yoga.

Yoga

In hatha yoga, it is not how well you twist yourself into a pretzel that determines a good asana, but how fixed and rooted you are, and how well you embody that asana. Sometimes an inflexible novice can have greater integrity in a yoga practice than a veteran of thousands of backbends and Downward Dogs. In fact, if flexibility and strength were the only benchmark of yogic excellence, gymnasts would be the supreme yogis of our world, as they are unsurpassed in these. But strength and flexibility are not the barometers of yogic mastery—they are its side effect. In just the same way, it is the Warrior's struggle for perfection, not its attainment, that is the ultimate heroic deed, and the Warrior's highest yoga.

Yoga means *union.* Union creates wholeness, and wholeness is the root of health. Healing comes when Warriors reconcile their deeds with the fact that it is impossible to be 100 percent right, especially in the modern age. Healing comes when Warriors are united, joined to their purpose, never wavering from it—and even should they slip, they strive to reunite with it. It is a special knack, actually a need, for Warriors to get themselves into perilous situations. How they handle these determines their excellence, not whether they are victorious. The Bhagavad Gita relates the counsel Krishna gave to his Warrior friend Arjuna as he was about to undertake the battle of his life:

> *Both of them are ignorant, he who knows the soul to be capable of killing and he who takes it as killed; for verily the soul neither kills nor is killed.*
>
> *The soul is never born nor dies; nor does it come about only after being born. For it is unborn, eternal, everlasting and ancient; even though the body is slain, the soul is not.*
>
> *Weapons cannot cut it nor can fire burn it; water cannot wet it nor can wind dry it . . . therefore you should not grieve.*
>
> *Your right is to work only, never to the fruits thereof. Do not be attached to making your actions bear fruit, nor let your attachment be to inaction.*

Whatever fight Warriors choose—be it nonviolent protest or a righteous war—they must remember their duty:

> *There is nothing more welcome for a Warrior than a righteous war . . . but if you refuse to fight then, shirking*

your duty and losing your reputation, you will incur sin, nay, people will pour unending infamy on you . . .

Die, and you will win heaven; conquer, and you enjoy sovereignty of the earth; therefore, stand up, ready to fight!

Treating alike victory and defeat, gain and loss, pleasure and pain, get ready for the fight, then fighting thus you will not incur sin.

Perform your duties established in equanimity, renounce attachment and be even-tempered in both success and failure; this equanimity is called Yoga.

Action with a selfish motive is far inferior to this Yoga of equanimity . . . for endowed with equanimity one sheds in this life both good and evil. Therefore, strive for the practice of this Yoga of equanimity, for Yoga is skillfulness in action.

SELECTIONS FROM THE BHAGAVAD GITA,
CHAPTER 2

This equanimity, whether in war or in nonviolent resistance, is key to the Warrior's ultimate survival and sanity. Learning to cultivate it takes steady practice and study, the path of evolution for the Warrior type.

WINNING THE WAR

Another way to support Warriors is to understand that it takes more than Warriors to win at war. It takes Educators to dictate the ideological battle with diplomacy, negotiation, and moral integrity. It takes Laborers to erect the infrastructures that build goodwill in lands ravaged by conflict. Building wells, housing the poor, and caring for the sick wins more hearts and minds than guns and tanks. It takes Merchants to create incentives for peace. Peaceful environments allow for the full enjoyment of life's luxuries, and this is impossible in a dog-eat-dog world of survival. It takes Outsiders to create understanding between warring parties, understanding that comes from intelligence gatherers (spies), translators, and cultural attachés.

Today's military leaders acknowledge that modern wars are not winnable by military strategy alone. They are ideological battles that involve complex variables including economic, religious, demographic, technological, and social factors. Each of these implicates the dharma types in specific ways that are beyond the scope of this book to detail. Ultimately it is up to you to express the grandeur and complexity of your dharma type in everything from making love to making war. Taking what you have learned from this book, living your dharma, and bringing dharma to people who are lost and confused can effect real global change.

14

Money and Profession

One way to understand your purpose is to ask, "What would I do even if I weren't getting paid? In a perfect world, would I continue to do what I am doing, or would I take up something else? What do I love?" In some way Outsiders would still seek to untangle the mysteries of the world and blend different disciplines to create something new. Educators would continue to pursue knowledge and counsel others. Warriors would tackle obstacles, challenge themselves, and fight for a just cause. Merchants would still involve themselves in commerce and social intercourse. And Laborers would build, work, and serve for the pleasure of the work itself, not its reward. Reward is one type's gratitude for another's contribution. What one dharma type can do other types cannot do as well, and every type is rewarded by its fellow dharma types in a reciprocal fashion—which creates social equality in a society that recognizes everyone's talents. Vivekananda, who at the turn of the century single-handedly brought yoga to the West, said:

> Caste is a natural order. I can perform one duty in social life, and you another; you can govern a country, and I can mend a pair of old shoes, but there is no reason why you are greater than I, for can you mend my shoes? Can I govern the country? I am clever in mending shoes, you are clever in reading Vedas, but there is no reason why you should trample on my head.[1]

We all give and earn reward by the natural operation of our dharma. Money and profession are therefore closely tied together.

MONEY

Each of the two pairs of mutually evolving types (Educator-Warrior, Merchant-Laborer) share qualities that make them compatible. Among these qualities is the attitude toward money. Educators and Warriors require less in order to live happy, fulfilled lives. Merchants and Laborers on the other hand, are blessed to enjoy more of the material good things in life, especially those that money can buy. Remember from chapter 1 that Merchants are associated with kama, desire, and Laborers with artha, survival and nourishment, among the four drives of life. While every type can survive with very little, we are considering what each type perceives as necessary for full enjoyment of life. Artha relates to security, and the land, houses, food, money, and family that provide this. Kama relates to enjoyment and luxury, which require the same things in abundance. As we shall see, every type has different ideas about what is necessary.

Educators

Educators require the least amount of money and luxury of all the types. This does not mean that they do not have expensive tastes, however. What an Educator deems necessary may seem wasteful to another. A 150-dollar dictionary and a mountaintop retreat may be indispensable to an Educator who makes a living writing books, though these would hardly seem necessary to a Merchant type who doesn't. Organic greens and costly dietary supplements may be de rigueur for another health-conscious Educator, where McDonald's would do for a Laborer type who is less concerned with the delicate machine that is the Educator body. Nonetheless, despite their specialized tastes, Educators still require less in the way of material resources than their dharma type brethren.

> "Those of you who uphold the pure precepts should not buy, sell or trade. You should not covet fields or buildings, or keep servants or raise animals. You should stay far away from all kinds of agriculture and wealth as you would avoid a pit of fire."
>
> SUTRA ON THE BUDDHA'S BEQUEATHED
> TEACHING (FOR EDUCATORS)

It is sufficient to supply them with what they need to keep Educators happy: a functioning vehicle, a roof over their heads, the tools necessary for their livelihood, and enough paid leave to keep them balanced. (Time spent in contemplation needs to be funded so that Educators can enjoy collecting their thoughts without thinking about their survival.)

Educators do not need to own material property, though they should control their intellectual property because when this becomes valued by Merchant culture it can lead to tremendous wealth, as in the case of Bill Gates, an Outsider playing an Educator.

In the everyday world schoolteachers who drive respectable cars, have decent houses, and have the wherewithal to care for their students have abundant means with which to lead happy lives. Food, shelter, and necessities should never be an issue for Educators. A society that cannot provide these for them is seriously deficient in priorities and teeters on the brink of moral corruption.

> Food, shelter, and necessities should never be an issue for Educators. A society that cannot provide these for them is seriously deficient in priorities and teeters on the brink of moral corruption.

Classically priestly Educator types begged for their daily food and wage. Today, this is not much different. Consider how often teachers, scientists, priests, and philosophers have to petition for funding from private and state institutions to support their continued pursuit of truth and enlightenment. We must not forget that this pursuit ultimately benefits society. Without advances in medicine and science, we cannot promote health. Without improved social consciousness, we cannot encourage peace and global understanding. Without increased awareness of the environment, we cannot live harmoniously in the world. And without spiritual understanding, we cannot truly fulfill our purpose in the cosmos. It is the Educator's role to provide these for us, just as a tree gives its shade equally to all who seek it. Educators are a natural resource and should be treated as such. Their fragile, complex natures require a dignified but simple upkeep; in return they freely offer their majestic insights and inspiration to all.

One of the problems Westerners have with the Indian caste system is that Brahmin (Educator class) families tend to command the respect and resources in their societies, generally leaving others owning little and slaving away at low-class jobs. This situation reflects the devolution and perversion of the archetype system. It is true that Educators should command respect in their culture—not for their power or economic influence, but for their abstinence from the same. Evolved Educators shy away from money and power because they are more concerned with ideas and ideals than with material resources. That is why those in the Brahmin caste are traditionally the beggars in society, not the working classes! Merchants, Laborers, and Warriors are assured of home and hearth because they have jobs. Educators have to rely on the goodwill of others, especially Laborers and Outsiders, who have a duty to take care of them. When they cannot produce this goodwill by making themselves useful in some way, they may starve. This sets up Educators to inspire their societies in the best ways they know how—by teaching, ministering, and enlightening others, whatever their actual professions. The Educator's reward for this may be money, but it may also be a bowl of rice, a "Thank you!" and a lifelong respect from the other types, who each give what they can.

When they are spared the need to compete for money, goods, and shelter Educators become fit to make laws and precepts, as they have little personal gain from the exercise of such laws. Educators have nothing to gain, and everything to lose, by setting themselves up as material masters of culture. Such positions are ill suited for them, unless an

Educator happens to be in a life cycle that sanctions these actions for a time. (See the next chapter for more on the life cycles.) Educators earn the esteem of their fellow classes by soaring like the Air Element above the influence of greed and gluttony. They require little in the way of wealth save what is necessary for the purposes of their dharma because Educators in any capacity are basically monks.

Be they scientists or teachers, Educators, like monks, should ideally wend their way in the world with the humility befitting their role as ambassadors of higher values. Educators in government may hold up social justice as their truth, while scientists may venerate the sanctity of ecological sustainability, but their dedication to these causes is no less austere and committed than a priest's devotion to God—the only difference is the subject matter they pursue.

When Educators follow their truth they are provided for by the powers they serve. When they do not, when they look with lustful or greedy eyes upon a person or object, they squeeze integrity out of their systems. When they seek to use their intellect for selfish gain rather than benefiting the world, when they introduce the oppressive caste structures that advantage them over others, their special dispensation dries up.

Educators do not need to maneuver and contrive to find financial freedom. Though neutral to the Merchant type, they essentially devolve when adopting Merchant values because these lead them away from their ideal of surrender. When they strive exclusively for money, power, and fame they can never attain satisfaction and end up losing these things in the end. Such temptations for Educators who think they can profit from the world using their intellect to scheme rather than to dream lead them down the wrong road, and eventually to self-destruction.

Warriors

Like their Educator partners Warriors require little in the way of luxury or comfort to be happy. Warriors can go for long stretches in extreme privation from food, shelter, and other necessities. However, because money is power in today's world, Warriors also gravitate to money as a way to secure their interests. It is inevitable that where power goes, Warriors will follow. But as we can see from the cycle of the ages in the first chapter, Warriors who resort to any means to secure power lose their inherent purpose, which is to protect others. Thus, in a competitive free market economy where Merchants rule the yard, Warriors can become hard-pressed to succeed, breaking the rules or taking shortcuts to get to the top. This, again, goes against their primordial instinct to uphold the rules, and as a result Warriors become shamed, often to the point of suicide, when they are caught compromising their principles in the name of profit. Many are the examples and cautionary tales of lost Warriors in the Merchant society. We will discuss some of these in the following chapter.

In the truest sense Warriors should be rewarded by money as an afterthought, or as an embellishment to their primary work. The actual value of a gold medal does not define the worth of an athlete's achievement—anyone can buy a gold medal on eBay or at some specialty store. What matters is the accomplishment it represents, the skill and work it took to get it. For Warriors that is the true reward; everything else is icing on the cake. Warriors should seek a worthy cause and let the rewards follow rather than plunging after the reward itself, which becomes meaningless when pruned of its real value. Fortunately for many Warriors today great prize money does go along with many of their achievements—from sports to medicine and the military—and they are taken care of by a society that values these. However, many heroes die penniless and unknown because their gifts are not as valued by the Merchant culture. Nonetheless, it is the inner pride and satisfaction of having lived his or her life with a purpose that sustains a Warrior type. Nothing else can provide that same rush, that feeling of aliveness, and the sense of a life lived to its fullest.

In the discussion of government in chapter 9 we examined why Warriors are more suited to public service than Merchants, looking particularly at their devotion to ideas, such as truth and justice, rather than material benefits. We discussed the fact that running a country is not the same as running a business because business has material wealth as its raison d'être, while a country has the health and welfare of its citizens as its primary goal. Thus we observed a basic division between Warriors and Educators on one side and Merchants and Laborers on the other, a division that has far-reaching applications, from government, health care, and money to religion and spirituality.

Educators and Warriors enjoy a bond on the level of ideas and concepts. This is why when dealing with money Warriors and Educators tend to sell ideas, while Merchants and Laborers sell products. Where the enterprising Merchant type may make millions by inventing the paper clip or the bobble-head, savvy Warriors promote themselves and what they can do for people, not what they can give people. Laborers and Merchants are better at working with materials to produce something useful; Educators and Warriors are better at organizing how such products fit into the social scheme.

TABLE 14.1. DHARMA TYPES AND WEALTH

DHARMA TYPE*	RULED BY	DURATION	REALM	WEALTH AS GOAL	SPIRITUAL SKILL†
Laborer	Emotion	Long-term	Objects	Yes	Works (service)
Merchant	Emotion	Short-term	Objects	Yes	Works (charity)
Warrior	Intellect	Short-term	Ideas	No	Wisdom (judgment)
Educator	Intellect	Long-term	Ideas	No	Wisdom (knowledge)

*Note that the pairs who are most like each other (Laborer-Merchant, Educator-Warrior) also evolve into one another. For this, among other reasons, these types are considered compatible.

†The spiritual skills, or yogas, prescribed for each type are in the Bhagavad Gita and other Vedic sources.

Thinking (Educator/Warrior) and feeling (Merchant/Laborer) extend to almost every area of daily experience, from helping us choose a profession to picking what to wear for the job interview. "I feel like you should wear that dress" is not an intellectual opinion but an observation from the speaker. Merchant/Laborer types tend to start sentences with "I feel," while Educators/Warriors might say "I believe" or "I think." Even when they say "I think," Merchant/Laborer types really mean "I feel," reflecting the two different ways these groups relate to the world.

> **Warriors are allowed to make life-and-death judgments. . . .**
> **Educators are far too separated from reality to make practical**
> **decisions, while Laborers are not broad and inclusive enough in**
> **their scope to make good political authorities.**

As related in previous sections every human being has multiple intelligences, which in this case break down into two camps: the body and the mind, the gut and the brain. The feeling group is better at listening to the gut, while the thinking group pays more attention to the head. One is not smarter than the other—they have different functions and different modes of communicating.

Merchants, famous for their street smarts and savvy, rely on their gut to make instinctual decisions. Warriors, on the other hand, must balance gut instincts with their principles if they are going to live up to the Warrior code. That is why Warriors are allowed to make life-and-death judgments—because they are in the middle of the feeling/thinking continuum that goes from Laborers (very kinesthetic) to Educators (very cerebral). Being in the middle, Warriors are designed to use both brains, the head and the gut, to make equitable, just decisions. That is also why they make ideal leaders, for they have both the idealist's acumen and the realist's practicality. Educators are far too separated from reality to make practical decisions, while Laborers are not broad and inclusive enough in their scope to make good political authorities.

Interestingly, other sacred sciences make similar divisions. In hand analysis this is tantamount to the difference between short and long fingers—long fingers connote deliberation and cognitive understanding, while short fingers connote action and visceral understanding.* If we look at the four elements, which are used in practically every esoteric ancient science, we see that Water and Earth mix well, just as do Air and Fire. There is compatibility between the types in each group and incompatibility, or at best neutrality, between the opposite camps.

However, these camps are not always clear-cut. The short-term/long-term duality has Warriors and Merchants together on one side and Educators and Laborers on the other. This short-term/long-term classification has several implications, including health and fitness, as discussed in chapter 8. For example, the short-term duo is susceptible to acute-onset illnesses, while long-term types are more prone to chronic disorders. Since this basic division can be used for diagnosis it is also useful for recommending lifestyle modifications. The short-term group responds to quick fixes and more intense and focused exercise and diet regimens, while those in the long-term group are better off with longer treatment and exercise regimens. In money terms Laborers and Educators are better suited to long-term strategies for wealth accumulation, all other factors being equal. Warriors tend to take more risks, and Merchants are more temperamental, which leads these two types to explore more lucrative but dangerous profit strategies.

Merchants

While Educators have to rely on the goodwill of their peers for sustenance, Merchants are blessed with greater potential for prosperity.

---

*In *hasta samudrika shastra,* the Vedic art and science of hand analysis, every finger is attributed to an element, beginning with the thumb (Space) on down. From the standpoint of biology and palmistry, it is the thumb that makes humans unique among mammals. We are Outsiders because of our opposable thumbs, our use of sex for recreation and pleasure, and our spiritual search for freedom—all qualities of the Outsider type. In this way every finger relates to a dharma type; it is not for nothing that hand analysts look at the ring finger (Merchant, Water) to discuss business, money, art, and creativity in a person's life.

This does not mean, however, that they are never poor. Because of their volatile personalities they may go through periods of success and privation in their lives, though the fear of loss and hope for gain tend to drive them back in search of security. This propensity has prompted the Merchant quip, "I have lost more money in my life than most people have made."

Because by nature they are given to wealth, Merchants more than any other type can share their prosperity with others. Their charity serves them in turn, for they receive back the gratitude and karmic merit of their giving. Investing in charity is no different than investing in the stock market, save that the returns are not as easily discernible: they are *adrishta,* invisible to the unaided eye. When you give to a cause, be it social or spiritual, you get a return on your investment—especially if the giving is done without unreasonable attachments and conditions. Merchants benefit from the very fact of giving, but like investing in the stock market when Merchants put money into disreputable ventures, knowingly or unknowingly, they do not reap the generous fruit that watering a good tree yields. Therefore they need to be smart and learn to help causes that uplift mankind, rather than serve the petty concerns that benefit a select, unworthy few. There is a difference between a special interest and the common good, and Merchants need to learn what seeds offer up fruit to feed the multitudes and what seeds grow a thorny, selfish tree—otherwise they might as well keep their money and resources for their own families.

> There is a difference between a special interest and the common good, and Merchants need to learn what seeds offer up fruit to feed the multitudes and what seeds grow a thorny, selfish tree.

Charity does not just mean handouts. It is giving opportunities to those who don't have them. It is giving others the chance for education, a dignified living standard, and self-help through entrepreneurship. Nobel laureate Muhammad Yunus is an example of a Merchant's ingenuity and generosity when applied to the good of the world. He popularized microfinance, the practice of private lending to poor entrepreneurs in developing countries, which led Bill Clinton, Oprah Winfrey, and news organizations around the world to hail this type of peer-to-peer lending as an easy and revolutionary way to help people help themselves. With a 99 percent payback rate, microloans are safer investments for Merchant types than the stock market or other financial gambles, and the return is more than monetary: the ability to change a family's fortunes, for the price of a dinner for two, can be priceless.*

Dr. Yunus believes that microlending is one of the steps to the eradication of poverty. As he says on his website, it is "a program for putting homelessness and destitution in a museum so that one day our children will visit it and ask how we could have allowed such a terrible thing to go on for so long."

Such an inclusive, optimistic vision typifies evolved Merchants' worldviews, for Merchant growth come through widening their familial net to see all people as their extended family. Having done this, Merchants do not need much else to invite grace into their lives. Educators have to sit for hours memorizing and cogitating, Laborers working and serving, Warriors practicing and perfecting, Outsiders roaming and seeking—but the Merchant need only extend a hand. Good works, good energy, and writing the check are the deeds that ensure a Merchant type's continued success!

> **"Poverty in the world is an artificial creation. It does not belong to the human civilization."**
> **DR. MUHAMMAD YUNUS, 2006 NOBEL PRIZE WINNER**

When they have made all the money they can make, what's next for Merchants? They can go on trying to fill their void in vain with

---

*Typically a microloan ranges from twenty to two hundred dollars and can be done from home. For more information visit www.kiva.org. For information on Dr. Yunus, visit www.muhammadyunus.org.

things, or they can give their things away. A dramatic example is Oskar Schindler, who upon making millions from war profiteering turned a corner and used his charm, popularity, and money to save 1,200 Jews from certain annihilation. His generosity is remembered to this day by the more than 7,000 grateful descendants of "his Jews." Such stories typify Merchants' ability to change the world for good—they do not have to be saints or live monastic lives but can use their God-given abilities to create new opportunities for those who have none!

Bill Clinton is another Merchant who worked to share his talents with the world, having perhaps done more after his presidency than he did during his tenure in the Oval Office to bring countries without clean water, food, education, and other opportunities into the twenty-first century. Such undertakings task all of a Merchant's resourcefulness, skill, and optimism but also deliver priceless rewards.

When Merchants fail to reinvest in their society, seeking power and wealth for themselves, they blight the Merchant name and condemn themselves to a lonely life, isolated from the community they are meant to support. As Merchants move toward Warrior values of power and ambition they devolve. Wealth is not a substitute for power. Real strength and authority are best evinced in Warriors, who have these as their birthright, just as the Educator has wisdom and the Laborer love. Real power cannot be bought, though that is exactly what the shortcut leaders of Merchant society attempt to do. This grabbing at power and resources leaves society more vulnerable and less secure, and eventually it impoverishes both the Merchants and their community.

Even Merchants lacking prosperity must understand this concept. They need to evaluate their behaviors and attitudes toward others and ask themselves, "Do I have charity in my heart?" Merchants who are poor may not have money to offer up, but they can still give of themselves—they can share their energy, skills, and time to reap the rewards of karmic merit. In the Vedic tradition this is known as karma yoga, the path of right action and good deeds. Evolved Merchants cannot help but become wealthy, for in sharing their energy with the world they inevitably receive the world's energy back many times over. Just as Nature nurtures the other types, She supports Merchants in their giving.

And once they flourish, Merchants need to avoid becoming arrogant and extravagant in their wealth. They must eschew the desire to lord it over others or demand unusual respect from subordinates and anyone who appears to have less than them. This is a clear case of devolution, which eventually spirals into destruction. When they are selfish they become poor in spirit and in wit, and eventually end up losing both. A lesson for poor Merchant types is not to repeat the mistakes that led them to this fate but to embrace, as difficult as it may be, their path of evolution in which Nature and the universe support their prosperity.

Outsiders

Since Outsiders value freedom above most things they are likely to spend money to achieve it. From buying loose-fitting clothes to secluded island retreats they spend money to achieve the isolation and expansion that their Space Element requires.* Freedom also motivates them to make money and work at professions that allow them maximal gain with minimal restriction to their time and liberty.

Outsiders may discover new ways of making money or have ambivalent attitudes toward money. Since historically they have operated on the fringes of society they do not have established attitudes toward money and need to let other types like Merchants or Laborers help them manage their wealth. Every other type understands the power and value of money—even Educators, though they are less concerned with it. But for many Outsiders money is a strange commodity. It is easy come and easy go. In Outsider professions money flows in unpredictable ways. A stripper may make one thousand dollars one night and only fifty the

---

*A sartorial note: Outsiders often prefer to wear black, the color of the Space Element. Not surprisingly, Outsiders of all stripes through history have embraced black as a way to rebel, blend, and hide from others, as in their biker, businessman, and ninja personae.

next. An astronaut may make nothing while in training but end up on a government stipend for life. Taxi drivers, independent contractors, musicians, inventors—all rely on an uneven or sporadic flow of income and duly attract Outsiders to such professions.

Not surprisingly, Outsiders' attitudes toward money can run to the extremes. They may be shockingly lax or conservative with their wealth. They may prefer to earn money in unusual ways; they may also prefer spending it on unusual things. On the one hand an Outsider bank robber might feel justified in stealing because of having gotten a raw deal in life. On the other, like Robin Hood, this Outsider may have little qualms in giving that money away, illustrating both the negative and positive traits of the Outsider persona: the ability to self-justify anything, and the gift of empathy with the suffering of others. Such unconventional attitudes are Outsider calling cards.

Outsiders may take on other attitudes when they are playing one of the other dharma types or living through another life cycle. Much of what we can say about Outsiders and money has to be in the context of the persona they take on. An Outsider playing an Educator will deal with money as an Educator, and an Outsider playing a Merchant will behave as a Merchant—the notable difference is that Outsiders can at any time revert to playing another role, or no role at all. In matters of money, as in everything else, Outsiders are unpredictable.

Outsiders may deal in foreign, mysterious, or even forbidden things to earn wealth. Because they are the most populous type, and because it is their dharma to bring new ideas to the world, the last two hundred years has seen an explosion of invention and new opportunities arising from enterprising Outsiders in every walk of life. From aviation and electricity to nuclear power and the Internet, Outsiders have pioneered new sources of wealth and opportunity for millions, even billions of people. This explosion has led some Vedic thinkers to speculate that we are coming to the end of the Iron Age of darkness into a new world age of light and wisdom. It is not clear whether these thinkers have also considered that the coming of a new age is always accompanied by great catastrophe—catastrophe brought on by the instruments that serve that very age!

Laborers

Classically, Laborer types worked the land to produce goods and services for the community. In today's world Laborers can work in any profession, but their affinity for land and property remains unchanged. Therefore, it is important for them to own their land as well as the tools and equipment they use in their daily work. Laborers are fond of their own things, and society, particularly Merchant types, must provide these for them. Since Laborers use their bodies to produce income they must also have security when they grow old. Being the longest lived of the dharma types they require some type of social assurance to ensure that they are cared for even in their eighties, nineties, and hundreds, when their bodies are no longer able to produce for them. The best security is having an extended family, with children and grandchildren to care for them, as well as free and clear property and possessions.

Laborers who own their land and provide for themselves are thus able to feed the masses and provide for others, especially Educator types, which is their duty (see chapter 9). They can do this with no loss to themselves because they produce more than enough to feed their community. In ancient days a farmer would bring milk to the local hermit to drink when family needs were taken care of. Because cows, trees, and crops produced an abundance of food, there would always be enough to go around. In another instance, a landowner would allow a solitary Educator or Outsider to use a lonely plot of land to live on. These days, Laborers' hospitality is still legendary, as they make the best restaurateurs, chefs, and hoteliers. While modern professions have taken them away from the land, the mores and values of the Laborer type remain unchanged.

Time and seniority play a crucial role in how the Laborer type is perceived in society. The longer the tenure at a job, the better the pay and benefits the Laborers receive. Thus Laborers tend to be loyal to their bosses and value long-lasting work relationships. Of course they also don't mind working long hours and overtime to earn that respect. Because time is the all-important measure of a Laborer's worth, elders are respected for their wisdom and experience, with Laborers tending to take care of their elders better than others because they know they will be cared for in turn when their time comes.

Lessons for All from the Laborer Type

Laborers are naturally devotional and have special lessons to teach the other types, like how to value the good things in life. Laborers have an attachment to things that define them—like their country, their house, their favorite chair, and the shirt they have worn since high school for good luck. A car need not be just an inanimate object for them but can be a personal, cherished part of their lives, especially if it reflects their personalities. Some people like trucks, others like sports cars; the vehicle people drive can say as much about them as the clothes they wear and the words they speak.

Laborers can teach Educators to name a favorite telescope or the dog-eared dictionary on the desk and to hold onto these as anchors to their dharma. Educators do not usually identify with inanimate objects and can find investing their personalities into a thing a useful way to hold fast to their purpose—even when they have forgotten it themselves. Educators can all too soon forget the people, places, and things that have touched their lives, feeling alone and cold like the Air Element that rules them. But when they recall the people they have known and the lives they have changed, they begin to warm up and remember their contribution to society. They must cherish their inner pictures and build an album of precious memories—not as a source of sentimental attachment, but as a way of remembering their own value to the world.

Laborers teach Merchants stability. In return, by the mutual interplay between evolution points Laborers receive valuable input from the Merchant type. Laborers are sentimental, while Merchants are excitable. These two types share an emotional nature: one attached to long-term emotional value, the other to short-term excitement. A Merchant may be dazzled by the newest BMW or stereo on the market, while the Laborer type cherishes a 1959 pickup and turntable. They are both deeply tied to the emotions that pull them to these things, but in different ways. For one the novelty may pass when the next model comes out; for the other, attachment is so comfortable that it becomes an unconscious part of life. This can play out in all sorts of ways, but in the final picture both benefit from a shot of the other's medicine to keep them emotionally balanced. For example, Merchants may find the prettiest spouse only to trade that spouse in for another four years later when the excitement has worn away. Likewise, Laborers may become so inured to married life that they treat their spouse like a piece of furniture: something they love and ignore at the same time. Merchants have to learn emotional stability and devotion, while Laborers have to find the spark of excitement in their lives.

Laborers teach Outsiders how to be relevant. By imparting the value of a good day's work, of honest self-reflection and the simple pleasures in life, Laborers show Outsiders how to be present with themselves and their reality. They also show that there is strength in solidarity, that sharing life with like-minded people makes its pleasures more precious and its pains more tolerable. Community is a refuge for furtive Outsiders, who may seek all their lives to find people who think like they do. Laborers show that the door is open and the Outsider is welcome inside.

Finally, Laborers teach Warriors the value of work for its own sake. Warriors who are busy with high-minded goals, perfecting themselves, and living for the just cause sometimes miss the obvious satisfaction of ordinary work and a job well done. Warriors share the Laborer's love of physical work, save that they are not inspired unless their efforts amount to some greater purpose. For Laborer types, on the other hand, work is its own reward. This is a valuable lesson for Warriors, who may be too busy planning their lives to actually get down in the mud and start building them.

Cautions for Our Merchant Society

Because we live in a Merchant society the Merchant ethic is widespread, which is why every type must be aware of the dangers as well as the glories that go with living in a Merchant world.

At their worst Merchant types can be mean and heartless. They can take advantage of the unwitting with their superior cleverness. Sacha Baron Cohen in his movies *Borat* and *Brüno* illustrated how inventively funny and excruciatingly heartless a Merchant can be at the expense of less clever, less articulate victims.

Usury, swindling, meanness, mockery, and other forms of belittling people form a dark streak in the Merchant personality. This is nowhere more evident than in relations with Laborer types. Though they should evolve into one another, Laborers often bear the brunt of the fallen Merchant's scheming tactics. From corporate treatment of employees to one-on-one relationships Merchants sometimes cannot resist taking advantage of Laborer types, simply because they can. A famous example is the relationship between Joe Frazier and Muhammad Ali. Friends at first, the Merchant Ali later turned on Frazier after losing to him in their first fight, resorting to excoriating diatribes and insults that caused a permanent rift between the two fighters. With his gift for gab, the otherwise elegant Ali smeared Frazier, ultimately tarnishing both of their reputations. The naive Frazier believed that his boxing in the ring would do the talking for him, but he was proven wrong, and their legacy to this day bears the bitter taste of hatred and regret.

> "In the ring Joe Frazier and Muhammad Ali were the equal of each other. Yet today, Ali has sold an 80 percent interest in the use of his name and likeness for commercial purposes for fifty million dollars . . . and Joe is living in a room above his gym in Philadelphia."
> THOMAS HAUSER, MUHAMMAD ALI'S BIOGRAPHER

Like Ali and Frazier, Merchants and Laborers need each other. Neither boxer would have been as great without the other. Their personal differences were based only on ego fixations—at the core the

Merchant needs the Laborer's down-to-earth stability and heart, while the Laborer benefits from the Merchant's self-promotion and vivacity. Nobody has more heart and more common sense than the Laborer type. Merchants, who think they have an abundance of both, are usually proved wrong by life itself, and that is when they need to lean upon the Laborer type for assistance. For their part, Laborers, who can be wrongheaded and stubborn, need to be cracked out of their shells by the eclectic and vibrant Merchant. Together, they better the world in unfathomable ways.

Earning Power and Consumption of Luxury

In a just society figure 14.1 reflects the earning power of the different types, though Outsiders can vary from top to bottom depending on which type they are emulating—Educators tend to earn least, while Merchants earn the most. But money and earning power must be examined together with the circle of duty to form a more accurate picture and set aright the obligations of one type to the next. Recall that Educators have a duty to Warriors, who have a duty to Merchants, who have a duty to Laborers and Outsiders both—Merchants are the only type with duty to two classes. We can now see why: since they are afforded the highest earning power and consumption of luxury they are best suited to share it with the largest demographic. By contrast Educators, who require the most support, are the only type who receives two duties, from Outsiders and Laborers (see chapter 9, "The Social Conscience of the Dharma Types").

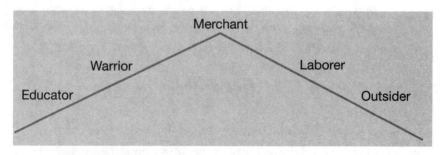

Figure 14.1. Pyramid of the earning power of the dharma types.

> "Pure, unencumbered, raw capitalism is never the answer for anything that involves a public mission."
>
> DAVID SIMON, *BALTIMORE SUN* REPORTER
> AND CREATOR OF *THE WIRE*

Another way to explain this is according to production output: the idea that labor output should cover the consumption of luxury. Educators have humble needs—they neither consume nor work to create much luxury. Accordingly, they have little control over the means of production. Warriors have more of a hand in the work of production since they are the overseers, managers, and executives, and they are afforded more luxury than Educators. But Merchants have the highest use *and* production of luxury, and they dispose of most of society's money and resources. Laborers, while intimately involved in the actual production, have less of a role to play in managing corporations and running the infrastructures of a capitalist society. Therefore, like Warriors, they are allowed less than the Merchant though more than the Educator. Though they do more actual work than any other type, Laborers are not afforded as much wealth in the dharma type model because inordinate wealth can actually backfire on Laborers, who need to take time out from working to manage their money. Managing money is no easy matter. Money is shakti, energy, and like raw plutonium it is difficult to handle when you don't have the tools and training to do so. It can become a hazard to people emotionally unequipped to deal with it, and many are the messes in society born out of the mismanagement of wealth.

Rules of the Money Game

Special rules govern how money moves—out of whose hands, and into whose pockets, it flows. Those who do not understand the rules are at a disadvantage in a capitalist global economy. A recent study showed that over the last century suicide rates across the globe skyrocketed during the tenure of conservative governments and decreased under liberal regimes. This occurred because conservative governments allowed so-called market forces to control economies, while liberal governments typically favored interventionist policies like public welfare programs and other forms of social security. Under conservative regimes those who understand the rules of the game necessitate less intervention than those who do not, a process that favors the Merchant type but disadvantages others who do not know how to play the Merchant game. Merchants are equipped to play the money game by both design and desire: they have more interest in and intuitive feel for how shakti moves and how to accumulate it. As a result Merchant governments are more likely to write the so-called free market policies that suit their needs, leaving other types to either play their game or suck it up, whence the inevitable rise in dissatisfaction among the rest of the population, as reflected by the sharp rise in suicide rates.

The result of such free market policies is that those without a grasp on money mechanics are disadvantaged. We have only to consider the global economic meltdown of the previous decade to see the side effects of people trying to play the Merchant game without proper training and knowledge. People sold on the capitalist dream were encouraged to overextend themselves, so much so that as they fell off the branch they took everyone else with them. While they have a share in the responsibility, ultimately those to blame are the masters of the money machine who lured them out on the limb in the first place—one cannot make the rules and then blame others for trying to play by them. The global economic disaster was caused not by renegades outside of the system, but by those who played within the corrupt rules of the game itself, which means that we must either change the rules or teach everyone else how to play.

> Values and ethics in the Vedic system are based on the tripod of karma, dharma, and duhkha, principles stating that a) what goes around comes around, b) there is a purpose to life—live by yours, and c) when you lose sight of a and b you inevitably suffer.

Consider the example of buying a car. Those who know how to negotiate, who also understand the wholesale value of a vehicle and its real market value, are better equipped to get a good deal than those who walk into a dealership without an idea of what they want, how much it is worth, or how to go about getting it. Regular folks do not usually have the bargaining acumen of trained salesmen or inside knowledge on financing, interest, and the real price of other add-ons. They need to know how to access such information if they are to avoid being ripped off. It is almost an American ritual for parents to take their grownup son or daughter to the auto lot to teach him or her how to bargain. But how are parents to do this when they never really learned it themselves? How are any of us to obtain this information if it is only available to the Merchant elite? The Internet has helped greatly, but ultimately it falls on Merchants to teach the other types how to prosper themselves and play the game, for the sustained benefit of both society and themselves.

> **Educators abuse with knowledge, Warriors with force, Laborers with strength of numbers, Merchants with cleverness, and Outsiders with deception.**

It is not just Merchant types who take advantage of others when the rules are stacked in their favor. A salesman is as likely to fleece a naive buyer as a trained boxer is to beat up an out-of-shape contender. When you are trained in the rules of your game you can take advantage of others who are not, unless within those rules is some form of ethic and moral integrity that protects the less advantaged. Values and ethics in the Vedic system are based on the tripod of karma, dharma, and duhkha, principles stating that a) what goes around comes around, b) there is a purpose to life—live by yours, and c) when you lose sight of a and b you inevitably suffer. By suffering you learn that the only way to attain durable fulfillment is to treat others as yourself, and to live the dharma of your type to the best of your ability. These three legs of the Vedic value system have survived for millennia, particularly because they underscore something basic and true to the human experience: namely, that no matter the government, legislation, or religious regime, without an inner understanding of this concept government, law, and religion are all bound to crumble from the inside.

Educators abuse with knowledge, Warriors with force, Laborers with strength of numbers, Merchants with cleverness, and Outsiders with deception. Corruption is not endemic to one dharma type, though it is apparent in Merchants today because of the abuses that have plagued money dynamics since the advent of Merchant society, and the Kali Yuga itself. Merchant training is essential for people who live in modern Western societies and capitalist countries. Understanding compound interest, lending, and credit is essential to building security and social status in a free market economy because the rules of the game will always favor those who do and disadvantage others who don't. Once you understand the game, you can enjoy it for what it is. Once you get that the game is not personal, emotional hang-ups can be taken out of the equation—when you understand that salespeople are punished for not getting the most out of customers, you can have compassion for both parties in a sales negotiation. In fact, once you get that salespeople are trained to leverage the most money out of you, you can begin to leverage them. Knowing the rules can help people turn the tables, leveraging Merchants' own need to sell against them in order to make deals that benefit both buyer and seller.

Dangers of the Money Game

Aside from the obvious dangers of financial ruin and even suicide, the subtle entanglements of the Merchant game are more insidious. Learning how to handle and invest money is key to getting ahead in capitalist societies. Merchants do their communities a service when they share the secrets of financial success with other dharma types—freely, openly, and without agendas. For many such education is a lifesaver, and in little time it can help a poor to middle-income family become more secure and self-sufficient. The danger is that once Merchant training replaces Educator principles learning tends to stop. Once people become wealthy enough, secure enough, and comfortable enough they may be lulled into believing that is all there is to life. They may pay nominal, if any, attention to learning the secrets other types have to teach, especially their own. This is because there is a lacuna, something missing, in the Merchant mentality that cannot be filled by material security alone—it takes the Educator's ideals, the Warrior's discipline, the Laborer's faith, and the Outsider's sense of wonder to complete society. A society perfused with only Merchant philosophy cannot remain happy for long. When the spiritual underpinnings of the human experience are forgotten or put away, such as when people begin to pay more attention to the size and shape of their car than what it is used for in the first place, people lose sight of their destination as human beings—which is not obtaining things, but self-attainment.

Though the rules are simple, Merchant training can be complicated. From getting a real estate license to investing in the markets, proper training can take months or years, requiring time and energy that could be devoted to other pursuits. For Merchants such investments of time ultimately prove useful to their quest for self-attainment because they lead to enjoyment and personal growth for them, as we shall see below. But for others enjoyment and personal growth come from different avenues, and it can be daunting to chase the Merchant's life while trying to be faithful to your own dharma. Recall from the Bhagavad Gita that it is better to be bad at your own dharma than to be good at that of another. The danger of the Merchant game is that you can become lost in its intricacies and forget your own path. Staying true to your own course and avoiding the power of money, which can steer you to places you do not really want to go, is crucial for surviving the Merchant age!

PROFESSION

Without passion and drive we cannot be successful at our professions. Each type naturally has passion for its own dharma: Educators for knowledge, Warriors for justice, Laborers for security, Merchants for prosperity, and Outsiders for variety and mystery. Dharma is the road we follow even when there is no monetary reward; it is what each type does naturally with its talents. To determine a likely profession we ask the same question that we did about money: "What would I continue to do even if I didn't earn money doing it?"

Whatever we devote our attention to grows. Whatever we spend the most time on becomes who we are. Since in the West an average person's profession is the mainstay of the day, it has the most to say about what kind of person we become, which is why one of the first questions people ask when they meet is "What do you do?" What we do is synonymous with who we are, which is why professions like Smith, Tanner, Porter, Chandler, Wainwright, and others became family names. Today the name John Smith does not identify its bearer as a blacksmith because we have lost the sense of dharma that goes with our professions, and most of us work at jobs that have little to do with who we really are.

A profession, the activity whereby one gains a living by contributing to the community, is different from a job in that it allows the widest avenue for personal expression and growth. But how do we know if we have a job or a profession? How do we know if we are growing or just decaying? Does our work afford maximal personal expression, or does it dictate someone else's rules for how we must express ourselves? The dharma types provide a key. Here is a summary of the ways that every class fulfills its needs for expression and growth through professions.

The **Merchant class** expresses best, and grows, when making money. There is no way around this—Merchants must make money, first for their own survival, then to nurture their families, and finally to care for their communities. This is their purpose, to be happiness brokers for the world by connecting people with each other and providing the clothing, shelter, goods, and services people desire. Personal growth comes in the commerce of goods, services, or even their own talents and skills. Their expression comes out in public performance, networking, social intercourse, and community service like volunteering, donating to charity, and other philanthropic work. Merchants find fulfillment and enjoyment in various forms of entertainment.

The Laborer class expresses through useful service. Laborers grow by growing something else in turn: by making or building things that are images of themselves. From erecting a building to raising children and family, Laborers' work is a creative expression of their dharma and represents evolution and growth for their type.

The Warrior class expresses and grows through competition and challenge. Warriors grow by testing their limits. They express themselves by completing feats and challenges. In proving equal to their challenges Warriors find fulfillment in their professions.

The Educator class grows by learning and best expresses by teaching. An Educator's desire to learn is ultimately a quest for self-knowledge and personal growth. Whether studying the cosmos and the stars or the atoms we are made of, an Educator's quest ends with wisdom about the self. This wisdom is ultimately the path of personal growth for Educators, and its transmission their greatest form of expression.

The dharma types can work any profession they choose: Laborer types can be teachers, astronauts, or farmers, but the way they do their job will be unmistakably stamped by their dharma type. Laborers will be more narrowly focused, diligent, and careful about their work than other types. Outsiders will accentuate their uniqueness, and Merchants their cleverness. Educators will try to offer good counsel, and Warriors will try to complete a challenge or compete for a goal. Let's look at an example of this through the lens of some professions, examining the same type of work through the eyes of an artist, a taxi driver, and an ayurvedic doctor.

As artists Outsiders are inclined to push the envelope of accepted aesthetic values. They may shock the public or bring in new styles of artistic expression. Being avant-garde, literally the "front line," they experience the hits and the highs of new discovery first. As in the case of Van Gogh, such discoveries may not be appreciated until well after their demise.

Educators, emphasizing truth and purity, will produce art for its own sake without the imperative of recognition or reward. Merchants, on the other hand, must be recognized and remunerated if they are to have satisfaction and fulfill their role to the world. Consequently, Merchant art tends to be the most circulated and recognizable.

Laborer art has form and function as its mainstay and can include everything from murals and stained-glass windows to cabinetry and sculpture. It appeals to the practical mind, is well made, and tends to be more lasting as a result. Finally, Warrior art is strong and has force, struggle, and character as themes, reflecting Warrior values such as self-sacrifice, honor, and valor. Warriors work in the name of an ideal, regardless of whether that ideal is recognized by the world.

When working as cab drivers Educators may point out landmarks and recite interesting trivia to their clients—they are less in it for the money than to meet and learn from interesting people and situations. Warriors in the same position would fight to get to their destination as fast as possible, even if they had to battle traffic with their accelerators, horns, and even their mouths!

Merchant cabbies, looking for the good fare, are happy to chat it up with their clients, taking a leisurely route to their destination and making it a pleasant and enjoyable experience, if painful to the wallet. Laborer types may not converse much, except to respond to direct queries. Having probably worked their seventh straight fifteen-hour shift they are more concerned with their family, paying the bills, and getting home to a good meal than any common courtesies their clients might expect!

Finally, the Outsider cab may look, smell, and feel exotic. Outsiders may play odd music, have varied decorations, or speak differently. Whether foreign immigrants or local locos, they will usually know uncommon and intriguing things about their city. Immigrants, who are either Outsiders or people in Outsider periods, stand out by their speech, mannerisms, and even what they eat, not to mention their personal expression through profession.

Each of the dharma types can work in any profession. How they do it and what they gain from it, however, varies. Ancient texts on ayurveda tell us that the science of life is to be studied by Educators for providing benefit to all creatures, by Warriors for protection, by Merchants for earning livelihood, and by Laborers for supporting children and the elderly. Each excels at a specific branch of this discipline (see table 14.2). Merchants may be masters at the alchemy of herbs and drugs, while Warriors may make the best surgeons. Educators do well in general medicine, theory, and education, while Laborers may excel at rejuvenation, massage, geriatrics, and pediatrics. Finally, Outsiders are challenged by diseases of the mind and disorders of unknown origin.

TABLE 14.2. THE EIGHT LIMBS OF AYURVEDA AND CORRESPONDING DHARMA TYPES

Internal medicine	Educator
Ear, nose, throat	Educator
Surgery	Warrior
Toxicology	Warrior/Outsider
Psychology/mental disorders	Outsider/Educator
Ob-gyn	Laborer
Rejuvenation	Laborer/Merchant
Virilization/Aphrodisiac	Merchant/Laborer

Anything that is outside of the mainstream—from psychosis to possession to incurable diseases like AIDS and cancer—proves fertile ground for the Outsider's interest.

The Types and Their Professions

Outsider: Any profession that involves *distant* or *foreign things* such as travel, foreign languages, and anthropology. *Fringe professions* that are less understood such as trouble-shooting, pornography, mysticism, new discovery, and the paranormal. Professions that no one else wants to do. Professions involving profound research and self-sacrifice, or that involve lying, stealing, or cheating like thieves, illusionists, assassins, spies, etc.

Merchant: Any profession requiring *entrepreneurial instincts, public performance,* or *publicity* such as sales, banking, pharmaceuticals, business/commerce, investment, promotion, entertainment, games and gambling, food and beverage, beauty, sex, fashion, and luxury.

Laborer: *Creating* things like community building, construction, engineering, agriculture, and obstetrics. *Specialized fields and trades* like detectives and private investigators, massage therapists, plumbing, aesthetics, makeup, carpentry, mechanics, real estate, etc. *Care and public welfare,* including crisis management, nursing, and emergency medical technicians. *Economics,* like accounting, financial services, banking, and bureaucratic government positions. *Service industry,* including restaurant and hotel, and manual labor. *Old things* like archaeology, geology, antiques, and history.

Educator: *Education and research* as in intellectual pursuits, the sciences, diplomacy, counseling, religion and spirituality, humanitarian professions, anthropology, authorship and literature, and the humanities.

Warrior: *Protecting others* as lawyers, law enforcement, firefighting, medicine, and the military. *Competition and power* in executive corporate and government positions, athletics, martial arts, leadership, and management posts.

Educators may teach ayurveda and its philosophy rather than actively practice it. They may focus on its spiritual components, where the Laborer would be more practical minded and interested in its immediate use. Warriors may work for the government to protect others by dictating health care policy or by performing emergency surgery on the battlefield. Outsiders may synthesize ayurveda with other practices to form unique offshoots.

Merchants may grow wealthy by preparing and selling drugs and concoctions. We see this today: one of the most profitable industries in the world is the drug company that supplies everything from aspirin to Zoloft to ease the pain and improve the pleasure of the American public. Thus, while different types may choose the same profession, they do it with profoundly different orientations.

Laborers tend to be specialists, and there is no one more diligent and devoted to their chosen profession than a Laborer type. Whether a brain surgeon or an electrical engineer Laborers love what they do and are particularly good in their niche. However, because of this narrow focus, they may not be as good in areas that require broad knowledge of diverse and varying subjects. As engineers they may specialize in electrical, mechanical, or other forms of engineering, but do not ask them about medicine or law because these are outside of their scope of expertise.

The Educator, on the other hand, being a Renaissance man or woman, knows a little bit about many things, in diverse and varying fields. What Educators do not know they are quick to learn, as intellect and understanding are their strengths. When Educators specialize they remain well rounded, retaining their intellectual curiosity about the universe. However, this overly liberal tendency to many interests can make them wishy-washy and unable to focus on one thing. They are also the least manually skilled type, and this impracticality can make them seem out of touch with ordinary reality.

Outsiders do not do well with a nine-to-five schedule. They need freedom, variety, and independence, gravitating to professions that allow them to make their own hours. Independent contractors, truck drivers, stunt people, actors, artists, writers, and musicians are some such examples. The common thread uniting Outsiders is their need to retain their individuality and freedom.

> **An evolved Outsider can use deception to give energy to rather than take it from the world.**

Outsiders are also world changers. Whether they do this as revolutionaries or as quiet agents for transformation depends upon individual circumstances—but Outsiders are put on this earth to reform and transform it. Just as Space is the most prevalent element, Outsiders are the most influential type for history and society, though ordinary society is usually ignorant of their contributions. The Warrior's duty to protect, the Educator's call to counsel, the Laborer's obligation to work, and the Merchant's drive to prosper are directives that are clear-cut and easy to appreciate, but few realize the crucial role Outsiders play in our daily lives, and the extent of their influence on world events. Whether winning the Cold War as spies and counterintelligence agents or World War II as code breakers and atomic bomb makers, the Outsider's invisible footprint on history is staggering to contemplate. The cracking of the German code in World War II prompted Winston Churchill to say, "Before Alamein we never had a victory; after Alamein we never had a defeat." Whatever their professions, Outsiders are the secret keepers of the world!

Each type has a positive and negative expression. The Outsider's negative emotion is self-deception. When this is turned around evolved Outsiders can use deception to give energy to rather than take it from the world. They may become illusionists or magicians, tricking observers for their pleasure. Many Outsiders also make great makeup artists, costume designers, and movie makers—anything that has to do with creating illusion and tricking the eyes of the observer. Outsiders bring new things to the world, like realms of fantasy and never-before-seen images, which makes them good fiction writers and storytellers. Anne Rice's vampire series and Isaac Asimov's outer space explorations are examples of groundbreaking ideas brought to the public through print. (Refer to table 7.2 on dharma type emotions on page 139 for more on how these may be expressed.)

Warriors are the natural doctors and surgeons of the dharma types. If medicine is a war against disease, no one is better fit to tackle it than the Warrior type. Warriors can make crack decisions, and life-and-death choices, in order to cut through afflictions. They also have the physical fortitude to battle for patients, even to their own detriment. It is the dharma of Warriors to fight and protect the weak and innocent, and medicine and wellness are fields that allow them to do so on a regular basis. When Warriors learn to integrate Educator skills their bedside manner improves, and they become friendly and understanding toward their patients.

The desire to fight on behalf of the disadvantaged also makes them great lawyers. Some people equate lawyers with sharks, but one must remember that in many countries the accused have no rights and often await their fates in jail without recourse to comfort or counsel. In these cases lawyers are the only protection the innocent, or the guilty, have. In this sense Warriors' obligation to help those who cannot help themselves, to fight for the rights of the underprivileged, and to give themselves for the cause of another are fully satisfied.

We can forgive lawyers who take the easy road to gain in Merchant society. If we can't forgive them, we can at least understand the pressure to conform to a system that promotes profit, not protection. In the long run both the lawyer and society suffer when he or she devolves into a moneymaking machine. But as long as the Merchant train grinds on, such disintegrations remain unnoticed; those who fall are crushed under its wheels and those who fail to stay aboard are left behind. At some point, though, as it loses its valuable members who are the operators and conductors, the machine itself crashes and becomes irreparable. At such a time it becomes necessary to reinvent the system and allow everyone to reboard and participate in steering society in the right direction, each according to his or her dharma type.

 HOMEWORK

Breaking down professions according to dharma type is useful, but ultimately people can work in any field that provides fulfillment and allows freedom for personal growth and self-expression. In the discussion of government in chapter 9 we saw how the armed forces branch into five limbs according to dharma type, and how these further split into individual subcategories. For example, while the Army, Navy, Air Force, and Marines reflect the Laborer, Merchant, Educator, and Warrior personalities, duties like tank operator, intelligence agent, and recruiter relate specifically to Laborer, Outsider, and Merchant types. We don't have to change our careers to find something that suits us; sometimes we just have to find the niche within our existing career that is appropriate for our individual dharma.

Whatever your profession, there is usually something in it for every type. It is not only Warriors who make great doctors. While Warriors have a talent for surgery, Laborers may be excellent pediatricians or nurses, and Educators might make great general practitioners. It is your homework today to think about your work—from agriculture to zoology—to discover how it expresses your dharma type. Enjoy!

15

The Life Cycles

We end this volume with a discussion of the life cycles, not because they are less important but because they are invaluable to getting the most from your dharma type. In the Vedic tradition first and last chapters are special because they create the first and last impressions in the reader. In chapter 1 we began with a survey of the dharma types, the basic nature of every individual at birth. In this chapter we discuss how that basic nature takes shape over the course of a lifetime as expressed by the life cycles. Practically speaking your life cycle determines what's going on *right now* in your life, while the dharma type outlines your basic DNA print at birth. Who you are is the dharma type; how you express who you are is influenced by the life cycle you are in.

For example, every woman has the potential to give birth, but that potential is only actualized during a specific portion of her life, between puberty and menopause. In addition, fertilization is only possible during narrow windows within her ovulation cycle every month. Nature works in cycles within cycles. Thus we cannot help but follow Nature's rhythms if we are to obtain desirable results, from having a successful pregnancy to creating a successful life. Like nature and nurture, the dharma types and life cycles come together to give us a complete picture of who we are and where we're going.

When people take the Self Test at the beginning of this book they usually select two types. One likely represents their dharma type, the other the life cycle they are in. Sometimes it can be difficult to separate *who* we are from *where* we are in our lives, our nature from nurture. This is especially true for people in Outsider periods, as these tend to be confusing to begin with. Outsiders, who can relate to every type, have a harder time finding themselves and people in Outsider periods are particularly challenged. The good news is that there are ways to map out the life cycles with clarity and insight. The best of these requires an accurate birth time and is read using the Vedic Life Map* or horoscope, which provides a snapshot of a person's dharma type as well as the past, present, and future life cycles they will experience.

> **"Not to know what happened before we were born is to remain perpetually a child. For what is the worth of a human life unless it is woven into the life of our ancestors by the records of history?"**
> CICERO

But even without Vedic techniques we can look at our lives to determine our current life cycle—are we in a moneymaking time in which prosperity, social intercourse, and enjoyment of life are primary motives? If so, we might be in a Merchant period. Are we devoted to raising a family and the quiet comforts of home, working hard to earn money but not ambitiously craving it? Then we may be in a Laborer time. Or are we ambitious, driven, physically active, and looking for promotion? This could signal a Warrior period. The Educator time is marked by self-cultivation, study, and an interest in humanistic concerns, while Outsider periods bring the unexpected. They put us in contact with the unknown, are unpredictable, and tend to keep us on the fringe of accepted social norms. Even people who gain fame and fortune in Outsider periods do so as rebels or distinct personalities. By looking at the karma we experience at any given time we can judge the life cycle we are in, and when it changes. Let's take a look at some examples.

---

*Visit www.spirittype.com for more information or to find a professional Vedic astrologer near you.

Joe was an Educator who loved to study and flourished early in school. At eighteen he lost interest in academia and found himself rebelling against his teachers. He began to resent the boundaries that restricted his self-expression and started to experiment with drugs and reckless behavior that eventually alienated people around him. When things at home began to feel stale he dropped out of college and went abroad to discover other cultures, to which he adapted quickly and felt a special affinity. He adopted many of their customs, and when he returned home he found himself somewhat out of the loop with his friends and family.

Can you guess what life cycle Joe entered at age eighteen? If you said "Outsider" you are on the mark!

After roaming the world for a few years Joe began to think to himself, "I'm tired of being poor and unsettled. I need to make money if I want to enjoy the good things in life!" He enrolled in several trade courses and became a successful design consultant to wealthy homeowners and businesses. Using his acquired language and cultural skills, as well as his natural ability to counsel and teach, he became a successful businessman for the next seventeen years.

It is clear that at this time Joe entered into a Merchant period. Here, his focus shifted to making money. However, because our basic nature stays with us, he could not escape the need to instruct and counsel others, though he found lucrative ways to do it. This is how the Merchant life cycle colored his Educator dharma type.

Let's look at another example.

June was a Warrior type who worked quietly to support her little girls. At a certain point in life she began to take an interest in self-improvement and started reading books on health, diet, and spirituality. She discovered yoga, which led her to take classes and eventually complete a teacher training course. She began teaching yoga and loved it so much that she quit her old desk job to teach full-time. Her renewed outlook and life philosophy started to rub off on her students, whom she taught by setting a strong example herself. Her main priority was to protect her children, and she often adopted this same attitude toward her yoga students, helping them to grow and transform through discipline, hard work, and a never-quit attitude.

Can you guess what cycle this is? If you said Educator, you are correct. Our Warrior June's interests naturally turned to education and self-improvement as the habits of her old cycle (perhaps a Laborer period) began to fall away. She became interested in knowledge and how to transmit it. She also began to empower herself, and because Warriors evolve into Educators her Educator period was particularly supportive for her, as we'll see below. Protecting people comes naturally to Warriors, who also like to practice what they preach, experimenting on themselves before subjecting others to their discipline. These were all hallmarks of her yoga teaching style.

The life cycle will not change your purpose, just its expression. Cycles different from your dharma type will express your virtues in different environments and different ways. This is where an Educator goes to Africa to teach English in an Outsider period, or a Warrior begins building housing for the homeless in a Laborer time. It is where an Outsider opens an import-export shop in a Merchant period, and where the Merchant enters politics to save the economy in a Warrior cycle.

The life cycle will not change your purpose, just its expression.

It is not difficult to tell when you enter various life cycles because your interests reflect the changing seasons of your karma. Below is a summary of what you can expect in each life cycle.

SUMMARY OF THE LIFE CYCLES

Outsiders

People in Outsider periods find it boring to live normal, everyday lives. They are keen on exploring the underbelly of existence, traveling, and discovering the unusual. Their education is interrupted, their living situation is in flux, and this period prevents their normal integration into the flow of society. This may cause suffering but can also become their strength, molding them into a *vichitra purusha*, a creature unlike any other. Coming and going within the community they can be disruptive, like a strange breeze. Whether that breeze wafts sweet scents or foul airs depends on their personal evolution, and what they have learned from life.

Outsiders often long to be normal. This is usually out of ignorance of their own gifts, and the fact that they would actually hate normalcy if they had it. If you are in an Outsider period and find yourself wanting the roller coaster to stop, remember that you are here for a reason and consider that if you shut your eyes to the experience you may never again see the sometimes strange and wonderful vistas that being on the roller coaster affords. That doesn't mean you have to become a carny to enjoy the ride; you do not need to be a rebel or an iconoclast to embrace Outsider virtues. Instead, you must make the most of what is available. Whatever the attitude, one thing is certain—no one is ever the same after a ride in an Outsider life cycle!

Merchants

People in a Merchant period become more interested in the finer things in life and how to acquire them. A natural sense of financial opportunity arises, and they are able to take advantage of it during this period. Out of fear of poverty and desire for success people in a Merchant life cycle drive themselves, working hard to attain financial security. Their web of friendships grows as they begin to network and get to know people outside their normal sphere, even if only superficially. They become more affable, attractive, and consequently better known in their community. Money is a big deal and the primary focus during this time. Everything revolves around the importance of financial security and the shelter, clothing, and sustenance it provides. The Merchant time is a great period for advancing your fiscal agenda.

Educators

People in Educator periods become role models for others, aspiring to truth and purity in their actions and beliefs. At this time they are interested in self-improvement, self-help, and the betterment of the world. They are more studious and open to learning both spiritual as well as practical, everyday matters. Knowledge becomes precious, as do ideas and ideals. They are likely to be attracted to intellectual people and pursuits.

Laborers

A person in a Laborer time is settled down and interested in work. Quiet service and a job well done become more important than self-promotion and deal making. Such a person becomes more devoted to family and strengthens close attachments. Life becomes uncomplicated and its goals clear-cut. The pleasures of working with your hands, sitting and eating, and existence itself become more deeply appreciated, as do hardships and tragedies. A Laborer life is more keenly felt, and that is why having a close-knit community of friends and family becomes monumental during a Laborer life cycle.

Warriors

Anyone in a Warrior period becomes a leader. Even though leadership may not be part of their natural disposition, people in Warrior cycles are thrust into roles that require executive abilities. People in their Warrior time become doers. They cannot sit and just let things happen but must be implicated in the flow of their destiny, instrumental in bringing about their desired outcome. They pick a cause and fight for it. Those in a Warrior time have definite opinions and are willing to defend them. They are protectors, sacrificing themselves for others, and will take on missions that put them in the line of fire. This may simply mean working at two jobs to feed a family or actually fighting on a battlefield. In either situation, people are not content with sitting still during their Warrior time and will take action to ameliorate their circumstances, or the circumstances of others.

EVOLUTION/DEVOLUTION

Now that we've surveyed each life cycle let's take a look at how these periods affect the dharma types based on their evolution and devolution points (see table 2.1, "Evolution and Devolution of the Dharma Types," on page 53). When a dharma type finds itself in a life cycle that is its evolution point it will tend to find success in that period, while such a type will experience obstruction during the period of its devolution point. A dharma type in a life cycle that is neutral to it will find itself neither terribly obstructed nor particularly supported. Let's take a look at what this means.

A Warrior in a Merchant period is not likely to do as well as a Warrior in an Educator period, all factors being equal, because Warriors devolve into Merchants, and Merchants into Warriors. Likewise, a Laborer is likely to find Educator cycles lonely and tough, just as Educators will feel unappreciated in their Laborer cycles. That is because they devolve into each other, and when a type sees its devolution period it can spell obstacles and difficulties. Here are some examples:

John is a Laborer who spent his high school and college days in Outsider life cycles. After graduation he got a job at a bank and soon thereafter began an Educator life cycle. Although he felt at home in his department, he was promoted to corporate trainer. This new job allowed him to travel and meet new people, but he preferred his old position and friends to the revolving door of new faces and new ideas every day. Although he made more money he felt lonely and isolated, unable to make permanent bonds with people, even feeling like an ascetic at times.

An Educator time holds some pitfalls for the Laborer type. The benefits of this period include learning new things, obtaining training, and being otherwise instructed. The dangers come when these Laborer types are put into positions that require Educator tasks they would rather not perform. In such cases they must excuse themselves from these positions if they want to keep their sanity and well-being, even if it means taking a financial hit.

Ultimately, Laborers do better without the headaches of having to deal with Educator issues. In fact, this may not be the most profitable time for Laborers as they may spend money on school, learning, and time away from the work that allows them to earn that money.

Conversely, Laborers entering a Merchant period will find the hustle and bustle of activity stimulating, not draining. Here Laborers see their gifts appreciated rather than misunderstood, and they feel more at home as opportunities allow them to fully express their talents and be remunerated for them.

Stacy is a schoolteacher, an Educator just finishing her Laborer period. She is soft-spoken and overweight, and her life has been marked by quiet service to her ESL kids: students learning English as a second language. Though severely trying at times this period has taught her that standard teaching protocols don't work, and she has worked hard to develop new, more successful techniques. Now, as she enters into her Warrior period, she feels compelled to share her discoveries so others can benefit from her work. She begins advocating for reform in teaching protocols, and the once quiet and unremarkable homeroom teacher now speaks with a voice that captivates thousands and demands appreciation. The new activity inspires her to renew her gym membership, and she finds that training her mind and training her body go hand in hand with building a positive new image, for herself and for children around the world.

Educators entering their Warrior life cycle are at the apex of strength. This is a time when their wisdom may become particularly popular and valuable to others. During their Warrior period Educators are encouraged to strike out boldly and put their ideas to the fore. They are disciplined, driven, and more likely to make their name than at any other time. Hence, this is a period for leadership, publication, and public acclaim.

Conversely, Educators in a Laborer period are typically more closed in and dedicated to their private work and the immediate affairs of family. Educators become more emotional and in touch with their feelings during this time. They also gain an added appreciation for the simple, concrete things in life—a home-cooked meal, a well-crafted object, and good company in general. Though not as philosophical and lofty, their ideas will carry weight and have more material applications due to this influence. There is a quiet enjoyment during this period. Because the Educator devolves into the Laborer type it is important to watch out for intellectual laziness, sloppiness, and unbalanced thinking.

Remember that life cycles rarely last a lifetime, and if you find yourself in a difficult cycle it does not have to be a negative experience. As an Educator you cannot ever *be* a Laborer personality. It is a time for research and investigation that will contribute to breakthroughs and insights in future periods. For Stacy, her Laborer time gave her the experience and endurance to observe how kids learn. And though it took a toll on her, she used it to inspire a new chapter in her life as her next period rolled around.

Every Educator must learn in order to have something to teach. The Laborer period is a time of learning, though often not by choice or in the manner that an Educator may prefer. It is a time of humility and quiet submission to the cycles of life, as it may be difficult for the clumsy Educator to fit into the Laborer's world. But the rewards are also there. The lesson for Educators is not to fit in but to learn from their dharma for their own benefit and the benefit of others. This is a time to swallow your pride, put your head down, and accept with faith and devotion what Nature gives you. You may not be seen for all that you are, but what you are seen for will be enough.

> Xu is a Warrior who has trained in kung fu since he first learned to walk. He spent his early days at his father's gym—eating, sleeping, and training. He cared little for talk and always felt that actions spoke louder than words. As Xu entered his Merchant period his father gave him the responsibility of running the gym and making it profitable. Xu experimented with many different things but found the headaches and worries of keeping his business fiscally solvent almost overwhelming. He began to cut corners and make mistakes, sometimes even cheating people. He began staying out late, drinking and carousing, leaving his training behind.
>
> Several years later as he began an Educator phase Xu's mind started to turn back to kung fu—this time not as a martial art but as a philosophy to help him deal with his elevated blood pressure, restlessness, and anger issues. He began to take retreats to sacred sites where he reconnected with the essence of his tradition, eventually returning to his gym to become a teacher, offering his students classes on a donation, pay-as-you-can basis.

Because Warriors evolve into Educators Xu's Educator period was fruitful both spiritually and intellectually. He began to read and study, learning the theories behind many of the disciplines he took for granted—the philosophy behind the practice. Xu may end up writing books or teaching his skills at this time and become honored by his students and readers. The emphasis here is on cultivating inner virtue and conscientiousness, not externally fighting for it. In fact, this is the stage in which Warriors learn the value of peace. They may let their physical skills lapse while developing other, more intangible attributes. Essentially, Warriors take on the characteristics of the Educator type, and because the two are compatible this is a most satisfying period. On the other hand, Warriors in Merchant periods tend to take on the negative qualities of the Merchant: loudness, instability, showiness, anger, and self-interest. Warriors can slip into egotism and pride when their Merchant periods roll around—attitudes they usually pay for later on since their dharma is about protecting others, not serving themselves.

 HOMEWORK

Take some time to think through how each life cycle affects the dharma types, with special attention to yours. There are twenty-five possibilities. This chapter is not about enumerating every period for every type but is a guide to help you integrate how different periods fit your life using your own imagination and what you've learned of the dharma types so far. Outlined below are some paragraphs to get you started. We will look at Outsider cycles first, since no type evolves or devolves into them. Then we will observe the Merchant cycle as an example of how you can do this for yourself.

THE OUTSIDER LIFE CYCLE

Educators

What do Educators do in an Outsider cycle? They still write books, but they are about the foreign and the unknown. They still study, though the subjects may be arcane or esoteric. Their mind is still occupied with self-improvement, though the route to it may circumvent the obvious and delve into alternative methods. Looking for Atlantis? Researching the Kabbalah? No subject is outside Educators' curiosity at this time, though the conclusions they reach may differ from what established research has to say.

At this time Educators perceive more keenly matters that may have long evaded investigation. Their mind is freed from the shackles of rote and established thinking to roam the expanses of the unknown. They may partake in mind-altering substances or go to excesses to obtain the object of their research, but in doing this they must be careful, for the limitlessness characteristic of the Outsider can also derange their mind's ability to stay rational, and therefore relevant.

People in Outsider periods become disaffected with the status quo. They need a break from the routine of their home and job, which is why many change professions and residences during this time. But relevance is the saving grace of Outsiders, who must construe their experiences into a model fit for public consumption if they are to be of use to themselves and society. Educators swimming in Outsider waters must take care not to drown in their depths or be carried away by their strange currents, lest they fail to return and share the treasures they have found—becoming adrift and alone, useless to themselves and others.

When they do return they are likely to bring back things never before seen. Their investigations and conclusions may bring about a paradigm shift in the world's consciousness and instigate new modes of thinking. Educators who enter into the unknown either disappear forever in its depths or, if they manage to reemerge, become permanently altered by their experience. From sexual escapades to psychedelic exploration Outsider periods redefine Educators' normally rigid boundaries and permit them to experience life with a curious admixture of depravity and virtue.

To maximize their stay on the border of the known Educators must stay true to their dharma type and continue to seek wisdom and self-improvement. As long as they do this they achieve their goal and attain fulfillment, no matter where their future may take them in other cycles.

Outsider Conditioning: Educator

Sometimes dharma types spend their whole lives in one life cycle, becoming so conditioned by it that they permanently take on many of its qualities. This is a rare and special occurrence that deserves exploration. An example of an Educator whose life has been conditioned by Outsider life cycles is shock rocker Marilyn Manson, who has been mostly in one long Outsider period. Knowing this helps us to understand that for all of his garish displays (Outsider) he is at his core *playing a role* and teaching people (Educator), presumably to be nonjudgmental and to relax their inhibitions. His Outsider persona is pointing out the flaws in our morals by invoking strong reactions, while his softer, sometimes geeky Educator side is at the same time shining through to temper these displays with a moral subtext. In this way understanding people's life cycles, and how their basic types orient to this, can give us crucial insight into their psyche.

Alanis Morissette is an Outsider playing an Educator who has been in Outsider periods most of her life. She will not see another period until her seventies. Themes of sexual experimentation, drug use, anorexia, and general exploration of musical, social, and personal boundaries characterize this curious Outsider-playing-Educator's search for meaning in the world.

Merchants

Merchants in an Outsider period may use their business skills in foreign or unknown markets. They may also take to dealing in drugs, crime, and other shadowy features of the Outsider element. They may become expatriated and begin life anew among different cultures. Merchant types perennially suffer from a sense of uneasiness, a type of emptiness that causes them to question their self-worth. In this period they may set out to find its source and fill that void with answers from the unknown.

Outsider periods temporarily dissolve the structures that bind Merchants, allowing them to penetrate into vistas far removed from their usual haunts. They may travel to new locales and experience a variety of entertainments, pleasures, and curiosities. In the end, these may serve them as they bring back their experiences to the normal world. They may find profit in new markets or by new strategies gained from their walk on the wild side.

There is one danger for Merchants in an Outsider period—with their already loosely defined moral structure they may be tempted to throw ethical considerations to the wind and cross the line of legal/moral decency at this time. As noted above, experimenting with drugs and sex may be too enticing to pass up. Merchant willpower is usually poor (except when pertaining to generating wealth, for which it is unrivaled), and this may cause Merchants to slip into behaviors they would not engage in under normal circumstances. But in an Outsider period they are temporarily out of sight of the Warrior's vigilance (in the circle of duty), cruising under the radar as it were, which allows them to do things they wouldn't normally consider.

Outsider Conditioning: Merchant

One example of a Merchant conditioned by her life cycle is Marilyn Monroe. Born a charismatic Merchant type, she spent her entire life in Outsider life cycles, thereby injecting a sense of the misfit (she was raised in foster homes), the iconoclast (she never settled for what Hollywood gave her), and the libertine (she sought freedom from and pushed the boundaries of sexual expression). In her desire for freedom she functionally became an Outsider to most everyone in her life, from the Kennedys to her Hollywood cohorts, and ultimately to herself as she sought liberation from limitation to the point of committing suicide. Even her death was tinged with the mystery and suspense of the Outsider personality, and the spectacle and notoriety of her Merchant archetype.

Elvis Presley is another charismatic Merchant who never saw another life cycle. Elvis came out of left field to redefine country/blues into something totally fresh, new, and dangerous—he was the face of rock 'n' roll. Thus, two of the most charismatic (Merchant) and eccentric (Outsider) personalities of the twentieth century, Marilyn and Elvis, both won peerless glory as well as infamy by spending their entire lives in Outsider periods.

Consider the parallels of Elvis and Marilyn's lives with that of Kurt Cobain, another Merchant who spent his life in Outsider periods, where the dangers and the laurels are many. For Merchants equipped with a working knowledge of the dharma type, and a map leading to evolution into the Laborer, the Outsider period can be most fruitful. But for those who lack the wisdom and support to point themselves in the right direction the freedom of the Outsider period can prove confusing, delusional, and even deadly.

By contrast, most people will see at least two different life cycles in their lives, and many may pass through all five. In Madonna's life we witness a cornucopia of change as she dances through Outsider, Warrior, Educator, and back to Outsider periods, hitting the height of her career during her Educator period and sustaining it over her lengthy Outsider cycle from the 1990s through today. This brings us back to the insight that each type will experience its most desirable effects during the life cycle of its evolution point and may undergo obstacles or difficulties during the cycle of its devolution point. As an Outsider functioning as a Warrior, Madonna found herself optimally set to enjoy success during her Educator period and will never see a Merchant period in her life.

Warriors

Warriors whose lord has been slain, or whose cause has been destroyed, must set out like mercenaries into unknown territory. This is their Outsider stage. Unrecognizable to their surroundings, their cause and credo may become foreign to the culture they live in, and their methods unorthodox or unpredictable. They begin to feel alone, to fight for different beliefs, adopting a new set of values. Yet they must not forget that knowledge and intelligence remain their integration points and let these guide them to a noble purpose in their lives.

The Buddha is an example of an Outsider playing a Warrior whose destiny was altered when he entered his Outsider period. Born a prince and intended for the throne, the Buddha's life dramatically turned when he left the kingdom in pursuit of Truth. Renouncing his former life, he became a full-time Outsider, performing rigorous penance and living in poverty and isolation—conditions utterly juxtaposed to the regal title he was born into. This influence remained with him even after he assimilated back into society, for he remained a Warrior rebel, unaccepted by most in mainstream brahmanical society.

> Outsiders have the power of surprise and innovation on their side, and when they have earned it, moral superiority.

His philosophy of nirvana, emptiness, clashed with the theistic view of the Brahmin culture current in India. Nonetheless, he became a champion of self-effort (Warrior) for those who wished to realize themselves, and he rejected systems and authorities (Outsider) for guiding aspirants to that end. Only a Warrior could have performed the severe penance that the Buddha did, going to extremes of fasting and asceticism. Only an Outsider could so reframe the current system as to bring about a total paradigm shift in religious thought. "There is no God! There is no soul!" Indeed only Outsiders, or those in Outsider cycles, know how to shock the establishment. Only Outsiders know how to create revolution. Compare from Matthew 21 Jesus's radical invective on the temple priests: "In truth I tell you, tax collectors and whores are entering God's reign before you!" Outsiders have the power of surprise and innovation on their side, and when they have earned it, moral superiority.

Outsider Conditioning: Warrior

James Dean is an example of a Warrior in a lifelong Outsider period. His iconic role in *Rebel without a Cause* was a fitting testament to the Warrior looking for his just cause. Remember that the goal for Outsiders is to find their purpose. When they are unable to do so they will push the envelope to connect to something bigger than themselves. Combined with the intensity and risk-taking nature of Warriors, an Outsider life cycle can be a dangerous time if it is not harnessed to a just cause, a noble path to guide and channel their energies.

Contrast James Dean's demise with Marilyn Monroe's to find

examples of failed coping strategies—one by a Warrior, the other by a Merchant. Finding themselves in Outsider periods, the Merchant Monroe turned to drugs and alcohol while the Warrior Dean sought out intensity and thrills. When Merchants cannot fill their emptiness by linking themselves to charity and giving they will seek to satiate themselves in the quickest manner available. When Warriors cannot give their lives to a just cause they will simply give their lives—by taking increasing risks until the risks catch up with them. These are snares that await the unwary who enter Outsider life cycles. But just as the jungle is treacherous, it can also yield untold treasure. There is a wonder in the world's hidden places that you can't find on the paved roadways of cities and towns. The most powerful medicine and the wildest adventure lie in the unmapped jungle depths or the rugged plains—the domain of the Outsider life cycle.

Yet such cycles do not have to be exotic. Like the three layers of skin that correspond to the Outsider (dermis, epidermis, hypodermis—see chapter 8) there are degrees of experience when it comes to Outsider life cycles. The relatively insulated hypodermis remains close to the body of society—this could be a scientist working on an alternative cure for cancer or a lawyer working with immigrants. They remain within society while brushing against the unknown. On the other hand the dermis, the outermost layer of the skin that is not connected to the life-giving capillaries of the body except by diffusion, corresponds to a more radical experience of the Outsider cycle. In such a time our scientist may indeed depart for the jungle to seek alternative cures for cancer, all the while learning new languages and absorbing new cultures. Counselors trained in reading the dharma types can help you determine if your Outsider period will be one of extreme adventure or quiet subversion from within—or something in between.

Laborers

Laborers may travel to foreign places for work during an Outsider period. This may be due to financial hardship or to a promotion through their current profession, depending on their fortunes. During the Outsider time they will experience an expansion of consciousness that is usually beneficial, as it opens them up to new ways of thinking, new cultures and traditions. Laborers cannot help but be enriched by this, except where such new exposure costs them insurmountable difficulties—if they are exposed to ridicule, shame, or discrimination. In such cases they are likely to develop a strong aversion toward the new, closing their mind in order to endure such hardships.

But Laborers and Outsiders share a special bond. They are both cut from the same cloth and have an affinity that helps Laborers weather any changes with their typical hardiness. Laborers are handy and possess practical skills useful anywhere in the world, which makes it easier to adapt to working conditions. On the other hand they are slow to take on new information, which may be a disadvantage for their introduction to societies that are radically different from their own. Whatever the situation Laborers in an Outsider period generally do well, as a little change is always good for the soul of a Laborer type!

Outsider Conditioning: Laborer

Paul McCartney is an example of a Laborer who traversed Outsider periods during the formative years of his life. From early childhood until his early thirties he entertained a life cycle that co-opted him and his fellow Beatles into a revolution that changed the world's musical landscape. Only Outsiders or those in Outsider periods can so alter the consciousness of society! Whatever your type do not fear the Outsider time, for it may be the most memorable of your life. McCartney later went on to experience Laborer and Merchant periods, but none were as transformative to the world scene as his Outsider time.

Bruce Springsteen is another Laborer musician who spent a great deal of his life in an Outsider period. In fact, as we have seen in our discussions of money and profession, Outsiders and those in Outsider periods tend to gravitate to jobs that offer just the kind of freedom, flexibility, and creative outlet that music affords, though you do not have to be involved in rock 'n' roll to be a rock star in life. Learn how to harness your Outsider periods to express the unique gifts Nature gives you, whether for a day or a lifetime.

> **Whatever your type do not fear the Outsider time,
> for it may be the most memorable of your life.**

Outsiders

Outsiders in an Outsider period are removed from the normal and mundane operations of life—they are in their own world. This may manifest in undesirable ways such as illness, during which they are forced to spend time in hospitals or at home recovering, or imprisonment, during which their actions are also extremely censured. Or it may occur in beneficial ways like travel, exploration, spiritual study, research, or anything that takes them away from the humdrum, mundane reality of their lives. Outsiders in Outsider periods rarely settle for a nine-to-five existence. Instead, they leave to explore the wild, eventually bringing some of it back to their society if they are wise to their dharma. Remember that Outsiders are never really fulfilled unless they digest, assimilate, and transmute their experiences. This is equivalent to the three levels of responsibility, ruth, and respect discussed in part 1.

Using the above examples this may be a person who beats his illness and writes a bestselling book about it. For the prisoner who does her time, it could be reaching out to her community and giving of herself to educate kids and help prevent crime. Or it may be the escape artist/magician who scours the globe to hone his skills and ends up with fame, fortune, and a show in Vegas.

Outsider Conditioning: Outsider

Many are the examples of Outsiders in Outsider periods, both glorious and tragic. Nicolas Cage spent his first thirty-four years in Outsider life cycles, thereby permanently imbuing him with an oddball, Outsider persona in both his movies and personal life. Jimi Hendrix wowed the world with his electric rock-god innovations but was carried away by his

Outsider cycle's excesses. From age seventeen to his death, Jimi both rose and fell in his Outsider period.

Bhagavan Rajneesh (Osho) is an example of an Outsider whose whole life was spent in Outsider periods. The ultimate iconoclast, this double Outsider even managed to piss off Ronald Reagan as he caught the attention of the American government with his lavish spending and antiestablishment message.

CYCLES WITHIN CYCLES

During long stretches of one life cycle there are invariably shorter-lived periods, or subcycles. Even for an Outsider in Outsider periods there are times of rest, education, goal attainment, and conviviality that correspond to Laborer, Educator, Warrior, and Merchant subperiods. These may last months or years, depending on the greater context of the main life cycle, and in longer cycles subperiods may indicate a temporary respite. For an actress in an Outsider period a Laborer subcycle may find her giving birth and taking time away from acting to raise a family. Let's take a look at an example to illustrate the point.

Juliet is an Educator who enters a long Outsider period. During this time she becomes interested in Italy and its culture. What begins with a few language courses eventually turns into an extended stay in Florence, where she takes a job at a coffee shop for a year to earn money and build roots while drilling her Italian grammar at home. This is her Laborer subcycle, which though not very glamorous lays the foundation and establishes her in her new home. After a while she meets a boyfriend and through him begins to expand her social circle. Suddenly, she finds herself delighting in shopping for new clothes, wearing makeup, going out dancing, and living the high life of a twenty-something in Florence. Having done the work of learning the language and its customs, she has given herself permission to have a good time and expand her network of friends. This is her Merchant subcycle.

After a year and a half of dating and enjoying her time in Florence she breaks up with her boyfriend but is offered a teaching position at the same time, one that moves her to a university in Milan. There she takes a post as guest lecturer as her Educator subcycle begins to exert its influence within the context of her Outsider life cycle.

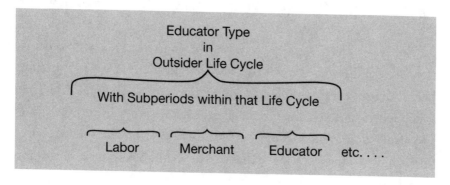

Figure 15.1. Example of subperiods within a life cycle.

Here we have a complex picture of an individual who finds herself in an Outsider life cycle, as represented by her interest in Italy and her eventual move there. While in Italy she sees various subcycles that color the expression of her long stay. In this example she goes from working to get by, to playing and enjoying herself, to settling down into a position suitable to her dharma type.

Life cycles and subcycles do not negate each other. As we can see from Juliette's vignette her Merchant subperiod of fun and romance occurred within the context of her longer Outsider cycle in the midst of new friends and foreign surroundings. Life cycles, dharma types, and subcycles do not cancel each other out—instead their energies blend to form a complete, fluid picture of one's life.

This example also illustrates that cycles often, but not always, are signaled by some event or change in life. In this case Juliette's study of and move to Italy inaugurate her Outsider period, in Italy her job as a waitress and quiet home study mark her Laborer subcycle, and meeting her boyfriend and expanding her social circle initiate her Merchant subcycle. Finally, moving to Milan to teach inaugurates an Educator subcycle.

In looking at life cycles and subcycles a rule of thumb is to start where you are—consider the most immediate influence and work your way up. During her Merchant subcycle Juliette was most immediately experiencing the Merchant energy of fun and friends, which was happening in a foreign country. Like Russian nesting dolls subperiods fit within the greater life cycle, just as the life cycle is subsumed by the dharma type.

Subcycles are optimally considered if you have an accurate depiction of your life map provided by a trained dharma type counselor. Practically speaking, simply knowing your dharma type and life cycle is enough to put you light years ahead of the curve in terms of self-knowledge and awareness of your life path. Adding the subcycles is a fine-tuning of that knowledge that can be useful but is not essential for getting the most from your dharma type.

THE MERCHANT LIFE CYCLE

Outsiders

Continuing with the homework assignment now, let's look at the Merchant life cycle as an example of how we can break down and analyze any period. Because Outsiders evolve into all four types they can adjust to a Merchant role fairly easily, unless they are playing Warriors, in which case their Merchant period may pose some challenges. Knowing that Merchant qualities must be developed during this time can help Outsiders focus their energy and keep them from feeling lost, as many Outsiders can feel when they do not know their place.

This does not mean that they will become card-carrying Merchants just because they have entered a Merchant period, for a type's basic qualities always remain, though in the background, to color its personality. It does mean that their Outsider dharma will be served by embracing a Merchant role for a while. They may become more socialized during this time, flowing smoothly with the culture stream, though this surface conviviality may come with an increased feeling of emptiness as the Merchant's sometimes low self-worth can exacerbate an Outsider's already heightened anxiety. This can be countered by staying grounded in dharma. For the Outsider playing a Merchant that means embracing charity, giving your energy and time to help others, and staying grounded in the three steps to integration as discussed in chapter 6. Meditation and natural supplements like melatonin, valerian, and other calming herbs also work well.

During Merchant periods Outsiders are interested in profiting themselves and may do so with novel ideas or products. They may become popular and well liked, and during this time they have license to have fun, entertain, and enjoy the Merchant lifestyle. Neither Outsiders nor Merchants are particularly concerned with repressive morals, and Outsiders in this time are more interested in a good time than in being "good." But they must be careful to maintain some moral order lest they walk away with lasting reminders of their mistakes, which may include police records, diseases, or physical and emotional scars.

Educators

Because Educators neither evolve nor devolve into Merchants this time is neutral for them. Educators are neither comfortable nor terribly bothered by the exigencies of the Merchant life cycle, and this is a time to sell and market their knowledge. Like Outsiders, Educator types find it difficult to know when it is appropriate to market their ideas. In fact, they may prefer to teach, study, and do what they do rather than actively promote themselves or worry about financial obligations. When Jesus sent out his disciples to teach and heal he did so with the command to "take nothing for the journey except a staff—no bread, no bag, no money in your belts" (Mark 6:37), very much an Educator sentiment. But a Merchant time affords Educators opportunities to harvest some rewards by using their smarts in different arenas. They may go into sales or investment or find other ways to financially benefit themselves.

This rest from Educator pursuits may in fact inspire fresh and new ideas when they move into different life cycles later, because Merchant periods are nothing if not motivating and exciting.

Warriors

The Warrior in a Merchant period is an instance of athleticism mixed with entertainment, a whirlwind mix of capitalism and pugilism that is at once brutal and exciting. In the best-case scenario Warriors earn money through their valor, power, and/or reputation, with their value recognized by Merchant society. Yet this is also the most precarious stage for Warriors, for Warriors in a Merchant period are also likely to lose their goal and purpose to Merchant temptations.

So what can Warriors do when there is no battle to fight? They can find a just cause to serve at home, which is what happens to athletes or soldiers who when their glory days are over become businesspeople, advisors, or workers depending on their life cycles. Here is the athlete turned sports commentator, franchise owner, or coach, or the retired boxer selling cookware to the multitudes. Whatever the case, for Warriors in a Merchant period the flashing red light is "don't sell out!" This is their only caveat.

Warriors entering into a Merchant time must therefore have an outlet for their skills—a just fight, a noble cause to embrace—in order to have inner satisfaction. If they fall into the trap of accumulating money and resources for their own sake, with no way to use them for a greater good, they risk descending into a Warrior hell. If, like the boxer selling cookware on TV, they are blessed with good fortune, Warriors should inject their earnings into charities and noble causes of their choice in order to leave behind a legacy worthy of them and to be truly honored for their achievements. Evolved Warriors in a Merchant period give up to 50 percent of their check to help others and are thus able to play the Merchant game to the max without being sullied in the process. In this way they can invest their total attention, energy, and skill into achieving fortune and fame without the emptiness that hounds the Merchant, and anyone traveling through a Merchant period.

It is the nature of Merchants to give back, to feed and clothe others when they can. Thus a Warrior in a Merchant time, while not able to save the world and protect the innocent in a Warrior fashion, may yet do so in a Merchant way. Therefore, giving back sooner rather than later is imperative. Since not everyone will become a millionaire in a Merchant period, this does not have to take the form of extravagant philanthropy. From volunteering at the YMCA to running a multimillion-dollar charitable foundation, the gifts Warriors give are commensurate to their abilities. What matters is that they give them, even if they have to do so in secret! Part of playing the Merchant game and making it interesting is not letting others know what you are doing. Part of giving away personal resources whets Warriors' appetites for more, whereas hoarding them dulls the edge of their competitive spirit. It is good for Warriors to always stay a little hungry, even amidst the feast of Merchant plenty.

> "Yon Cassius has a lean and hungry look;
> He thinks too much: such men are dangerous."
> WILLIAM SHAKESPEARE, *JULIUS CAESAR*

The Warrior's nature is to fight and die for a cause—in fact, Warriors must always be ready to do so, for death may take them at any moment. That is why Warrior cultures stress present moment awareness and steady vigilance as tools for enlightenment. These are ways to keep Warriors centered in reality and to help them avoid being swept away by pride, lust, and anger, which are easy traps for Warriors in a Merchant time. Life then has sanity and balance, and even should death sneak up it can be faced with full readiness rather than succumbed to in surprise—and Warriors then have the power to enter the next world on their own terms, with no regrets.

The collapse of Enron a few years ago gave us a tragic example of a Warrior corrupted by the Merchant system: A former captain in the U.S. Air Force, John Clifford Baxter was a top Enron executive and, by all accounts, a man of utmost integrity. After the public debacle that followed Enron's bankruptcy he killed himself, writing in his desperate suicide note, "I've always tried to do the right thing, but where there was once great pride—now it's gone," a tragic example of a Warrior who lost his way. Warriors must remain centered during the Merchant period and give away their earnings, time, and energy, not just to their families, but to benefit those who can't help themselves. This gives them a noble purpose and prevents tragedies like this from happening.

Merchants and Laborers

Now take a moment to imagine how the Merchant will take to a Merchant cycle. Will this be a time of improvement or decline? Will Merchants and Laborers feel comfortable or awkward in this period, and if so, why? How will they express themselves? In fact, for Merchants and Laborers this period is one of opportunity and improvement. Merchants will find their skills expressed to the fullest and are likely to benefit through them, just as any dharma type will in a self-same cycle. The wind is full in their sails and they should feel no compunction about being themselves, as the world is supportive of their self-expression. They should feel more charming, social, and involved with others. Money, goods, and opulence await them here, just as they do Laborer types, who will feel like they are on center stage, earning the deserved rewards of hard work.

> **For the Labor type, the reward of good work is more work.**

NEUTRAL DYNAMICS

Let us now examine an instance of a neutral life cycle. Since we have seen Educators in a Merchant time, we will consider the period between Warriors and Laborers.

In a Laborer life cycle Warriors put down the sword and take up the spade. Here their strength, skill, and leadership ability are put to use coordinating and building things, rather than destroying them. They find respect in working hard and in the camaraderie of being part of a group, though they are not always appreciated for their full worth as Warriors. Their skills and training may become rusty, their weapons unnecessary, and during this time Warriors' swords become paperweights while their basic work ethic is put to use.

For the Laborer type, the reward of good work is more work. But Warriors seek a definite goal, an end to achieve—they need a mountain peak to scale; the slow journey of ten thousand miles is not as interesting for them—and therefore they may grow bored doing Laborer-type work and feel their talents are being wasted. Conversely Laborers in a Warrior time become impassioned and fervent fighters for the rights of others: civil rights and community activists whose voices are finally heard, defending the causes they believe in. The immovable object now becomes an irresistible force in their Warrior period.

The only danger here is that Laborers may become politicians rather than activists and take the wrong road to betterment, because it is difficult to keep one's integrity when playing the politics game. It is not easy to enter the matrix without becoming affected by it. Some historians have proffered that George Washington was the only unsullied president, having never campaigned or even desired the office—everyone else had to play the game of government and compromise himself thereby. Such are the caveats for Laborers in a Warrior time.

Laborers may also never find lasting contentment in a Warrior period. Like a boxer who must fight to defend his title, Laborers cannot sit back and enjoy their laurels during this time. Thus, there is ambivalence: great achievement mixed with some dissatisfaction. There is action without rest and recovery, which Laborers normally enjoy.

SHARED LIFE CYCLES

Have you ever noticed that your friends change over time, and the people you considered yourself inseparable from are now distant memories?

Or are you the type of person who has had the same friends all of your life? Much of our compatibility with friends and lovers has to do with the life cycle we are in. People in the same life cycle share a common framework. People in different, incompatible cycles tend to drift apart. People we wouldn't normally speak with sometimes cross our paths because they are on the same journey we are. Sometimes we get to know people on planes, trains, or buses whom we would never have met if it were not for sharing a space and a similar destination. The same is true for sharing life cycles.

One of the methods for determining compatibility is the life cycles people share. True Outsiders will get along with other types in their Outsider cycles. They will enjoy the common ground of shared experience. On the other hand, two Educators who normally under-stand each other may not get along if one is in a Warrior period and the other in a Merchant time. Though Educators share similar values, the expression of those values will differ according to the energy of the cycle they are in.

CONCLUSION

This work has been the foundation, a stepping-stone to understanding your dharma. What happens when a dharma type does not live out its dharma? There are examples everywhere of people not fulfilling their potential. Sometimes family responsibilities necessitate taking on any paying work to feed, clothe, and house your family. Difficult economic conditions such as the "downturn" of 2008 also do not seem to promote free movement toward a dharmic lifestyle. However, these obligations are also a dharma, a duty we have to our families and society. Living your dharma type potential and carrying out your obligations to the world are not mutually exclusive—they go hand in hand. In fact, the current economic depression affords us an oppor-tunity to step away from previous jobs and commitments to analyze our lives. Such times can be ripe opportunities to shed ourselves of superfluity and ask the question: "Who am I, and what am I here to do?"

During good economic times we tend to coast along, comfortably numbed by a good paycheck even while working in areas that do not befit our optimal self-expression and personal growth. But we are more than just moneymaking machines. We all have a higher destiny we must try to live up to despite war, pestilence, and other conditions that bar us. In fact, it is during crisis that we look most at ourselves. It is during times of distress that we have the opportunity to redirect our lives in the direction we wish them to go.

During the Rwandan genocide people were forced to become either Warriors fighting to survive or Outsiders running for refuge. When basic survival needs are not met there is little space for the dharma of your type to shine. But even in our hardest times, we in the Western world do not face such overwhelming challenges. Whatever our circumstances we still have the opportunity to make our essence shine if we have the motivation and, more importantly, the tools to do so. It may take work, however.

> **Great creations grow out of great conflict;**
> **this is true in art as in life.**

Everyone has a duty to family, society, and the environment. The higher dharma of the dharma type can only express when these obligations have been satisfied and leave us time to pursue our individual destinies. There is no shame in working to feed our kids, but resourceful people will seek a way to do both: to live up to the potential of the dharma type while fulfilling duties to family and society. They will work at two jobs until they finish that novel or complete that business plan. They will juggle responsibilities to others and find time to be responsible to themselves, even if it means temporary hardship and setbacks. Great creations grow out of great conflict; this is true in art as in life.

TABLE 15.1. SUMMARY OF IMPORTANT ELEMENTS
OF THE DHARMA TYPES

	LABORER	MERCHANT	WARRIOR	EDUCATOR	OUTSIDER
Season	Spring	Summer	Summer	Autumn	Winter
Yoga Body	Food/ Flesh Body	Sensate Body	Vital/ Breath/ Energy Body*	Wisdom Body	Bliss Body
Intelligence	Emotional	Aesthetic	Energetic	Intellectual	Radical/ mystic
Element	Earth	Water	Fire	Air	Space
Duty To	Educator	Laborer/ Outsider†	Merchant	Warrior	Educator
Priority To	Merchant	Warrior	Educator	Laborer/ Outsider	Merchant

*Note that the Breath Body corresponds to the Fire Element. Like oxygen in an internal combustion engine that helps ignite gasoline and create fire, prana (chi) is responsible for creating the processes whereby the energy systems of the body create force and transformation.
†Merchants, who have the greatest capacity to provide support, are the only dharma type with duties to two types, while Educators, who need the most support, are the only type to receive two duties.

There are many reasons not to live up to your highest potential. In the worst extremes, we see cases of serial killers who cannot express their natural selves but in the darkest and most tortured ways. But for the most part people "live lives of quiet desperation," as per Thoreau, hiding their worth and covering it with platitudes and good excuses. It takes great courage to stand up and say, "This is who I am!" with dignity and pride, and to let the chips fall where they may. It takes a calm surrender to the Nature that made you to accept who you are and create the most of your opportunities. There is one thing that you do better than anyone else in the world, and your dharma type is the key to finding it!

Notes

2. EDUCATOR: ENLIGHTEN OTHERS

1. Emmet Fox, *The Sermon on the Mount: The Key to Success in Life* (San Francisco: Harper Collins, 1989).

4. MERCHANT: CLOTHE, CONNECT, AND ANIMATE OTHERS

1. Willam Blake, *The Marriage of Heaven and Hell* (1793).

5. LABORER: NOURISH AND SERVE OTHERS

1. William F. Buckley, Jr. and John Dos Passos, *Up From Liberalism* (New York: McDowell, 1959).

6. OUTSIDER: INNOVATE, REBEL, AND FREE OTHERS

1. Erin Gruwell, *Teach with Your Heart* (New York: Broadway Books, 2008); and Erin Gruwell, *The Freedom Writers Diary* (New York: Broadway Books, 1999).
2. Arthur Ashe, *A Hard Road to Glory: A History of the African American Athlete in Basketball* (New York: Harper Collins, 1993).

8. FIVE PATHS TO WELLNESS

1. Gary Wills, *What Jesus Meant* (New York: Penguin Books, 2006).

10. ELEMENT, SEASON, AND TASTE

1. Linton Kwesi Johnson, "Seasons of the Heart," in *Mi Revalueshanary Fren* (Keene, N.Y.: Ausable Press, 2006), 81.

11. INTELLIGENCE, SECRET FEAR, AND SPEECH

1. Gabriel Byrne, radio interview, *Fresh Air,* NPR, April 30, 2009.

12. MUSIC, MYTH, AND POODLES

1. Alanis Morsette, "Thank You," *Supposed Former Infatuation Junkie,* CD, Maverick, 1998.
2. J. K. Rowling, *Harry Potter and the Deathly Hallows* (New York: Scholastic, 2007), 718.

13. SPORT, WAR, AND WARRIORS

1. *The War Tapes*, directed by Deborah Scranton, 2006 (documentary).

14. MONEY AND PROFESSION

1. From *The Complete Works of Swami Vivekananda,* vol. 3, http://www.ramakrishnavivekananda.info/vivekananda/volume_3/lectures_from_colombo_to_almora/vedanta_in_its_applications_to_indian_life.htm.

Suggested Resources
on East/West Wisdom

Dr. Vasant Lad

www.ayurveda.com

Dr. Lad is perhaps single-handedly responsible for training more Westerners in authentic ayurveda than any other teacher. His institute is a haven for all who thirst for Vedic wisdom, and a port to higher knowledge. He teaches with compassion and an uncanny understanding of a student's needs.

Robert Svoboda

www.drsvoboda.com

The original ayurvedic Westerner, Svoboda holds the distinction of truly honoring India's spiritual traditions in his books as well as in his life. A must read for those wanting to explore ayurvedic alchemy and the mysteries of sacred India.

Hart deFouw

www.vedicvidyainstitute.com

What Dr. Vasant Lad is to ayurveda, deFouw is to jyotisha—a living, breathing embodiment of the art and science of Vedic astrology. He is the first Westerner to authentically imbibe and carry on a

Vedic tradition normally inaccessible to Western students; his books and classes on jyotisha make for tough reading but set the standard in authentic instruction.

Robin Gile
www.robingilepalmistry.com
Author of *The Idiot's Guide to Palmistry,* Robin is a practicing palmist and archetypal symbolist in the Albuquerque, New Mexico, area. Few can match his talent and uncanny insight born of forty year's experience.

Graham Hancock
www.grahamhancock.com
This far-out journalist cum spiritual seeker has trekked the globe looking to uncover man's ancient civilizations and their connections to the modern world. He is voracious in his thirst for knowledge and truth: an Outsider-Educator combination that makes us stand up and take notice. Even if you don't agree with his conclusions, his body of work cannot be ignored.

Pavel Tsatsouline
www.dragondoor.com
Pavel is a Master of Sports, the title of highest achievement accorded in the old Soviet system—akin to a Ph.D. in both athletic understanding *and* practice. Revolutionary in his approach, he transformed the Western fitness scene by introducing the kettlebell and other little-known training secrets to America. He makes difficult concepts simple to digest and is as compassionate in his delivery as he is brutal in his excoriation of what doesn't work. A true Warrior-Educator evolution. Check him out!

John Douillard
www.lifespa.com
John Douillard is a true admixture of East and West, a triathlete turned

doctor turned ayurvedic physician. His insights on modern Western integration of ayurvedic principles, especially in athletics, are unique and enlightening. Read his books.

B. K. S. Iyengar
www.bksiyengar.com
Well known to the West, Iyengar is largely responsible for making yoga safe and understandable to the Western practitioner—all without diluting the essence of his tradition. Iyengar is one of few among the yoga multitude who has kept his sincerity, integrity, and tradition intact over the years. For that, he remains a jewel to yoga culture.

Krishna Das
www.krishnadas.com
Not an author but a musician, KD is the East-West link to devotional Indian music and chanting. By the grace of his guru, he carries the spark of an ancient tradition in a modern Western voice that's guaranteed to make you sing along (just don't send him your speeding tickets).

For more information, or to find a dharma type practitioner near you, visit **www.spirittype.com** or write **siddhadeva@yahoo.com**.

Index

Page numbers followed by *t* indicate tables.

aboriginal societies, 37, 59, 206
ADD (Attention Deficit Disorder),
    154
aesthetic intelligence, 251
ages, four (chaturyuga), 31–39
agni (fire), 152, 222
Air Element, 28, 224–27
Allen, Woody, 46
Amen, Daniel, 152
America (United States)
    blacks in, 135, 308
    democracy in, 198–99
    entertainment in, 37, 213
    as a Merchant nation, 77–78, 213
    pets in, 295–96
    retirement in, 236
    vegetarianism and, 245
Ammachi ("hugging saint"), 96
anatomy
    Educators and, 147–49
    Laborers and, 149–50
    Merchants and, 150–52
    Outsiders and, 145–47
    overview, 144–45

Warriors and, 150
    See also specific organs
animals, 293–301
anxiety, overcoming, 133, 156
archetypes
    described, 2, 3
    Hollywood using, 285
    importance of, 10
    traditions of, 5
    See also dharma types; myth
artha, 24, 325
Arthur, King, 207, 208, 213
artists, 350
Art of War (Sun Tsu), 315
Ashe, Arthur, 130
ashrama (stages of life), 230–31
Asimov, Isaac, 355
astringent taste, 242, 243, 247, 248
astrology, Vedic (jyotisha), 161
astronomers, 160
Atharva Veda, 196
athletes, 67, 311–13
Attention Deficit Disorder (ADD),
    154

BOOKS OF RELATED INTEREST

Numerology for Decoding Behavior
Your Personal Numbers at Work, with Family, and in Relationships
by Michael Brill

Seed Sounds for Tuning the Chakras
Vowels, Consonants, and Syllables for Spiritual Transformation
by James D'Angelo, Ph.D.

Chakra Frequencies
Tantra of Sound
by Jonathan Goldman and Andi Goldman

Your Emotional Type
Key to the Therapies That Will Work for You
by Michael A. Jawer and Marc S. Micozzi, M.D., Ph.D.

The Science and Practice of Humility
The Path to Ultimate Freedom
by Jason Gregory

The DNA Field and the Law of Resonance
Creating Reality through Conscious Thought
by Pierre Franckh

Wheel of Initiation
Practices for Releasing Your Inner Light
by Julie Tallard Johnson

The Zero Point Agreement
How to Be Who You Already Are
by Julie Tallard Johnson

INNER TRADITIONS • BEAR & COMPANY
P.O. Box 388
Rochester, VT 05767
1-800-246-8648
www.InnerTraditions.com

Or contact your local bookseller